SILK

Aarathi Prasad is a writer, broadcaster, and researcher. She is the author of *In the Bonesetter's Waiting Room: Travels through Indian Medicine* (Profile, 2016) which was a BBC Radio 4 Book of the Week and won the Popular Medicine Award at the BMA Awards 2017; and *Like a Virgin: How Science Is Redesigning the Rules of Sex* (Oneworld, 2012), shortlisted for the Salon Prize and translated into Italian, Bulgarian and Dutch.

Born in London to an Indian mother who wore only silk saris, and a Caribbean father who loved the natural world, Aarathi was educated in the West Indies and the UK. After completing a PhD in molecular genetics from Imperial College London, she later trained in bioarchaeology. She works as a Senior Research Fellow at the UCL Institute for Global Health, focussed on sustainability and urban health in Kenya, and as part of an international team excavating and analysing ancient DNA from funerary sites in Spain, Rome, and Pompeii.

Celebrating
30 Years of Publishing
in India

SILK

A History in Three Metamorphoses

AARATHI PRASAD

HarperCollins *Publishers* India

First published in Great Britain by William Collins 2023

First published in India by HarperCollins *Publishers* 2023
4th Floor, Tower A, Building No. 10, DLF Cyber City,
DLF Phase II, Gurugram, Haryana – 122002
www.harpercollins.co.in

2 4 6 8 10 9 7 5 3 1

PISBN: 978-93-5699-479-9
EISBN: 978-93-5699-480-5

Typeset in MillerText by Palimpsest Book Production Ltd,
Falkirk, Stirlingshire

Printed and bound at
Thomson Press (India) Ltd

MIX
Paper from responsible sources
FSC® C010615

This book is produced from independently certified FSC® paper to ensure responsible forest management.

Dedication

For my ancestors, women silenced through fates not of their own choosing. For my great-grandmother, the brilliant and beautiful Sundaravalli, daughter of, and mother to, professor men, but denied an education herself; my grandmothers, Ranganayaki, who kept the perfect penmanship she learnt at school until the age of 13, when she was taken out to be married, and Jiriah, born in a mud hut and into a life of penury in the Caribbean, to parents who had been trafficked there as indentured labourers. For my mother, Nalini, who began the spectacular work of breaking our chains. And for my daughter, Tara, who I trust will keep breaking them.

CONTENTS

Introduction 3

Part I – MOTHS

1. The Wondrous Transformation 19
2. Inner Workings 29
3. *Bombyx* 40
4. The Long Road 55
5. Saturniidae 63
6. In Ambon 76
7. Indus 84
8. *Antheraea* 93
9. Muga 105
10. *Attacus* 130
11. The Works of Industry of All Nations 136
12. Wardle 143

Part II – SILKEN SHELLS, GOLDEN ORBS

13. *Coquillages à Soie* 169
14. A Tangle of Threads 176
15. SLKY 189
16. Italo 195
17. Pinnidae 206
18. Upon the Usefulness of the Silk of Spiders 222
19. Araneae 231
20. The House of the Spiders 241
21. *Nephila* 253

Part III – REINVENTION
22. The Khan's Underclothes 271
23. Conscription 277
24. Tombstone 289
25. Mimic Men 301
26. The Silks of Nearly Anything 314
27. Smarter Silk 323

Acknowledgements 335
List of illustrations 339
Index 343

'. . . nature does not limit itself to a few examples, even of its most singular productions.'

– René-Antoine Ferchault de Réaumur, 1711

'On Monday . . . I bestowed dresses of honour on the Afghan Yusufzai chiefs who had accompanied Shah Mansūr; I gave Shah Mansūr a silken robe with rich buttons; presented another with a robe of waved silk, and gave another six persons robes of silk, after which I dismissed them. It was settled that they should never enter the country . . .'

– from the memoirs of Bābur, founder of
the Mughal Empire, 30 May 1619

INTRODUCTION

THE COLLECTIONS AT LONDON'S NATURAL HISTORY MUSEUM CONTAIN three Lepidoptera floors, within which are eighty thousand drawers arranged in long corridors of tall, grey metal cabinets, extending from the floor to the high ceilings. They are kept in low light and clinically regulated temperatures. Lepidoptera, from the Greek for 'scale' and 'winged', is the name of a so-called biological 'order', which is one rank above a 'family' – this one comprising the 133 insect families which include all the world's butterflies and moths. Among them are 157,000 species. The ancestors of these winged insects are now known to have lived alongside early dinosaurs two hundred million years ago; and their fossil caterpillars with the characteristic spinneret – their silk-spinning organ – have been found sealed within 125-million-year-old amber from Lebanon.

Inside those characterless filing cabinets, starkly labelled for their categories and subcategories, are a series of unexpectedly beautiful wooden boxes and cases that contain Lepidoptera specimens going back nearly three hundred years. Some are encased with their ephemera – leaves and stalks of the plants on which they depended – faded labels, a vast variety of stages of their life-cycles and ingenious cocoons constructed by caterpillars using anything from fabrics and twigs to porcupine spines. Many of these specimens are the very first of their types to be catalogued by the celebrated European natural historians of the seventeenth to nineteenth centuries. On the second floor of the museum's Lepidoptera archives, next to a study room with trays of dissected insect genitalia on the workbenches, are a series of cabinets in which I am particularly interested. They contain the moths historically employed in the production of silk.

One specimen of the Chinese silk moth dates to 1758. It is the same one that was examined by Carl Linnaeus, the scientist who made famous the two-name system by which all animals and plants are still classified today. This was *the* 'type specimen', the animal that helped him to determine the fundamental characteristics of every moth of its type; the type he would call '*Bombyx mori*'. It was an insect that had become small, pale and flightless through the generations of selective breeding that set it along a path to complete domestication, and made it synonymous with the production of farmed silk. The first of its two names Linnaeus chose from a Greek root that indicated that this was an animal that produced silk. The second told of the silkworm's favourite food source, which were the leaves of the *Morus* tree – Linnaeus' *Morus alba* – otherwise known as the white mulberry. Both the insect and its food plant had started life in China's northeast, many millennia before, somewhere around the middle reaches of the Yellow River.

The silk of this moth had fascinated me for many years. As a small child I watched the threads it produced being woven into long, narrow fabrics on hand looms in the south of India, intricately interlaced with fine gold wire. I grew up around a mother and many aunts who only wore that fabric on special occasions. On religious festivals, I saw those women dress statues of their gods in silk.

Later, out of curiosity, I bought *Bombyx mori* eggs so I could see for myself how they made those threads. My caterpillars hatched, tiny at first, dark in hue, writhing as a mass in a brown cardboard box I kept by my fireplace. I fed them from a tube of mulberry leaf paste, but whenever I was in a park I'd look for a mulberry tree hoping I could take them fresh leaves as treats. As they grew, I watched as they exuded fine, white, luminous silk that held them securely to the surface of their box; as they fattened; as the dark little larvae developed a bluish-white translucency when they became plump and round. I liked holding them, because they felt soft and rubbery like partially dried glue. They had ten fat little back legs that I knew would be lost when they became moths. They wiggled when they rolled. The transformation they were moving slowly towards would be astonishing.

I read that seventeenth-century anatomists studying insect metamorphosis had cut them open right about now, stunning the scientific world by revealing pre-formed adult parts underneath, so I watched their translucent skin to see if I could spot wings. I imagined taking a scalpel, pressing down until it burst through the buttery softness and peeling away their outsides, but I couldn't do it. Like fat puppies, they sweetly rolled over when I moved them until one morning they stopped writhing, stopped eating and climbed upwards onto the paper tubes I'd left them. There, they started weaving what looked like a random mass of string in every direction. By night this mess of stray pieces formed a scaffolding that held aloft perfectly oval pods. At first, these were like the thinnest of veils through which the caterpillars at work were visible, writhing and turning their heads in slow motion as they worked up successive layers into their precisely shaped cocoons. By morning they were ensconced, and I could no longer see through to locate them. And so I said a final goodbye. They seemed simply to have gone to sleep in cradles of their own making, swaddled in kilometres of pure white silk, packed tightly into a ball with a surface like the moon.

One month later, moths a pallid off-white dissolved the cocoons at one end and slipped out of their chrysalis cases. They measured not much more than two centimetres long, with a wingspan only half a centimetre wider than its length. They were cute, but not beautiful. Their only markings of interest were the sparse dark veining to the wings, which rapidly whirred at times, as if they were about to take flight. In reality, they could not fly to any degree. In their adult form, *Bombyx mori* neither eat nor defecate, nor do they do much at all as moths, except to mate and die.

I have heard it said that scientific study can take away a sense of wonder, because science reduces a miraculous organism into mere mechanical parts. I have never found that to be true. Perhaps I find miracle in mechanisms. But, however I looked at them – these insects, their metamorphosis, their silken threads – all were still *miracula*, true 'objects of wonder'. The facts remained that the fine silk protein strands those caterpillars make from nothing more than a diet of mulberry leaves are somehow extruded from their bodies as threads of extraordinary strength and beauty; that those threads possess remarkable characteristics that science has struggled to replicate. I spoke to engineers and biologists about new experiments being conducted with silk, designed to develop wonderful new applications in medicine and in technology. And yet, all I then really understood of the material was nothing deeper than this: that silk is a precious – and a mysterious – thing. That it possesses unique properties that people have long used to heal and to protect. That it is spun from threads made through the metamorphosis of a silkworm. That both the silkworm and the technology to cultivate it had come from China, and entered all other countries along the Silk Road, once upon a time, though, outside of legends, no one seemed to be sure entirely how.

It was for this reason that I began exploring the cabinets of the museum, and through that search, found myself embarking on a journey in which I learned that there had been a greater, far more nuanced story of silk. Because there in those long, dim corridors, as I pulled the metal shelves forward to inspect the specimens, innumerable long mahogany boxes labelled in elegant cursive scripts began tipping forward. Inside were cocoons spun by the caterpillars of moths that lived some 150 years ago. Their labels, which stated their origins, caught my eye. Some were, of course, from China, of the purest white, and crafted by that most well-known source of silk, *Bombyx mori*. But there were others, too, of which I had had only the vaguest idea. Theirs were cocoons in shades of beige, yellow and brown, in shapes and textures I had not expected to see: elongated, loosely knit, some messy, others rough to the touch. One in particular looked as though it had been crafted from pure gold, as if spun of fine wire into a net of filigree, its colour so astonishingly bright it must have looked quite the same on the day it was placed into the museum's collections.

That golden-hued silk cocoon had not come from China, the handwritten label stated, but from Assam, in India's northeast. Many of the moths too – wonderfully coloured, some enormous – had also originated from various locations in the north or east of India. And then there were yet other silk moths from China, large, and of different hues, and, therefore, clearly not *Bombyx mori*. Alongside those, a larger number still had come from many other countries, from Greece to Iraq, Albania to Madagascar,

Turkey to Mozambique. None of these were domesticated, at least not entirely, as *Bombyx mori* had been.

And yet here these silk-producing insects were, pinned through their abdomens, their cocoons spilling out of boxes, their silk folded neatly into the smoothest of skeins, some wrapped for safekeeping between the pages of Victorian newspapers bearing advertisements for remedies for colic and diarrhoea and cholera.

Beautifully designed damask and embroidered fabrics that had been made from them tumbled out of the pages of a sample book entitled 'WILD SILKS'. I unfolded a handwritten note from one of the boxes. It was crumpled. A rough vertical tear had split it entirely in two. I pieced it back together. It said this:

> *Silk – Cocoons of a silkworm called* Eria *– It is principally reared by the Cacharis on the castor oil plant. About 200 maunds of cocoons are made annually. Of which 1/14th is sent to market and sold at ~~Rs~~ 20/- per maund. The silk is woven by the women of the producers' families. There is no export trade in this article.*
>
> *Paris Exp. 1878*

I did not know exactly what these strange silks, their moths and boxes upon boxes of cocoons had to do with a nineteenth-century exhibition held in Paris. But it quickly became clear that at that time European manufacturers were discovering that there were more silks – ancient silks – than they had imagined, fabrics that had long been in local use in many parts of the world. It opened a new world of biology for its natural historians, as knowledge of their lifecycles and their use was drawn from local peoples, other wonderful varieties of animals that made silk began pouring into the West, animals very different from the famous Chinese moth.

These were collected as marvels to be shown in the imperial exhibitions of the age, alongside other strange and curious things gathered from new colonies Europe had been accumulating across the world. What was more, silks were not just sourced from silk moths, either domesticated or wild, but from other organisms, too. Principal among them was an enormous mollusc that sat, immobile, on the floor of the Mediterranean Sea, from where it was harvested for its meat and its threads; as well as a startling type of spider, reports of which had begun flooding in from Africa, the Pacific and from the Americas. Its silken threads bore truly extraordinary biological properties that meant they would far surpass the strength of that of any other animal.

. . .

Silk has not, of course, been the only fabric we have co-opted from the animal world. And humans are not the only animals to have exploited products made in the bodies or by the efforts of others. Cuckoos usurp nests; wasps lay their eggs inside the bodies of other insects for their own larvae to feed on; parasites can alter the behaviour, and even the sex, of their victims using chemicals; other insects farm fungus and different animals for their own ends, much as we do. But over human history, our use of the natural world has not merely been motivated by our biological needs, but augmented by our cultural ones, from the foods we eat to the clothes we wear – or the fact that we choose to wear clothes at all. In the vast expanse of time between 200,000 to around 12,000 years ago, if we covered our bodies, we would have done so in animal skins, or using foraged plant fibres of bark, grasses, or root fibres. The earliest evidence that humans used more complex, woven materials of our own making dates from the Neolithic, in the period known as the Early Food Producing Era, between around 9,500 and 7,500 years ago, when small, more settled farming and hunting communities emerged. Although it may have begun in that way, farming was not simply about getting enough to eat. Excess food could be stored and traded. That was when another revolution was able to emerge through new uses of animals, and from new kinds of plants, making possible long-lived commodities for trade, like wines and cheese, and new materials for clothes and crafts.

Varieties of flax, for example, probably first cultivated for its edible oily seeds, could be selected by farmers for linen, by breeding the plants that produced greater amounts of fibre, and doing so expressly for the making of fabric. There would also be cotton, the South Asian *Gossypium arboretum* and southern African *Gossypium herbaceum*; *Canabis sativa* for hemp; and *Boehmeria nivea* of the nettle family which produced ramie fibres used in eastern Asia. There was also the selective breeding of animals, particularly sheep, that had longer and woollier hairs, for the manufacture of textiles. It was in the Neolithic that *Bombyx mori* was made too. The capacity to do this implies the peoples who produced plants and animals for clothing had more land, and more resources than they would have needed simply to feed their families and communities, more space to grow flax or cotton or mulberry trees. Crafting any of those fibres into textiles also required women who had enough time to dedicate to weaving. Crafting cloth was intensive work, highly skilled labour which needed to be learned. In return for that space, and time and skill, these plant and animal threads opened routes with the potential to transform economies, that took smaller scale Neolithic societies towards urbanism, towards growing trade networks. These products were commodities through which wealth could be accumulated, transported, and because of their value, monopolised, by emerging elites. Social and economic identity and status – even military hierarchies were built on these early cloths. Among the ruins of the Bronze Age Minoan settlement of Akrotiri, on the Greek island of Santorini, destroyed by a volcanic eruption around 1700 century BCE, are two frescos illustrating the clothed versus the unclothed in battle scenes. They bear silent witness to a military – and cultural – defeat by elegantly dressed soldiers of the naked opponents who drown in the sea, or are killed in battle wearing only roughly shorn animal pelts. Or as Mark Twain reputedly wrote, 'Clothes make the man. Naked people have little or no influence on society'.

But fabrics have hierarchies too. Some in particular were, for many millennia, to clothe the few, those with greater means. It is no surprise that these were the fabrics whose passive threads could be woven to bear a mystical air of perhaps not having been created by any ordinary means, or those with the magical splendour of finer, ethereal cloths that took more skill to fashion, or that were harder to acquire. Fine cotton with its lightness of weave, and asbestos, which could be cleansed in fire, had been two of these, which were very expensive. But above all others, no fabric had the lustre or mystery of silk, nor incited global movements on the unprecedented scale this cloth inspired. In trade, as it was for gems and spices, even small amounts of it produced large profits.

In the early Chinese empires, silk was the most precious of all textiles. It could be exchanged for other items of high value, used as tributes and bounties, and supplemented coins and metals as currency. Sometimes, governments would use it to pay armies. In general, it would be their major item of trade in the markets at the country's frontiers. But its value went beyond the financial. Silk was imbued with as many forms as the metamorphosing insect that had created it, and as much power. It was offered up during seasonal sacrifices. It was an object of spirituality, transformation, ritual. Of beauty, and of protection. 'How naked its external form, yet it continually transforms like a spirit', wrote the third century BCE philosopher Master Xun of the *Bombyx mori* silkworm. 'Its achievement covers the world, for it has created ornament for myriad generations. Ritual ceremonies and musical performances are completed through it; noble and humble are distinguished with it. Young and old rely on it; for with it alone can one survive.' These were the realms of the silkworm and its silk, for this was a cloth at the heart of economy, and of society.

. . .

When I first started thinking about silk, I had imagined only the silk of *Bombyx mori*, a silk with one source, one story, one path. It had intrigued me that its silk was probably the only material that has lived so long, remained in continuous use, that has been invented and reinvented. Here was an ancient material with a surprisingly technological future; a substance made by an insect to protect it from predators and disease; that, once in human hands, became a material for the most luxurious of clothing, and that was now being trialled for ingenious applications, in medicine, technology and as a sustainable material to help mitigate the planetary catastrophe we now face. But what quickly became clear to me was that the knowledge and use of silk, in all its wonderful varieties, is a global story. Quite naturally, people everywhere had watched and studied their world in different ways, and engaged with it to their benefit. Where there was an animal that made silk, those threads were used in interesting ways. But it is not always easy to find, in equal measure, the voices of all people, so that we might understand their knowledge of, and the history of their relationship with, silk. We have European colonial writings on their discoveries, and the correspondences of western men of science that allude to local peoples and their practices at the time at which those records were made. There are few records from the local, or indeed, women's, perspective left to piece together. Many indigenous women and men who informed the study of silk-producing animals in various ways remain nameless.

Accepting those limitations – finding, and retelling, the global knowledge of the cultivation of silk – is to complete the story of a material of which only a part is generally told. But it is also to widen the common lens through which we view the development of modern science, which itself collected learnings from all over the world, and not always in ways that brought mutual benefit. I wanted to get to know the naturalists who travelled the world in pursuit of new knowledge, to understand what drove their obsessions – for such was their passion – and to paint a picture of the landscape of the history and context in which this was done. It was not always an easy history to research or write; it is, in places, replete with injustices of the worst kinds. I have tried to reflect both passions and prejudice. As a biologist, it has been the bewildering ingenuity of the silk-producing animals that has given me the greatest pleasure and sense of wonder. But the biology and ecology of the animals that make silk, and the distinct, extraordinary properties that wild silks have are also of vital importance to its future applications, because understanding variety, and, through it, working out local solutions to the technological and environmental challenges we face, has never been more vital.

Because there is not just one silk, there is not just one story of silk. Not one road, one people who found it, nor who made it. Not one country can lay claim to its source. In silk is science and history, mythologies and futures. Through accounts of the scientists who have studied silks, and the animals from which they have been drawn, what follows are stories of its three metamorphoses: caterpillar to moth; cocoon to commodity; and simple protein chains to threads with very extraordinary capabilities.

PART ONE

MOTHS

'. . . the earliest allusion to the mulberry and silk met with in the ancient writings of the Chinese is in the *Historical Classic*, a work which existed before the days of Confucius, because it is quoted by him . . . we have the allusions referred to recorded in the section called the tribute of Yû, who flourished 2,200 years before Christ. In his days the mulberry is spoken of as a well-known production, and silk obtained therefrom; so that it must have been discovered before his days. The usual tradition is that it was discovered during the reign of Hwângté (B.C. 2640), by his queen.'

– Tseu-kwang-k'he, *Nung Cheng Ch'ilan Shu/Complete Treatise on Agriculture*, 1640

1

THE WONDROUS TRANSFORMATION

IT WAS 1699, ON A THURSDAY IN THE SECOND WEEK OF THE COLDEST February Amsterdam had experienced for five or six years. At the periphery of the town's narrow houses mounds of snow congealed. A thin ice covered its canals. On that day, two months before drawing up her will, 52-year-old Maria Sibylla Merian advertised for sale a large number of her most beloved possessions. Among them: an artistic and curious work produced on the highest quality vellum pages, decorated with images of rare herbs, flowers and fruits, accompanied by observations on 'bloodless small creatures'. One hundred etched copperplates. A catalogue of flowers, coloured and complete with botanical descriptions of the plants it contained. Several hundred further pages painted with flora of the East and West Indies. A singular crocodile, snake, iguana, or small turtle sourced from those new colonies; and a variety of animals she had collected in Germany, Friesland and Holland over forty long years.

Here were works exquisitely etched, drawn, coloured or preserved by Merian, assisted by her daughters Johanna Helena, by then 32, and

Dorothea Maria, ten years Johanna's junior. Advertised in a local Dutch newspaper, the *Amsterdamsche Courant*, the announcement itself was an investment of almost two guldens, one-third, maybe, of a master artisan's weekly earnings. On top of that, Merian had to pay for the care of her younger daughter, who was still unmarried, and the rent for a share of a house that was also her studio, only recently built near Amsterdam's newly dug canals, just south of the centre of the growing city.

Merian had to be in Amsterdam. The city brought merchants from all over the world. In it were shops selling exotica, carried on ships travelling in from Asia, Africa and South America loaded with wares. More than Paris, more than London, that was where those who loved art enough, and were wealthy enough to collect it, came. For a woman who for years had worked in isolation on the metamorphosis of the silk moth, it was also a good place to find natural scientists, and it was a good place for a natural scientist to be.

Merian was the eighth child of a stained-glass designer-turned-engraver whose forebears were sawyers and timber merchants in Basel, but who was born in Frankfurt in 1647. It was a city then enclosed within two formidable walls and fairy-tale towers topped with battlements, though none of these had averted its sacking at the hands of the Swedish Empire less than twenty years before her birth. In more peaceful times, it was known for its half-timbered houses built upon bases of red sandstone, the very first Jewish ghetto, and fairs that drew traders of books and spices, grain and fish, horses and silk. Merian's father had relocated to Frankfurt having perfected a precision in drawing images in reverse, a skill much needed in topographical engraving. He had become famous for these maps and town and city views, but also fashioned illustrations for books he published on medicine, science and technology, alchemy, the military, works of unorthodox theology and volumes of the accounts of Europe's recent voyages of discovery to the Americas, Africa and Asia. His were among images of the world that would influence the European perception of other cultures until well into the eighteenth century: savage violence meted out by native peoples against innocent colonists as well as against their own fantastical beasts tormenting the rivers of exotic lands; 'Indians' plagued by the devil; African chiefs wearing Amerindian feathered skirts; and the tyrannies of the Spanish Catholics feeding slain Amerindian women and children to their dogs.

But in the years approaching 1650 Merian's father had been suffering from an illness that would soon take his life. By the time his grave was dug in his adopted city, his young daughter was only 3 years old. A little over a year later, her mother married another artist, this time a painter and art dealer, trained by one of Germany's best contemporary artists in the portrayal of still-lifes, birds and flowers. It was he who taught Merian watercolour techniques, how to grind pigments, to prepare canvases and vellum, to colour prints, layer by intricate layer. She absorbed all this while her half-brothers, who had taken over her late father's printing house, taught her the skills he could no longer pass on: the mastery of engraving, etching and the making of prints.

It was this fortunate intersection of education and talent that meant that, by the age of 28, Merian was publishing her own engravings: plates of a book of flowers that would run into three volumes over the next years, books she used to teach drawing to women who were noble or else wealthy, as well as her skills in the embroidery and painting of silk fabric. At 38 Merian took condign umbrage against her husband and moved her family to Friesland, a province in the far north of the Netherlands. There they joined a religious community of staunch disciples of Jean de Labadie, the founder of Labadism, a pietist sect, the son of a soldier of fortune who had taken a musket shot to the arm, a rapier to the face and an elevation to petty nobility, which had added the prefix 'de' to the family name.

Before his birth in February 1610 Jean had caused his mother pain so intense his father feared for her life; as a baby he was expected to live no more than a month; as a child his growth was so stunted that he was once mistaken for a waif and dressed in red so he could be seen among the grass and flowers. At school he faced warring gangs of boys who concealed weapons under their gowns or else favoured the welcome of new students with extortion or a severe thrashing. In the years before Jean started formal schooling, two such students had even been executed for murder. Somehow his military father still hoped Jean would aspire to a similar career. Perhaps not surprisingly, he instead showed an early penchant for all things pietistic and spiritual. In the hands of his god and in defiance of his midwife and the best efforts of his fellow students, de Labadie managed to live until the ripe old age of 64. When he died in 1674, his legacy included the community in which Merian would live for the next six years of her life. Housed in the stately home of three aristocrat sisters, it was one largely kept solvent by the donations of its patrician or monied members. And yet it eschewed pride and worldly vanities, expected personal, mystical prayer and utter devotion, was based upon an absolute equality between the sexes and required the sharing of personal wealth with the brother and sisterhood of the commune.

To fulfil the latter, Merian had handed over a collection of her drawings of flowers. The King of Denmark bought fifty of her works and had them hung above his staircase at Rosenborg Castle in Copenhagen. Dispensing with these flower paintings had required no great sacrifice, divine or otherwise. Painting them had increasingly become a pursuit for which she cared little. Almost from the moment she had arrived in Friesland she had instead sought out caterpillars in the surrounding countryside, to collect and breed, to add to the body of work in which her real passion lay. Merian's interest was not in the flowers, so sought after, that had paid her way. It was in the natural history of insects, and specifically in their metamorphoses.

The precedence of taking on floral works that more easily earned her an income meant that the interval between the start of her entomological diary, a study book she began in 1660 when she was 13, until the time she would publish her first insect studies, had been extraordinarily long. Having 'retreated from the company of people and engaged in this study', she was finally able to produce two volumes in her thirties, each one with fifty plates engraved and etched to form the verbosely named *The Wondrous Transformation and Particular Food Plants of Caterpillars*. Merian was a methodical woman with an innate curiosity. Each book contained years of repeated observations, detailed studies or time-consuming breeding. By invitation or by paying a fee she was also able to study dead insects in the cabinets of curiosities of collectors of naturalia, of anatomists and physicians, missionaries and merchants, of producers of luxury fabrics woven of the silk of metamorphosing insects, and other researchers on the metamorphosis of caterpillars. But there was only so much those animals in bottles or pinned through the abdomen onto stiff card could reveal to those collectors; she debated with those men based upon her own observations made of insects while they lived. It was why, of all of these naturalists, Merian had been the person able to depict the transformation of these animals in their entirety. By the end her caterpillar volumes catalogued her study of nearly two hundred complete metamorphic cycles. It showed moths and butterflies, their caterpillar larvae, the plants on which they depended for food and protection, whether these were flowering, or fruiting, how they supported egg to caterpillar, cocoon to pupa,

pupa to emerged adult in flight, or at rest. She had made sure she had seen how they lived, behaved and died.

Within those descriptions would come the detail of their 'astonishing changes', during which she 'kept them all in boxes, and showing them to anyone wishing to see them', their life histories: how, where, and at what point in the year they developed; their segments, claws, hairs; when they were active or at rest; how they fed; their legs, eyes, wings, feelers; and their markings, features and patterns of colour for males and females where she could. These animals delighted her. Of the legion insects she raised or observed, she wrote of how she 'could not marvel enough' at their 'beautiful shadings and contrasting colours' that she had often used in her paintings.

'But after I discovered the transformation of the caterpillar some years later . . . it seemed a very long time until the beautiful [moth] came forth. Thus, when I did obtain it, I was filled with such great joy and was so pleased . . . that I can hardly describe it.' Although by the time her caterpillar books were published she had studied and drawn many insects, at the head of all of these Merian had placed the silkworm.

'Most esteemed reader and lover of the arts', her *Wondrous Transformation* began, 'while I have always endeavoured to adorn my flower paintings with caterpillars . . . and small creatures of that kind . . . I have also often taken the trouble to collect them; until eventually, by observing the silkworm, I became aware of the caterpillar's changes and began thinking about them, and whether that very same kind of transformation might occur in others as well. Since then, after diligent and painstaking investigation, I concluded that their manner and type of change is nearly identical; the difference is that silkworms spin useful filaments while . . . others spin themselves up like a silkworm and produce exactly the same kind of capsules encased in silk, although not as strong as that of the silkworm.'

By then, her extensive observations had shown her that the metamorphosis of the silkworm easily exemplified the metamorphoses of similar insects. By using the already 'familiar so-called silkworm . . .' she felt, 'almost all the transformations and changes of . . . caterpillars . . . will be more readily understood'. It was why 'I made this noble transformation myself as copperplate No. 1 for my first caterpillar book and described it in the greatest detail (without mentioning its fine uses . . . but as a model for instruction).' But it had been these fine uses – the production of Frankfurt's silk by these 'noblest' caterpillars 'that almost everyone knows' – that had made it so easy for Merian to record the silkworm's metamorphosis from the start. She was able to observe the cultivation of silkworms because of the 'people who keep large numbers of them', including through her own stepfather's brother, who was said to have worked in the city's silk industry.

If the publication of the book itself had taken decades and no small sacrifice, setting down the beginnings of the silkworm, as Merian recorded it, would have required no small amount of courage. Silkworms, she wrote, 'like all caterpillars, as long as the adult insects have mated beforehand, emerge from their eggs, which have the appearance of tiny millet seeds'. It was a statement quite at odds with the ideas of many men of science, including some of her contemporaries, who were quite willing to concede that insects might equally have arisen from inanimate matter, mud or decaying flesh. That was based upon an idea with ancient roots that would prove extraordinarily persistent; two hundred years after Merian's works, a contemporary of Charles Darwin would even be arrested for heresy for suggesting that they had not. But time and time again she had seen that their formation was not spontaneous, and she drew what she observed. 'One can soon tell whether something useful will come forth from [the eggs], . . . nothing will come from any that are collapsed, or crushed, or appear like empty husks, for they are spoiled. Now . . . they should be kept in a . . . warm [place] . . . Then the little worms, which chew their way out when ready, crawl out of the aforementioned dots.'

Having chewed through the remnants of their eggs, these little worms emerged like thin squiggles, just a few millimetres long. Treated 'very gently, because they are so delicate', the tiny larvae ate through the softest, young mulberry leaves – their preferred food – steadily growing, then, four times, pushing 'off their skin completely . . . just as a person removes a shirt over his head'. In each stage the caterpillar would raise its ever-larger head to the sky as if praying, but in which it was really just waiting, immobile, for its progressively tightening and drying skins to split and release what had formed underneath. Through it all it would have exuded fine, white, luminous silk, otherworldly threads also stuck fast to the copious green-mulberry leaf pellets of excrement turned black through the passage of the gut. From these cycles, the repeated moultings of shed outsides and new growth, it would emerge not just larger, but softer and paler each time. Finally, at about two inches long and the weight of four lumps of sugar, it adopted a bluish-white translucency, with ten back legs that would be lost when it became a moth.

When the time came, around a month after they had hatched, the caterpillars would stop moving, stop eating and climb to a suitable space to spin: on 'small branches from trees, or a little paper house like a cone'. 'Its colour, ordinarily white, is becoming yellowish, shrunken, and swinging its head back and forth and somewhat transparent because it is preparing to spin its cocoon. It spins very busily and remains hard at work until it completes its entire cocoon', and within twenty-four hours becomes entirely ensconced into a silken 'oblong . . . white, yellow, or greenish envelope'. 'After completion of this, it becomes a date seed [pupa] in order to change into a moth.'

This pupa wrapped so neatly inside its cocoon Merian carefully cut out; just as she had described it, the immobilized, transforming caterpillar resembled the reddish-brown seed of a date. It was out of these pupae that the adult form emerges around a month later, moths a dull white in hue that vomit up a fluid that dissolves one end of their cocoon to allow them to emerge. They slip from their bindings, and as they go, discharge a reddish-brown waste liquid that will stain its cocoon long after the moth departs.

These moths are small: including their wingspan, around two centimetres wide and tall. 'When it has come forth, it needs half a day to get clear, dry wings, or its finished form. It has only six legs, two brown [antennae], two small brown eyes, and four white wings . . . The male is more delicate and smaller than the female, which has a fatter body, the male a thinner one.' These females are so enlarged because they carry up to five hundred eggs. In their final adult forms, all that is left for both male and female moths is to mate, lay new eggs and die.

The transformation of the *Bombyx mori* silkworm, made by Merian as copperplate No.1 of her first caterpillar book.

If in the seventeenth century the silkworm had been known to almost everyone it was because, by then, Europe had been its home for just over a thousand years. It would take another hundred years or so after Merian published her caterpillar books, until the Swedish taxonomist Carl Linnaeus and his followers used her depictions of the natural world to name at least one hundred species. Merian had never separated the insects she studied from the plants upon which they depended, plants which would come to define them. Linnaeus himself would give the silkworm she had observed in Frankfurt the scientific name *Bombyx mori*. *Bombyx*, denoting that this was an insect of the family of moths called Bombycidae; and *mori*, honouring, as Merian habitually had for the species she recorded, that this caterpillar's natural food source were the leaves of *Morus*, the mulberry tree. The industry that centred around the silk of *Bombyx mori* brought wealth to western Europe: to the fairs of Frankfurt, and to its great producers, France and Italy. But it had not just put the metamorphosis of this particular insect at the heart of European trade. The fact that it was bred for so long in homes and factories specifically for its silken cocoons had made this caterpillar so docile and prevalent and immobile that it would also quite seamlessly become the focus of intense scientific study. And so, while over long years Merian bred and observed caterpillars by eye or magnifying glass to capture how insects developed through mysterious transformations, other scientists began more intimate studies under new microscopes, flaying open their bodies, stage by stage, as the first attempts were made to dispel these mysteries entirely. To figure out what exactly was happening inside the caterpillars and their silken cocoons that allowed them to change so entirely beyond recognition, these worm-like larvae that somehow transformed into moths with whirring wings.

2

INNER WORKINGS

MARCELLO MALPIGHI WAS BORN IN 1628, SOME TWENTY YEARS BEFORE and five hundred miles south of Merian. It was the year of the publication of William Harvey's *De motu cordis*, in which Harvey, who was 'Physician Extraordinary' to King James I of England, took a fresh stab at describing the circulation of blood, dispelled the long-held idea that it was continually formed anew from digested food, and demonstrated that the primary function of the heart was not in fact the production of heat. In the meantime, King James himself had been busy appointing a silkworm adviser-in-chief and a keeper of the king's mulberry gardens. He had planted four acres of mulberry trees near the site of the future Buckingham Palace, and had himself penned a preface to a silk-worm book in which he offered magnanimous and friendly encouragement to the landed gentry to plant yet more 'food of the wormes . . . that they may be nourished and maintained'.

While James prescribed ten thousand mulberry trees for each county of England, his queen, Anne of Denmark, sat for a stony-faced portrait grandly outfitted in an elaborate grey silk dress of the late Elizabethan age, its mutton-leg sleeves fully embroidered with wriggling silkworms of gold and silver thread biting at mulberry leaves. She had commissioned an up-and-coming architect named Inigo Jones to design for her an elegant silkworm house two storeys high, with oval and arched windows, a frieze and a large west window with the queen's coat of arms beautifully painted in glass.

To these monarchs, bringing silkworm cultivation to England was a 'question of so great and public utility to come to our kingdome and subjects in general . . .' that they were quite 'content that our private benefit shall give way to the publique', for 'such a work can have no other private end in us, but the desire of the welfare of our people.' It was an ambition which had seen huge success in France, which England sought to emulate. But in Jacobean England it would ultimately abjectly fail, just as it would in the king's new colony of Jamestown, Virginia; though there, the mulberry was superseded by tobacco, that other lucrative leaf which would be even more enthusiastically adopted in England and its colonies.

But Marcello Malpighi had the good fortune to be born neither in the England nor the America of the Elizabethans, but to a family of landowners in Italy, in the small town of Crevalcore, northwest of Bologna, which some say had been hit by a meteorite some thirty years before. Whether or not that was the case, Marcello's future fame as his town's most eminent citizen was by any reckoning a meteoric rise of his own. One of nine siblings, he had been required to abandon his studies to assume their care when both his parents met an untimely death. Despite this setback, the grief at the death of his wife just a year after their marriage, a disastrous fire in his house that destroyed manuscripts and equipment, and having suffered ill health for much of his life, Malpighi had somehow managed to go from a boy raised on the family farm to probably the most extraordinarily productive and the most luminous anatomist of his time.

It would be Malpighi who would complete William Harvey's missing link on the circulation of blood to the lungs, which he did by dissecting frogs, dogs and the oblong lung of a tortoise. He was the first to lay his keen eyes on the capillaries and alveoli of the lungs; to find significant new structures in the kidney, spleen, liver and brain, among other organs; to see red blood cells under a microscope; to attribute the colour of blood to them; and to conduct the first microscopic studies of the development of the chicken embryo and the anatomy of plants. As a doctor, he would also be issued a personal invitation to become physician to Pope Innocent XII – a high honour he tried to refuse, but was compelled to accept. As a result of this forced transfer from Bologna, Malpighi arrived in Rome with a bitterness unassuaged either by the reward of a status equivalent of the clerical Monsignor, or an elevation to the upper echelons of the Patriciate Roll of Rome. Despite his innumerable achievements and his prescience in thought – or perhaps because of both of these things – Malpighi's work was routinely attacked with a curious mixture of suspicion, opposition and no small amount of professional jealousy. The suspicion arose because he thought independently, which is to say that, just as Merian had, Malpighi observed, recorded and recast old ideas, presenting different results from the highly respected but scientifically outdated scientists and physicians of ancient and classical times. And the criticisms would be levelled towards his scientific approach, because few could then see how the new microscopic detail of organs and tissues might have any utility for improving the medical treatments of the day.

Malpighi, meanwhile, was undeterred. 'Nature in order to carry out the marvellous operations . . . in animals and plants has been pleased to construct their organized bodies with a very large number of machines', he wrote, 'which are necessarily made up of extremely minute parts so shaped and situated as to form a marvellous organ, the structure and composition of which are usually invisible to the naked eye without the aid of the microscope . . .' He continued to push at the limits of what was known, or taken for granted. As for the bitter disputes, these would become something of an ongoing occupational hazard, with origins that were occasionally not even professional in nature at all. Once, in an altercation in 1659, Malpighi's brother made the grave error of fatally stabbing an opponent who happened to be the eldest son of another scientist. Perhaps they were less susceptible to acts of physical violence, because these lettered men wielded the pen as a weapon, albeit one more devastating than the sword. It was engaged to great effect in the family feud that ensued, with the wronged scientist committing to a savage, lifelong criticism of Malpighi's works as the hostilities smouldered on.

In the meantime, one small reprieve to his angst came in 1669, in the form of his honorary election to the ranks of the esteemed Royal Society of London, a standing he would share with Isaac Newton, Giovanni Domenico Cassini and Christopher Wren, and one which raised him to international scientific fame. It had also made him the first Italian among their number (Cassini being elected in 1672) and one whose methods and studies resonated perfectly with the Society's motto, *Nullius in verba* ('Take nobody's word for it'). Although the insect books of 'that curious person Madame Maria Sibylla Merian . . . in great forwardness, and highly approved of by all who see it' were advertised in the Royal Society's journals, that motto was a call to men – for the

Society admitted only men – who were curious about the workings of the world to test their ideas, to do the experiment, discover the facts: in short, to not take anyone's word for it. Among this group, Malpighi's work was much admired, as expressed in their letters inviting him to send them his manuscripts of research. 'To no one . . . observing the structure of the human body does Nature seem to have revealed her secrets as fully as to her beloved Malpighi' their secretary once wrote, 'so too our Royal Society embraces no one with greater affection'.

Once submitted, most of his anatomical studies would go on to be published in their journals, recorded for posterity. Over the next decades he published prolifically. And then, on 19 November 1694, aged 67 and still not released from the personal service of his pope, Marcello Malpighi suffered an apoplectic fit and died. His end had come as he feverishly worked to finish a further series of manuscripts that he realized he would never be able to complete. Having anticipated such an eventuality, Malpighi had the forethought to bequeath these unfinished works to the Royal Society with the specific intention that they should be completed and published, but only after his death. Three years after his remains were laid to rest at the church of Santi Gregorio e Siro in Bologna, this last work finally emerged. It was called *Opera posthuma*, and it was even more forthright, more polemical, than the works he had been criticized for in life. Within it, Malpighi had not neglected to include a particularly long and bitter letter of response, a last rebuke to the criticisms levelled at him by the scientist father of the man his brother had dispatched nearly four decades before. It had been his only recourse to retaliation; a revenge served very, very cold. But Malpighi had always been a man of astonishing patience. To look into organs and tissues and see their finest detail had required long hours spent in deep concentration over a single magnifying lens, or bent over the eyepiece of that compound microscope Galileo had developed in 1609, but which Malpighi would become one of the first to use for biological studies some fifty years later.

In 1667, he had decided to take on a request from the Royal Society to work on entire organisms far, far smaller than those he had reported on before. If, as their letters of adulation implied, nature had revealed her secrets more fully to Malpighi than to others, they would have known well it was because of the pain he was willing to endure in peering into her most inaccessible parts. It was also why he would give the scientific world the first systematic dissection of any insect. That insect would be *Bombyx mori*, and Malpighi would work for an entire year taking it apart. What the Royal Society had asked of him was permission to continue their correspondence, to have more of what Malpighi could give them, but this time, particularly where his studies might concern 'plants, or minerals, or animals and insects, especially the silkworm and its productions . . .' such questions needed to be revisited; received wisdom said that insects had no internal structures apart from the gut. The Society had made the mistake of posting that letter to Messina, Sicily, where he had held a short posting as Professor of Medicine, but it eventually found its way to him in Bologna. By this time, he had already begun some small-scale studies of silkworms, which were among the 'animals whose parts are made with such skill and such wonderful minuteness that they escape the senses and the dull understanding of my mind'. Though the metamorphosis of the silkworm may have been captured in beautiful detail by Merian seven years earlier, the minute changes to its insides – which was Malpighi's interest – were still a mystery. *Bombyx mori* had arrived in his country some five hundred years earlier. Italy had become the largest producer of European silk;

Bologna, he said, abounded with them. His reply signed off with a promise that he would work on the study of their anatomy in early spring. In Italy that would be March, April and May, in the months just preceding the hatching of the tiny silkworms from their millet-seed eggs.

On 18 February 1668, almost exactly one year later, Malpighi's new communication on the silkworm was read at the Royal Society. 'The silkworm . . . is the most well-known insect among our countrymen', it began, much as Merian had, '. . . in which so wonderful Metamorphoses happens, and the work of nature so shines forth, that it is necessary to consider the unique aspects of its life'. In order to do so on a microscopic level, in *De Bombyce* he had described not only the silkworm but had placed it alongside other animals, to attempt to compare their bodies in as fine detail as his microscope would allow. There were locusts, butterflies, stag beetles, crickets, bees, wasps, and even a slug. All in, the final document amounted to forty-eight drawings with almost sixty thousand words of text. Only two of these drawings dedicated themselves to depicting the whole, perhaps living insect: one, a silkworm caterpillar, and the other, a male moth, both long familiar in form.

Like Merian's study, it had begun with the eggs and hatching of these caterpillars, observed their changes of colour; then proceeded 'to the growth of the young worm, the various trials in feeding it with diverse other leaves but those of mulberry, their sickness . . . the casting of their skins' and 'an account of the production, structure, food, growth, sicknesses, workmanship, changes, generation, and death of the silk-worm'. But in Marcello's study the Royal Society would also discover an 'anatomical description of all, even the minuter parts of that insect and the varieties of them in the several changes it undergoes'. Through the microscope, *De Bombyce* had pictured this caterpillar outside and in, from the fine hairs that cover its body to the organs, glands, tangles of convoluted tubes hidden inside, cut out and arranged to demonstrate their inner workings. As the Royal Society must have hoped, the real novelty of Malpighi's work had come in the form of illustrations of the insides of a body never before seen, internal parts out of the context of their bodies, the intimate structure of the viscera, all shown in detail that was unprecedented. If Merian had brought the stages, changes and behaviours of a metamorphosing insect together to show the whole, Malpighi had taken that insect and sliced it into the sum to its parts. Doing that had been 'extremely tiring and laborious', he wrote, 'because of the novelty, minuteness, fragility and entanglement of the parts'. But the difficulties had not come from those things alone. The peculiarities of working with insects and their parts not more than a few centimetres long, of being the first to work with structures so small, had 'therefore made it necessary to develop entirely new methods' before he had even begun. He had 'pursued this exacting work for many months without respite'. But because of it, by the autumn, Malpighi found himself with eyes that were inflamed and fevers that would not abate.

In his writing of *De Bombyce*, Malpighi did not disclose how he had carried out his work in miniature – an oversight, perhaps, but one that made his remarkable dissection somewhat mysterious. Still, his first cut to the silkworm might well have been after pinning its head and tail down, drawing a sharp blade through its body as if making a straight cut through a long cake, allowing the eye to see, in the section, the map of the layers of the organs and systems therein.

Malpighi's anatomical studies had already looked closely at the systems of circulation of blood and of oxygen in different bodies. There, in his silkworm at its largest, most mature stage, the first thing that would have drawn his eye may have been a long tube running the length of the back. In life, this would have carried blood flowing forward towards the head and backwards through the body cavity, circulating throughout the cavities and appendages, transporting nutrients and removing waste products as it flowed, filling most of the space not occupied by the internal organs, and pumped by a heart pulsating rhythmically with a frequency that slowed as the caterpillar matured and dropped before each moult. It stopped in extremely high or low temperatures, and fluctuated with movements.

In the silkworm's anatomy, Malpighi's study would describe the shape and size of its nine distinguishable segments, the nine spiracles, small holes through which it breathes; its head, eyes, the teeth that cut by a sideways motion, rather than up and down; the hairs of its body, its legs and claws and their posture and motion when it spins a cocoon. He described a new, rosy-coloured skin under the old skin to be shed, how the wings are already in place – though out of sight in the growing silkworm, 'latitant under the second and third [segment] of the worm', before even it begins weaving its cocoon; the muscles, vessels, the caterpillar's nervous system, which in his observations connected to no brain at all.

That fact that he illustrated no brain, and his suggestion that 'the heart, which reaches from the head to the tail, being of a strange figure and rather many hearts, than one . . .' – that there were a number of hearts inside the silkworm that simply were not there – would prove glaring faults in his otherwise intriguing body design. In his pursuit of fine detail, he responded simply that there had not been space on the page to feature a brain. As for the many hearts, perhaps he thought this was the case because once its heart had stopped beating, the dead caterpillar could no longer tell its dissector that the steady wave of contraction he must have seen pulse, almost beat – as it progressed from the back to the front of the silkworm – was merely its one living heart filling with blood. Remaining were the silkworm's digestive and excretory systems, composed of plumbing he identified that would later carry his name: the Malpighian tubules, which branch off from the silkworm's intestinal tract carrying water and waste.

The one thing Marcello had not had to discover was the source of the animal's silk, because the pair of tubular silk glands running the length of the worm were large enough, and long enough, to have already been located around seventy years before. This was a tube, after all, not unlike a salivary gland, that stretched to ten times the length of its caterpillar, fully grown, and that accounted for half its weight. But his microscope helped him see its detail with more clarity than anyone had before, closer to understanding that two of its three regions were replete with territories specialized for the massive secretion of silk proteins, that, after a cocoon had been spun, self-destructs. Sketched out in his book were the hidden mechanics behind the production of silk, a 'woof of vessels containing the Silky juice in the sides of the Belly about the Ventricle', those convoluted tube-like glands that turned forwards and backwards, ascending and descending through a caterpillar's elongated form. Just one part of the stunning difference between the insides of the larval and adult forms of a creature that had long been remarkable for the changes it underwent on the outside, and for what it was able to produce. His lengthy introduction to *De Bombyce* had opened by laying out in detail the history of *Bombyx* silk, and its economic importance – a consideration which would not have escaped the notice of the Royal Society, so named because by then it had been granted a royal charter by King Charles II, successor but one to King James I. Marcello pandered to such economic concerns in words, as scientists are wont to, but with his own inflamed eyes set firmly, and solely, on its biology.

His wonder at finally taking apart the viscera and peering inside the diminutive caterpillar must have been indescribable. But it was inevitable that the entry point into the study of the metamorphosis of all animals would be this domesticated silkworm. It was abundant. It could not fly. It was kept only because of the desire for the silk that emerged from inside its convoluted glands; threads it made solely for the purpose of its transformation. It was there to be observed by those who cared to study it. And so, from the sixteenth century, *Bombyx mori* would become a fortuitous model for an unanticipated amount of European scientific discovery – microbiology, immunology, physiology, zoology, evolution and genetics – at a time when enormous paradigm changes were also taking place towards new understandings of biology, and, as Merian would come to invent through her obsession with the lifecycles of her caterpillars, an entirely new study of ecology, the intimate relationships between ecosystems in the natural world. At that time, the metamorphosis of silkworms was a prodigious mystery. In some ways, it still is.

3

BOMBYX

Around four hundred million years ago, soil-dwelling insects evolved in the earth's shallow, warm and oxygen-starved swamps. These forebears did not undergo metamorphosis. Back in the era of giant insects, around three hundred million years ago, in a period called the Permian, around 90 per cent of all insect species perished in what has come to be known as the 'Great Dying'. While that most severe of all known mass extinctions of insects happened around them, some of those insect ancestors evolved into the only invertebrates to have powered flight with wings. This allowed them to hover, to feed, to mate. To glide with wings outstretched. To close their wings when at rest. Flight demanded power, steering, control of speed. It demanded stabilizing the body angle, keeping steady. Not pitching. It required working with forces well in excess of what they would have been subject to had they been like an aerofoil, a fixed wing of an aeroplane. It saw them develop a variety of mechanisms to generate vortices, accelerating air over these wings and shedding them as the air moved down, below and behind them as they flew. All that required well-developed muscles and seamlessly adapted wings.

With this innovation, these insects were the first of all animals to take to the air. They would own the skies for over a hundred million years until the pterosaurs appeared in the Late Triassic. Within the first one hundred million years of their origin, winged insects had acquired the features that would allow them to live in almost every habitat on earth. Small in size, their ability to fly provided a means to avoid being caught by predators, to move rapidly between areas in which they might find food and to spread as widely as they could across geographies. The varying forms of the wings of different pterygote insects were probably determined primarily by aerodynamics, to reduce drag on the body. But other factors, those that were dictated by their environments – their ecology – would also push for such variety: whether they fly fast or slow; the predators they have; or whether there is a need for camouflage.

Moths and butterflies have exquisite wings. They belong to an order of insects known as Lepidoptera – so called because of the *lepís*, the 'scales' like flat plates that clothe their *pterón*, 'wings', and which are responsible for their colours. They are ancient: the oldest Lepidoptera appeared at least two hundred million years ago. In the wild, all have the capacity for rapid flight. That is why the bases of their wings are broad, compared to the narrow wing bases of slow-flying insects like damselflies.

But despite its sheer beauty and wondrous advantages, flight also posed problems as it began, specifically to the development of the wing, which, in these diminutive pterygotes, needed to be as light as possible. The strategy of incomplete metamorphosis was seemingly first adopted in order to solve problems that came with developing wings that were both delicate and efficient. And it was from this partial transformation that complete metamorphosis followed. Now, instead of starting as small external winglets made ever lighter by killing cells off, for silkworm caterpillars wings began forming inside their bodies, at first unable to move, but later morphing into articulated wings as larva finally moulted into moth, wrapped as a pupa, mummy-like in its cocoon. And so it was the evolution of flight that ushered in the metamorphosis that would provoke from humans such wonder, delight and discovery, and that initiated the journey of insects like silkworms towards their triumphant, total transformations. The success that came with complete metamorphosis continues still. Over two hundred million years later, holometabolous insects are the most diverse. It is they that account for up to 60 per cent of all living organisms.

The population explosion enjoyed by insects that became able to most drastically shapeshift was helped along by the very fact they were able to produce more than one form. Before, a young insect that looks and behaves just like its adult form was a potential competitor with their own adults for food. But instead, with complete metamorphosis, all growth would happen in a new larval form, completely separating the resources needed for growth from those needed for reproduction. Because if an animal were to decouple the abilities, needs and development of its young from later airborne adult forms, to so enhance differences between its life stages, then voracious caterpillars could occupy a different niche in the environment. There, they would be well fed, protected and at no time in direct competition with their adults. As for young of the insects like silk moths, whose larval form would look entirely transformed when it came to be an adult, tucking away the beginnings of their wings inside the worm-shaped bodies of their young would allow them to burrow for safety, as some wild silkworms do, or to live inside fruit and other sources of food without detection.

This is not to say that there were no disadvantages to complete metamorphosis. Lying immobile in the transformation stage directly between larva and adult, metamorphosis came at the cost of great vulnerability to predators, parasites and pathogens. During pupal life, *Bombyx mori* pupae are immobilized inside their silken cocoons. Some other wild silkworms, the larvae of fleas, caddisflies, and some bees, wasps and ants, construct underground cells, cementing soil particles around them, or chambers of wood fragments or leaves, or even the spikes of porcupines glued together around their bodies to form an impenetrable case. The silk that makes that case is not just made of the proteins that form the silken threads, but also substances that seem to be able to destroy the proteins of microbes that might damage it and harm the development of the insect as it metamorphoses. But specific changes also happen inside, in the developing insect's immune system as they lie still. Now, the immunity of the pupae strengthens to protect them from infections over weeks and months. Even the tiny microbiota that live in their gut – important in their own right for resisting infection – change as they transform from caterpillar to moth.

In an animal that morphs so dramatically from young to adult forms, the question of how exactly this metamorphosis evolved – of what came first, caterpillar or moth – is still a contentious one. It seems likely that an adult form with mouthparts which was itself able to feed on plants preceded the voracious, wriggling larvae, meaning that, rather than beautifully winged adults, it was the caterpillars that were the real innovation. Here were remarkable organisms able to produce liquid proteins inside vast and convoluted tubular silk glands; to pull them into a chain through an internal press, have them rapidly dry into luminous threads when exposed to air. That the threads of *Bombyx mori* were so coveted, so fine, had been because of another long road in their evolution, this time engineered by farmers who lived somewhere around China's Yellow River, sometime in the Neolithic, between 7,500 and 5,000 years ago.

Due south of the lower reaches of the Huang He – the Yellow River – lies Henan province, situated on a central plain in a landlocked region, around six hundred kilometres from the Yellow Sea. It is a temperate land with torrential summer downpours that inundate its soft soil, tinted a dark brownish yellow by the rich minerals of riverine silt that gave the waters their name and the surrounding land its abundant fertility. From the sandy soil of the Yellow River basin grow apples and jujube fruit, pears and walnuts, chestnuts and black fungi, a highly prized green tea, and the watermelon first cultivated in the rich silt of another great river five thousand years ago. Just as in Egypt the Nile nurtured formidable cities and cultures, at around the same time the Huang He would become the mother of Chinese civilization, and Henan's well-watered lands the heartland of many splendours designed by the people who would live there: exquisite jade carvings, the tri-coloured glazed pottery of the T'ang Dynasty, Chan Buddhism and the Shaolin temple, perched upon a rocky peak in the foothills of the Song mountain range. But before all that, the ancient peoples of Henan had begun crafting the genes of a small brown moth until it became pale, pallid and flightless, with larvae that were fed on the tender leaves of the white mulberry that would see them, in time, produce a silk beyond compare.

Just east of the great river's Luo tributary, thirty kilometres due north of Mount Song lie the remains of an ancient city, at a site known as Shuanghuaishu. South of the village of the same name, it sits on a plateau raised above rugged, scrubby cliff sides. The view from that tableland is now interrupted by a major highway. But beyond that, the expansive flat, green arable fields still meet the yellow silt of the wide river, much as they might have when the settlement was first built. This Shuanghuaishu is said to have been an ancient capital, dating to 3,500 years ago. Over time, it would extend to more than a million square metres, and was set within three layers of defensive moat-like walls. It was a city that boasted well-planned rows of residences, potters' workshops, networks of roads and ritual sites, as well as three large, remarkably orderly cemeteries. In them were the skeletons of its former residents, still laid neatly in much the same positions in which they would have been when their bodies were lowered into their graves. As the many terracotta pots and remains of its people and animals surfaced during the city's excavations, another curious object also slowly emerged from beneath its yellow soil.

This was a carving that portrayed a silkworm, beautifully wrought, neatly segmented, and at around six and a half centimetres, close to what would have been such a caterpillar's fullest length. Its head was raised, possibly capturing the moment it moulted that final time, or at the point it would have secreted silk thread to build its cocoon. It was not the first such artefact to be found. By the time the excavation of Shuanghuaishu began in 2013, ornamental silkworms cast in gilt bronze or carved from jade had already been recovered from graves in the region. None were quite as old as this, but nevertheless some dated back three millennia. The use of jade in that part of China was already five thousand years old by then, first crafted, as it was, by a people who also lived around the upper-to-middle course of the Yellow River. Often, jade was carved into chisels, axes and other simple tools, but also into ornaments, of which many are in the shape of the larvae of insects. Some were cast as chimeras, with the head of a dragon and a caterpillar's body. Those who made them must have keenly observed the transformations of animals, but also venerated their metamorphoses from larva to mature adult. Because, over millennia, such silkworms crafted of stone or metal would continue to be buried with the dead, perhaps with a prayer that death was merely a kind of sleep within which we might transform, from whose bindings we, too, might escape.

This Shuanghuaishu silkworm, however, was remarkable, because it was made from neither jade nor metal, but carved from a ten-millimetre sliver of the tusk of a boar. Dated to around five thousand years ago, it was the oldest such object yet found. The hand that made it would have belonged to someone who lived during the final days of a Neolithic society that has come to be known as the Yangshao culture. They lived at a time of climatic optimum; that is to say, these were people who had the great good fortune of enjoying their rivers and their lands just before a prolonged period of oscillations of painfully cold and arid episodes. Before that, before their steady decline as the environment deteriorated, theirs were populations that remained sparse, static and largely in good health.

They fished and hunted deer and small mammals, brewed beer of barley and rice and millet, grew wild peas and tubers; kept sheep and goats, pigs, chickens and dogs. But half of their diets came from agriculture, from the millets of different varieties they farmed. In their settlements, storage pits for the grains they harvested were ubiquitous, suggesting that although by then millet had already been domesticated for a millennium and a half, and the people of the Yangshao culture were not the first farmers in that fertile region, it was during their period that agriculture intensified, with traces of increased cultivation found at nearly every settled site in the region. What has also become evident is that their cultivation was restricted neither to crops nor the usual variety of farm animals. Because at around the same time these were the people who would take the first steps along the long road that culminated in the complete domestication of a silkworm.

Exactly which silkworm was portrayed by the hands of the carver of that boar tusk is not clear. Though it was a carving that resembled the caterpillar of the domesticated silkworm of *Bombyx mori*, that would be a remarkable fact given its extreme age. But from the lands around ancient Henan, fabrics of silk themselves have also been found, in funeral urns that contained the dead. These include a fragment found around the skull of a child placed there nearly 5,500 years ago; the remnants of woven silk fabric reported just southwest of Shanghai, dating to a thousand years later; and remains from Qianshanyang, another Liangzu Neolithic site in the Zhejiang province of southern China a thousand years after that. Only one of these has been confirmed as the silk of *Bombyx mori*, woven in a tabby weave, and dating to between 2650 and 2850 BCE.

Although there are now more than a thousand strains of *Bombyx mori* kept across the world, and this caterpillar is the the creator of the vast majority of silk used today, not only was modern *Bombyx mori* not the only silkworm known to the Neolithic people of China – but for some part of the two thousand years during which the early Yangshao culture thrived it would not even have existed at all.

Other silk moths were most certainly present. In 1926, Chinese field archaeologists were working at Xiyin Cun, another Yangshao culture site around two hundred kilometres west of Shuanghuaishu, when they unearthed a small object, semi-oval in shape, hollow and slightly crushed at one end. It was found to be half of a silken cocoon that had been neatly – that is, artificially – cut in two by a sharp object. The other half was nowhere to be found. At first it was reported to be a cocoon of *Bombyx mori*, and excitedly declared to be evidence of the deepest antiquity of China's production of silk of the domesticated silkworm. That find dated to 3500 BCE, around 5,500 thousand years ago. But then its silk was analysed, and it was found instead to have been the creation of another silk moth, this one a wild species also native to China. White with tiny black flecks, its caterpillar closely resembles the form of *Bombyx mori*. This was a silkworm that also fed on the leaves of the white mulberry, that can also wrap its pupa in threads of white silk. The scientific name it would be given was *Rondotia menciana*. In Shanxi, the place where its ancient cocoon must have fallen and become buried 5,500 years ago, its silk moth now no longer exists.

. . .

In 1758, when that 'prince of botanists' Carl Linnaeus had finished figuring out the origins of, and relationships between, the animal groups at his disposal, he named them accordingly and set them out in the tenth edition of his great work known as *Systema Naturæ*, or the 'System of nature through the three kingdoms of nature, according to classes, orders, genera and species, with characters, differences, synonyms, places'. Linnaeus had formed around one hundred of these classifications using Maria Sibylla Merian's studies, forty years after her death. Others would have come from collections, and the exotic samples sent by his group of 'apostles', a team of his students trained and dispersed to the distant lands Europeans were fast occupying, and where many would perish under burning fevers of tropical diseases of which they knew little. Among the samples Linnaeus would acquire from their efforts were plants, animals and insects brought from North and South America and Japan; from India and Indonesia, from Linnaean apostles assigned as surgeons to the Swedish East India Company and the Dutch East India Company; from Turkey, Syria, Egypt, Libya, Tunisia, Senegal, South Africa and Sierra Leone. All of these would be brought into Linnaeus' earlier hierarchical rankings of other natural things, of which he had already named nearly eleven thousand plants.

'The knowledge of the self', Linnaeus wrote, 'is the first step towards wisdom . . . A man surely cannot be said to have attained this self-knowledge unless he has at least made himself acquainted with his origin'. In this edition of *Systema Naturæ*, he would also firmly apply that now familiar system of a first and second Latin name to categorize his collection of known animals. Not without controversy, among them he included humans, with varieties of 'European white', 'American reddish', 'Asian tawny' and 'African black' under the grouping 'Homo', of which he himself was the so-called 'type' – *the* specimen that has exemplified our animal since. Linnaeus would apply the same concept to the origin of insects. 'Men, and all animals, increase and multiply in such a manner, that, however few at first, their numbers are continually and gradually increasing. If we trace them backwards, from a greater to a lesser number, we at length arrive at one pair . . . Such numberless swarms of armed insects fly about the earth, that their species are more numerous than all the ground produces. These, in their infancy, are disguised in the form of caterpillars, in which state each has its proper plant assigned it, which it is appointed to inhabit and feed upon . . .'

Among the more than eighty groupings of insects Linnaeus came to classify, he had included the moths of the Lepidoptera. Stacked below them was a family he called *Bombycidae*. It was a name which may have come from the Latin writers of classical Rome – *bombycinae* was one of the terms by which they referred to silk – or else Linnaeus might have taken inspiration from the word *bombykia*, used in ancient Greece to describe cocoons made by silkworms that were unravelled for their threads. Either way, the family was named for the fact that its insects produced silk that was used in the making of fabrics. Principal among these, then, was the only insect to be entirely domesticated by humans, that which was, in Linnaeus' world, most famously co-opted for human use from a wild, ancestral moth.

In China, its silk must already have been in use by the time it began being farmed – it is hard to see quite why a silkworm would have become domesticated if the technologies to create the world's finest silk fabrics had not already begun to be developed. Such an ancestral silkworm would have fed on the leaves of the white mulberry, because this plant, too, was bred and cultivated so that its branches became low-lying, allowing farmers to more easily harvest the insects' cocoons, and so that the leaves became even more highly nutritious for the silkworms. It was because this mulberry was the 'proper plant assigned it' that Linnaeus assigned this silk moth the scientific name *Bombyx mori*.

But the silkworm that was first domesticated, some of whose offspring would eventually become this *Bombyx mori*, does not appear to be the one whose cleanly-severed cocoon was recovered from under that ancient settlement just north of Henan. Though that *Rondotia menciana* of Shanxi, with its ochreous-yellow wings that silently develop inside its white, speckled caterpillars, is a close genetic relative, the most likely origin of *Bombyx mori* seems to have been a different moth: one smaller, darker, whose twig-like caterpillars were masters of camouflage and preferred living solitary lives. The transition of this insect, which was a Chinese variant of a wild moth found across Asia, in Korea and Japan, from northern and southern China to the far eastern regions of Russia and to India's foothills of the Himalayas, was initiated around 7,500 years ago. Known as *Bombyx mandarina* Moore, it is one of the eight species of Linnaeus' *Bombyx* regarded as 'true silk moths'. The threads of its cocoons are of a fine-quality silk, thinner than that of its wild relatives, and both lighter and stronger than the silk fibres that would come to be from the cocoons of *Bombyx mori*.

Genetic studies suggest that the stages of this millennia-long breeding of the wild species that brought it to domestication were completed sometime between 4,100 and 5,000 years ago. Historical records from that point, taken from the accounts of the Shang Dynasty, corroborate this later date, with four-thousand-year-old silk remnants emerging from the banks of the Yellow River in Shanxi province. But older findings of silk also exist, and continue to be found: five-thousand-year-old silk fibres, fabrics and ribbons from Zhejiang, southeast of Henan; silk fabrics found in Henan province dating to five to six thousand years ago; spinning tools, silk fibres and fabrics, and an ivory mug with images of silkworm caterpillars from along the area around the lower Yangtze River. What is unclear is what stage of domestication such artefacts represent: the wild silk of *Bombyx mandarina*, or *Bombyx mori*, in any of the intermediate stages along the changes that occurred as it took shape. But it does appear that silk of some stage of domesticated moths was being created as long as five thousand years ago, and that the domestication that would create *Bombyx mori* quite neatly coincides with the husbandry of other livestock during the Neolithic agricultural revolutions that were taking place around the world in the preceding millennia.

That domestication of animals and plants – including the plants that such animals were dependent upon – was one of the most extraordinary and important transitions in human history. More than fifteen thousand years ago, ancient hunter-gatherers developed long-lasting relationships with the wolves which would one day become our dogs, domestications that may not have always been deliberate, but that slowly, over millennia, would come to include many animals, farmed and familiar: the horse, cattle; and the sheep, goats, pigs, and the chickens found at Shuanghuaishu that slowly changed through repeated inbreeding and outbreeding with wild ancestors. Guided by the materials that could be produced from them, the sheep that were predominantly hairy ten thousand years ago became woollier when they started being bred two thousand years later. Like *Bombyx mandarina* Moore and the threads of its silken cocoons, the animals and plants chosen for domestication must have already been valued, already used for what they were able to produce or provide. On balance, domestication would make them all more useful, more docile with humans, less aggressive with others of their own kind, or better at doing, making or providing more of what we wanted: meat, milk, clothing, transport, affable companions at the sides of herders and hunters.

Domestication led to the cocoon shell of *Bombyx mori* becoming ten times heavier than that of *Bombyx mandarina*, creating a silken thread that would reach up to a kilometre or more from a single cocoon. It enriched the genes that increased quantities of the *fibroin* protein from which silk threads are crafted, and the *sericin* cement that makes up a third of the silk, enveloping fibroin fibres with successive sticky layers, to bind its threads and form the cocoon. This increased the more scant, less reliable amounts made from the wild *mandarina* moth in the forests of northern China and across the countries of its wider habitat, where before it would have taken much labour to gather it from the wild.

This genetic engineering, started by Neolithic Chinese farmers, and the technology that would be developed by their descendants, made the new silk not just easier to control and harvest but to spin and to dye into vibrant colours, and so increased its usefulness, its beauty and its value to humans. The silkworm's domestication also created a supply of by-products and waste products that could now be readily obtained at different stages of silkworm rearing: eggs, larvae, pupae – and faeces, used in traditional medicines, in dyes, fertilizers, and flavouring; and, as for the pupae, eaten for its protein.

Domestication also made the caterpillars easier to rear. While *Bombyx mandarina* caterpillars naturally moved from place to place in search of the mulberry leaves on which they needed to feed, the domesticated young, provided with steady supplies of food by human hands, became more inactive, making no attempt to escape. The solitary caterpillars of the wild moth that feed by night and remain motionless for long periods, stretching taut the front part of their bodies during the daytime to expertly mimic twigs, became *Bombyx mori* larvae that wave their heads liberally and wriggle happily in close proximity to others. It was a change that made it easy to rear large numbers of them in restricted spaces, in which they no longer needed to protect themselves from being spotted by wild predators. *Bombyx mori* adults cannot fly, though males flap their wings when they sense the presence of a female, while *Bombyx mandarina* adults, both male and female, had strong wings for flight, coloured in shades of a nutmeg-brown which camouflaged them against predators. On the way to becoming domesticated for human use, captive *mandarina* moths lost their colour camouflage, any fear of predators and humans, and, with only vestigial wings remaining, the ability to fly. The *mori* became less able to perceive odours in its environment. It became sluggish, clumsy and blind. Changed from mulberry pest to peon, it became incapable of surviving in nature. It is easy to manipulate, requires assistance even to reproduce and is now completely dependent on humans for its own survival.

No one knows for certain whether the domestication of this ancestral moth took place at more than one ancient site , or where precisely in China the process was begun. What is certain is that by China's Bronze Age, nearly four thousand years ago, the domestication that led to *Bombyx mori* had become highly developed, and the weaving of its silk was already of an impressive quality, with high thread counts, untwisted threads of cross-warps and crepe still evident in the weaves of the fabrics they produced when they were uncovered from the Bronze Age Shang site of Taixicun, in the North China Plain of western China. But it would not be until after the sixth century CE, that is, more than five thousand years after people in the lands around the Yellow River transformed the *mandarina* into the *mori*, that this insect would reach the lands far to their west.

If this silkworm had found its way to Europe, eventually into the studio of Merian and onto the dissecting table of Malpighi, it could only have been because it had been carried there from China. What route that took, how and in whose hands those blind and docile caterpillars might have arrived is shrouded in layers of tales almost as convoluted as the pair of tubular silk glands Malpighi unfurled; no less tangled than the copious threads that would be extracted from its precious cocoons.

4

THE LONG ROAD

AN OVAL OCEAN OF SAND EXTENDS IN ALL DIRECTIONS FROM THE heart of the Tarim Basin. It is pushed and pulled by wind and water, and settles at over a thousand metres high. Layer upon layer, it has coalesced into one of the largest sand seas in the world, a terrifyingly inhospitable expanse surrounded by immense mountain ranges. Below it lie the sharp peaks of China's Kunlun Shan and Altun Shan; above, the heavenly Tian Shan; and, to its west, the snow-covered Pamirs, that knot of mountains fortressing Central Asia from South Asia, and South Asia from East Asia. India lies to its south, the lush Ferghana Valley of Uzbekistan, Tajikistan and Kyrgyzstan to its north and China to its east. For the journey of *Bombyx mori* from its Chinese birthplace in the country's northeast, this position is significant. It was this region, its oases, now vanished under the mighty ridges of desert sands, daunting even to the bravest of camels, that seems to have been the first place outside China where the *mori*'s eggs would have been warmed and watched by careful women until they hatched into blind caterpillars. It was here that white mulberry trees were planted so that the young insects might eat until they became large enough to wrap themselves in their secretions of silk and where these cocoons would be gathered up and unravelled to produce fine fabrics. Many peoples would settle there. By the first century BCE, it was along the routes west into the Gobi and Taklamakan deserts of the Tarim Basin that China built garrison towns, resettling farmers from their former range in the heartlands around Henan, farmers who would have long been privy to the secrets of the domesticated silkworm.

Along the southern rim of the Taklamakan Desert, not far from the town of Niya, the remains of a cocoon of *Bombyx mori* were uncovered at a site that had been home to a thriving community between the first and fourth centuries CE. Close by, a curious, ghostly orchard emerged from the dunes. In it were the desiccated trunks of no longer living white mulberry trees, perhaps four metres tall, stripped by the aridity that afflicted Niya's once thriving farms and vineyards formerly irrigated by meltwater from mountain glaciers. Its river courses and deltas were plagued by desertification when the Tarim River abandoned its original course, leaving the region uninhabitable. But in that green oasis belt also once stood Loulan and Karadong.

Loulan, as the Chinese called it, or Kroraina, by its local name, began life around 300 BCE, flourished during the first and fourth centuries CE and disappeared completely around 600 CE. Its many dwellings, administrative buildings and rubbish dumps, and its burial grounds, were all abandoned to the encroaching sands. But the aridity of the desert also meant its ruins had kept its treasures safe, so that they were almost perfectly preserved when they were rediscovered around a millennium and a half later. There were fragments of carpets, still impressively coloured, and even the stiffened bodies, still clothed, of its beautiful-faced dead. Dating from the second century BCE onwards, under its sands were also found textile fragments, worn-out and discarded clothing and burial garments still largely intact. These were made of wool, plant fibres, leather and fur, and there were also silk textiles of plain and patterned weaves, richly coloured. There were, too, bolts of plain-woven yellow silk, perhaps collected as tax, that could not be carried away by the excisemen because of their bulk. Just over a hundred kilometres west of Niya lay Karadong, the site of a large fortification and substantial houses built of poplar wood. It stood just north along what remains of the Keriya River on the route across the Taklamakan. It was a site at which bared mulberry trunks were also found, as well as recovered fabrics woven with the silk of *Bombyx mori*, specimens that date from the third century CE until about a hundred years later.

Though desolate today, the Tarim Basin – encompassing an area around the size of modern Egypt – had once been the site of nearly forty city states. Among these were major trading posts, vital for merchants of various origins to rest before resuming their journeys to all points of the compass. In the early centuries CE, major trading routes between China and the West would approach and depart the river oases of this desert basin across long distances. They could be found along the upper Indus and what is now Afghanistan; down, past the Hindu Kush towards India, over the Indian Ocean, and then across the Red Sea towards the Mediterranean Rim. Many migrants settled there, too, from China, but also India, and people from the areas around what is now Uzbekistan, to the north, and Afghanistan, to the west. Some of the silks found around the Tarim Basin would have been those that continued to be imported from the east, those smoothest of silks made by the dextrous hands of Chinese experts, who by then had been creating it for around three thousand years. Those have been found in the Tarim, and also in other lands that neighboured China, from steppe burials in what is now Russia, dating to the fifth to third centuries BCE.

But the fragments of silk fabric were evidently not from China, or at least were not crafted as if they were. These were irregular, formed from discontinuous threads, and at the time Karadong's textiles were abandoned were probably quite newly made in the settlements along the Keriya River. The cultivation of silkworms and the processing of their threads may only have been learned by the people who lived and worked at those crossroads relatively recently, but the differences in the quality of the silk first made outside China may not have been that marked because it was a newly adopted technology in those lands. Nor would it have been that the new silk makers lacked the skill, though they will have had more limited experience with raising the insect, and with working its long, fine threads. Instead, the silk cocoons cultivated in their new home seem to have given rise to broken threads, rather than the single long strand that emerges from the caterpillars' immense tubular glands. That continuous strand secreted by the silkworm to wrap around itself could only have remained intact in one particular circumstance – if the moth being moulded inside the pupa was never allowed to emerge from its protective cocoon. The stifling or heating of the pupal stage of the domesticated silk moth so that it could not break apart the cocoon had been an age-old Chinese innovation; that, and the use of an alkali to strip the silk's fibroin protein of its gummy sericin glue, was what had given the fabrics they created their coruscant, fluid-like gloss. It was also what made the silk more able to take, and hold, the dyes whose colours were still apparent after nearly two millennia under the desert sands.

The people of Karadong, it seemed, had not adopted any one of these innovations in particular. Instead of killing the pupae inside their silken cocoon, the moths would have been allowed to emerge and live their short adult lives in which they might have mated and produced new eggs, some of which would hatch into caterpillars and continue the production of silk. That silk, however, would be damaged as the moth pushed its way free. And broken silk meant that woven textiles in which those tiny breaks and reconnections of the thread would be perceptible interruptions of what could easily have become a seamless cloth. Perhaps this was thought more beautiful; perhaps it produced the cashmere-like texture already more familiar to them. But it is also not unlikely that the preservation of the silkworm's metamorphosis was a decision taken, perhaps enforced, because of the creed of its state rulers. The towns uncovered from the Tarim's sands all included Buddhist stupas and relics. Karadong itself had been home to two Buddhist shrines, among the oldest discovered outside India, just to its south, where Buddhism was born, and from where its core principle of not harming living things – including the silkworm – was spread.

In among the vicissitudes of the fortunes of empires, of trade deals and conquests, the silkworm may then have passed from Central Asia just west to the Kushans, whose empire encompassed northern India in the first to third centuries CE. Then moving to Mesopotamia, spanning what is now Iraq and Syria by the fifth century, at the moment at which long-distance trade began to flourish through the Achaemenian Empire, which stretched from Turkey to India, and from Central Asia to Egypt. Along went the silkworm to Sasanian Iran, whose lands stretched west from Afghanistan across to the Mediterranean coast, covered large parts of Egypt and ran somewhat diagonally through Turkey, and nearly all the way to Istanbul, then called Constantinople, which was the capital of the Byzantine, or Eastern Roman, Empire.

The people of Sasania may have long been content with the plentiful import of bales of silk cloths, still accessible from their eastern neighbours, rather than breeding *Bombyx mori* themselves – because the silkworm itself reached Iran rather later than its silk, starting, it seems, in the sixth century, up along the borders of the Caspian Sea. Four hundred years later, it had spread across most of the regions of the Iranian Plateau, with the tiny eggs of *Bombyx mori* still being taken there, even then, from Merv – at one time the world's largest city, in what is now Turkmenistan – a majestic place with palaces and pavilions, gardens and ice houses that was famous for watermelons, chilled drinking water, its soft cottons and its fine silks. At one time it contained perhaps a dozen great libraries consulted by astronomers and mathematicians and doctors, and, no doubt, its natural historians interested in small insects, because translations of Aristotle's most famous works would have, in all likelihood, been housed there, too. And it may also have been from that great city's silkworm stocks that in the mid-sixth century trading Christian missionaries from the church in Central Asia acquired what would become Europe's first *Bombyx mori* eggs. These, it is said, the monks brought to Constantinople, and with these tiny seeds the technology needed to initiate a silk industry in Europe went west, too.

Come the seventh century, the Islamic Empire would see the establishment of silkworm rearing across North Africa and all the way to Spain, which, later, in 1530, the conquistadors would take to Mexico. At around the same time, in the sixteenth century, in the hands of the Ottoman Empire, the silkworm would spread widely: across Turkey, Cyprus, Greece and Bulgaria. The first documented attempt at growing the white mulberry in Europe was in

Tuscany in 1434, although silkworms seem already to have reached Sicily via the Arabs some five hundred years before that, in the tenth or eleventh centuries. Not until the thirteenth century would the breeding of silkworms be established in Malpighi's Bologna, at roughly the same time as it also began, if more modestly, in France. Over the next two centuries France's production scaled up impressively, piquing the interest across the English Channel of King James I of England. He would attempt to take silk production to his new colonies in North America, but would have little, if any, success in either the New World or the Old.

And so it is that the many silken fragments pulled from the sands around the Tarim Basin tell the story of at least one of the paths that would take *Bombyx mori* out into the world, from its eastern origin, towards the countries to its west. The peoples of that region set it on a route from the north of China that would make this silk worm the only insect to ever be truly domesticated, and the first to be dissected, eight thousand kilometres away and 4,500 years later, in the north of Italy. By then the breeding of this insect had already long been established further east, taken with skilled people who migrated from China to the Korean Peninsula by the second century BCE. And at around the time that the oases of the Tarim Basin traded and thrived, in the third century CE, the cultivation and care of the silkworm had also been taught to China's nomadic neighbours, when silkworms and the white mulberry tree were gifted to peoples in the eastern Eurasian Steppe to their northeast, around what is today Mongolia.

But this *Bombyx* created by the human hand was not the only insect to make such a silk, nor was its silk the only cloth from an insect to have been used in the ancient world. Across the globe were other animals creating other tantalizing threads. When the time came for Europe's western nations to take up arms and seize territory, the size of which would finally surpass the Mongols' – along with enslaved peoples and sugar, gold and diamonds, tea and tobacco – they would also spark a search for types of silks that, until then, they had known absolutely nothing about.

5

SATURNIIDAE

IF THE YEAR 1699 HAD OPENED WITH SOME UNCERTAINTY FOR MARIA Sibylla Merian, summer would come like a balm to the brain of the bored entomologist. By June, Amsterdam's skies had cleared to blue, the air warmed as best it could and in place of her fine images of the flowers and insects of Holland and Friesland were now two passages on a ship departing for the New World. Through those pleasant days and mild evenings, Merian, with her daughter Dorothea, prepared the accoutrements two women needed to live and work over the next years. Their studies would now be made under the weight of a wet, overpowering heat they had never before experienced. Many were the travellers who had set out on similar journeys but never arrived; even more who had arrived and were never to return. Some were lost at sea, others to parasites that could not be seen or fevers that would not abate. From the perilousness of such an adventure, they would be protected only by Merian's freshly drawn-up will and the most earnest prayers of both women.

Their adventure over some sixty days and seven thousand kilometres had a singular aim. After four decades of study in the western European lands, Merian had already produced copious observations on those insects that populated the places with which she was familiar. Early on, that work had also included the migrant Chinese caterpillar that had so lucratively wrapped itself in silk. Now, something else attracted her eye. In Holland, in her city that welcomed ships from across the globe, she had been 'astounded to see what lovely creatures were brought back from the East and West Indies . . .' These had been kept in the collections of mercantile and scientific men, and those other types who speculated in the hope of gaining the spoils, and destroying the souls, of distant lands. Many had brought insectile trophies home. Of them all, Merian felt particularly honoured 'of being able to see the precious collection of the Most Honourable Mr Nicolaes Witsen, Burgomaster of the city of Amsterdam and Administrator of the East India Company . . .' Witsen's reach was extensive. He was a statesman and a patron of the arts. Like Merian, he had collected natural objects since his youth. Unlike Merian, he was a man, and one who had been admitted as a Fellow of London's Royal Society of esteemed scientists, which gave voice to his interests, and brought recognition and support – without requiring him to sell his possessions. But in one sense the study of the animals he collected had a glaring flaw. Like all the other 'countless insects' at which Merian marvelled, those in Witsen's grand collections were generally quite dead before they had even been loaded onto a merchant ship or into a frigate's hold. That fact did nothing to further her research, because as much as she was able to admire them in that state, 'their origin and reproduction were lacking, that is, how they transform themselves from caterpillars . . .' It was this omission which inspired Merian '. . . to take a long and costly journey, and sail to

Suriname in America (a hot and wet country, from where these gentlemen received these insects) in order to . . . carry out more accurate observations'.

. . .

With her luggage readied, her younger child and a magnifying glass close at hand, Merian departed over the slick, white-capped waves of Amsterdam's harbour on that busy seaway out of the Dutch Republic. Their journey took them first to the wind-bound sea channels of the island of Texel, past the Isle of Wight, the storm-worn point of Portland from whose glowing stones London's St Paul's Cathedral was still being built, and out of the English Channel into the treacherous, sloping swells of the Bay of Biscay. After a week or so, they would have rounded towards the rock-bound Cape Finisterre with its deep-blue coloured sea swallows – storm birds that skimmed the horizon and foretold impending tempests. A brief respite at the Canary Islands refreshed the ship with supplies and vegetables. That was followed pleasantly by the temperate relief of the tropical and trade winds that blew east, and with it, the delightful sporting of dolphins and dorados that followed in the wake of vessels. After that, the weather would become increasingly warm, a portent for Merian that, not at all as she had intended, she would later find herself 'obliged to come home earlier than I thought . . . since the climate in that country is very hot, and the heat did not agree with me'.

But the end of this particular voyage was in sight. Now, Merian's ship had only to yaw past the guano-covered black tops of the Constable Islands that emerged like cliffs from the waters; and then round Devil's Island, whose perilous currents and treacherous rocks demanded a considerable diversion for the sake of sparing seafarers' lives. But already, from there, Merian's eye would almost have been able to pick out the coast of South America.

For their new settlements, ships like the one upon which Merian had sailed brought items that plantation houses needed to make the rainforest feel more like home: fabrics and utensils, furniture, glass and china plates. Hams, preserved vegetables and livestock: pigs, sheep, ducks, geese, fowls and turkeys. Medicines, though probably of little use in the tropical New World. Wine and port and cider to at least restore the spirits. Fresh supplies of the tools and such materials of which Fort Zeelandia had been built: cobblestones, bricks and nails. Despite the unrelenting heat of Paramaribo, a place one well-travelled Englishman once avowed that he would 'not willingly incur the responsibility of sending a friend, or even an enemy – unless he happened to be a mortal one . . .' Livestock fattened on the flat, temperate wealds and wolds of the Dutch countryside would also be sent to graze new pastures carved out of swamp forests and the lands that flanked the great Amazon.

Still, after the discomforts of so much time spent below deck, Paramaribo's heat also brought the fragrances of the land; of lemons and limes, oranges and grapefruit that wafted from the expanding plantations now lining the banks of the Suriname River, intoxicating smells in the warm, humid air. As for the town itself, Paramaribo was laid out by the Dutch in the kind of neat order that the snaking vines and the weeds and creatures of the tropics perpetually sought to disrupt. Despite the profligate industry the colonizers forced on its people, Suriname's nature still held some liberty. Luxurious greenery encircled the town with woody and heady perfumes, and within the forest lived parrots and the crocodile-like tegu lizard, scorpions, brightly hued lizards, enormous spiders and strange toads, armadillos, snakes, armies of ants, and new insects about whose metamorphoses European science knew nothing at all.

This was what Merian had been looking for. In Paramaribo, she, Dorothea and one or two servants moved into a small house in a district not far from Fort Zeelandia. Through its unglazed windows to the rear she could look upon her garden, with trees and crops, medicinal herbs and spices that she drew in all the varieties she saw. There, what caterpillars she found she observed and recorded as religiously as she had the insects she had discovered in Europe. Like those around the garden's *Battattes*, the sweet potato she had never before seen but which the locals 'prepared like the beetroot', and 'also stewed with meat', upon which she observed the metamorphosis of 'a lovely golden beetle'. 'A tree that grows as tall as an apple tree in Germany . . . called by the Indians after its fruit Guaiaves' – the guava. On it, Merian 'found many of these large caterpillars . . . and fed them with its leaves'.

'They are white with black stripes and have on each side fifty shiny red beads. Mr Leeuwenhoek thinks that they are eyes. Until now I have been unable to confirm that they are eyes. Because then, in my view, they should be able to discover their food from behind and from the side, which I have so far not been able to establish, and they are never covered with an eye membrane. When they are fully grown, they make a large grey cocoon . . . and then they turn into pupae, as I saw happen on 20 October 1699, from which on 22 January such white moths emerged, adorned with black stripes . . .'

Then there was a tree that produced a fruit 'called Banana in America. It is used like an apple and has a pleasant taste, just as apples have in Holland. They taste nice both cooked and raw. When they are still unripe, they are light green. The ripe ones are lemony yellow inside and outside. They have a thick peel like lemons. They hang in bunches . . . The bunch is as large as a man can carry . . . On this tree I found this light green caterpillar, which I fed with its leaves until . . . it shed its skin, became a pupa, and . . . changed into such a beautiful moth.'

Through her magnifying glass, Merian looked closely at the males and females for each specimen, and at each of their stages of growth. She observed the wings, antennae, the form and coverings of the legs, the patterns of colours that adorned them, 'the dust on the wings' that 'appear like fish scales', or 'like roof tiles lying in a very orderly and regular manner'; and the copious hairs of the moths, the 'translucent glassy butterflies with scales'. In this way, having exhausted what might be found close to their Paramaribo home, she and Dorothea would begin visiting the sumptuous plantations nearby, with their beautiful gardens overflowing with even more new and wondrous fruit, all fed by the Suriname River.

The Dutch established plantations to grow coffee, cotton and cocoa and enslaved local people, plus a few thousand others brought from Africa, to work them. In the years that followed, Suriname's enslaved gained tortures in the place of reward, treatment that was notorious even by the standards of the time. The profits for their masters were immense. From Paramaribo alone, some 16,000 barrels of sugar, 12,000,000 of coffee, 750,000 of cotton and 600,000 of cocoa were loaded onto ships heading back to Europe. Entire economies now depended on humans bought or captured and the children born of them.

If there was any point in comparing the brutalities inflicted on peoples whose liberty or lands had already been lost, then the slavery in Dutch Suriname would become one of the most emblematic in the Atlantic, almost spectacular in its brutality. Many of the enslaved sought to escape into the country's interior, with their masters' mercenaries in hot pursuit. Branded as rebels, their fate would often be death, and no easy one. In one instance, eleven such 'rebels' were retrieved by detachments of military and plantation hands. One man was strung up alive on a gibbet by an iron hook stuck through his ribs; two others were chained to stakes and burned to death by a slow fire. Six women were broken alive upon the rack with an iron bar, and two girls were decapitated. Iron sprigs were driven under the nails of hands and feet, four strong horses were fastened to arms and legs to pull bodies apart, the clanking of weighted chains on the ankles of a woman, who swung limply from the branch of a tree to the rhythm of the final lashes of a lacerating flogging.

'As for old men being broken upon the rack, and young women roasted alive chained to stakes', in the words of an eyewitness, 'there can be nothing more common in this colony.' The horrors inflicted, added to the tyrannies of whipping and chaining and other depravities that routinely occurred throughout many plantations, were meant to induce others who were enslaved to submit to their fate. Instead, it enraged both those in captivity and others who had fled, so that the colonists who had come and seized and occupied lived in continual terror of invasions. Yet many who depended on the suffering of their labourers for an income continued in their behaviour with impunity, because the governance of humans, bought, sold or captured, was dictated only by the vicissitudes of capricious plantation masters, or the whims of turpitudinous overseers.

Through the plantations and beyond, Merian 'entered the forest to see what I could discover', including caterpillars and the strange plants on which they fed. Enslaved Amerindians and Africans gave her the names of those plants, their uses in medicines, or as food; told her what was toxic, or how to make them safe. There were leaves that she learned were applied to wounds, some to stop worms, or itching, others said to stave off diseases of the lungs.

One of the medicinal plants that most intrigued her, from which, early in 1700, she collected sea-green caterpillars from whose pupae grey moths emerged, was one whose seeds were 'used by women giving birth to carry on the labour'. The women also told her of a more tragic use of 'Flos Pavonis [peacock flower] . . . a plant measuring nine feet tall', that 'bears yellow and red flowers'. She wrote that 'the Indians, who are not treated well when in service with the Dutch, use it to abort their children, not wanting their children to be slaves, like them. The black female slaves from Guinea and Angola have to be treated very kindly. Otherwise they do not want children in their state of slavery and will not have any. Indeed, they sometimes even kill them because of the harsh treatment commonly inflicted on them, because they feel that they will be reborn in a free state in the country of their friends, as I heard from their own lips . . .'

For a scientist attempting to understand the cycles of life of unfamiliar plants and insects in an unfamiliar place, Merian could not have carried out her Suriname studies without relying upon the knowledge of the people who knew the forests well and who formed her team. Though Cornelis van Aerssen van Sommelsdijck would support the publication of her Suriname studies, she found her own community of little help, finding that they showed no interest in the new world around them even out of curiosity, particularly when such knowledge offered no financial gain. When she walked through the thick rainforest, with its clouds of tiny black flies that ripped at the skin, enslaved people cleared her path and brought samples she wished for: 'since one cannot cut off any plants there because of the heat, or they would wither at once, I had my Indian dig it up by the root and carry it home, and plant it in my garden . . . Because the forest is so densely grown with thistles and thorns, I had to send my slaves ahead of me with axes to hack out an opening for me, to get through it all, which was still very troublesome.' Other colonists she met there, she wrote, '. . . do not feel like investigating something like that. Indeed, they mocked me for looking for something other than sugar in the country. Yet there were more things to be found (in my opinion) in the forest, if it were accessible.'

Merian did find more things. By the end, she would have 'some 90 observations of caterpillars, worms and maggots . . . and also how, shedding their skins they change colour and form, and ultimately transform themselves into butterflies, moths, beetles, bees and flies'. All, she had placed with 'the same plants, flowers and fruits that they feed on'. As well as these, she had also 'added the reproduction of the West Indian spiders, ants, snakes, lizards, wonderful toads and frogs, all painted and observed from life by myself in America, except for a small number, which I have added based on the accounts of the Indians . . .'

In among the 'lovely creatures' she gathered and painted, Merian had also discovered new, wonderful moths that in just over one hundred years' time would be scientifically classified under a family named Saturniidae by a middle-aged Massachusetts doctor and librarian of Harvard University. These moths count among the largest insects in the world, with eggs that might be as large as half a centimetre, caterpillars reaching around twelve centimetres long, and adults with a wingspan twice as wide as two splayed human hands. Only twelve species were to be found in all Europe. But there, in the tropics and subtropics, vast numbers flew freely, and nowhere more so than around the northern coastal areas of South America. In the space of just two years during which she wandered only the wild places that surrounded Paramaribo, Merian was able to collect, observe and paint eight types of Saturniidae moths.

Here were sharp-spiked black and white striped larvae that became smooth, bright yellow caterpillars camouflaging themselves perfectly with the bright yellow flowers of the palisade tree, and metamorphosed into light-brown moths with wing tips tinged a rosy pink. Enormous Saturniidae cocoons on gum-producing trees that grew wild on Lucia van Sommelsdijck's La Providentia plantation. Light-green caterpillars adorned with extensions like feathers crawling upon the blood-red, leather-like flowers of the banana tree, that 'changed into such a beautiful moth'. Navigating the curvature of a new 'large and delicious fruit . . . called Pompelmoes in Suriname . . . less sweet than the orange and not as sour as the lemon' – the grapefruit – were 'green caterpillars with blue heads, whose bodies are full of long hairs which are as hard as iron wire'.

But then Merian found the curious caterpillars that lived on orange trees 'like the tallest apple trees in Europe'. These were: 'green with a yellow stripe across their body. On each segment they have four round orange-yellow beads with small hairs on all sides. On 18 February they made an ochre coloured cocoon . . . on 11 March lovely large moths emerged, with a patch like Muscovy glass on each wing. They flew rapidly. Three days later they laid ten small white eggs.'

It would be almost sixty years before Carl Linnaeus would place moths into an 'Order' called the Lepidoptera, those insects with wings covered in tiny scales. From there, some would find their home in a superfamily lineage called Bombycoidea, further divided into ten families. In Germany, and in Suriname, Merian had handled, admired and studied moths of more than one of these families. But it would be inside the little bodies of only two – in the Bombycidae, with which she was familiar, and the Saturniidae, the caterpillar that Suriname revealed to her – in which snaking tubules and glands would shape and mould the sericin and fibroin proteins to emerge as splendid cocoons of the finest silk.

Had Merian not made this onerous and dangerous journey she would not have known that one of her wondrous new moths, with such wings patched as though with glass, could produce silken cocoons. She gave it no particular name, but she would be the first naturalist to report its existence to Europe. And her eye for silk was trained. She had handled the fibres of *Bombyx mori* that had named the entire Bombycidae family, and she knew it intimately, because she embroidered fabrics with their threads. Deep in the forests of Suriname, this particular Saturniidae, she began to see, was also able to make something beautiful. What was more, it could make it in abundance. Merian's appreciation of its value may well have been honed through her contact and conversations with her enslaved helpers, because she saw the people of African or Amerindian origin already using the threads of that cocoon – or perhaps others like it, how 'the maidens string . . . full brown seeds which have a very strong musk scent . . . on silk threads and bind them around their arms to adorn themselves . . .' If the enormous profits from sugar had not excited her in the least, the potential of the silk that her newfound insects wove was an entirely different matter: 'These caterpillars are found frequently. They become so fat that they roll. They appear three times a year. They spin a strong thread, which led me to think that it was good silk. Therefore I gathered some and sent it to Holland, where it was considered good. So if someone wanted to go through the trouble of collecting these caterpillars, they could produce good silk, and make a large profit . . .'

But, in the end, the forests in which she spent two years were filled with other insects that had not been so congenial to her purse, to her studies, or to her health. Near the banks of the rivers and creeks where settlers arrived and stayed swarmed clouds of mosquitos especially fond of keeping company with strangers at night which would have sucked the blood of Merian until they were barely able to fly. The large blotches and itching they left in their wake were intolerable, but, worse, they may have been the source of a tropical disease that it is believed she contracted, so that when she left it would be earlier than she had imagined, and in great haste. On 18 June 1701, two years after they had arrived, Merian and Dorothea made their way back to the Netherlands on the merchant ship *De Vreede* – 'Peace'. But just as their plantation had seen little providence, so her ship met with little tranquillity. No sooner had it set sail than *De Vreede* ran aground at Paramaribo. Its cargo was unloaded and passengers – sick or healthy – disembarked so that the vessel might be refloated. Caterpillars and pupae became separated from their adults as Merian's carefully packaged specimens got jumbled up. Arguments flared among rattled travellers. The departure was delayed by close to a month, until the extra expenses of the set-back could be covered. When the women finally managed to draw closer to home, they met with seas preparing to face the looming threat of a new war, which frightened civilian ships and delighted privateers. To avoid the cannonballs of frigates and the greedy hands of pirates, *De Vreede* would have taken the long route, along the west coast of the British Isles, all the way up and around Scotland, before it could finally dock again near the salty marshes of the Wadden Sea. Here, Merian and her daughter could once again breathe the bracing autumn air of the Dutch Republic.

For the lungs of the third woman who disembarked with them, that cold, spartan landscape, that air of expanding brick-built cities must have come as much as a shock as the hot, wet, fragrant, insect-filled skies of Suriname would have been to Merian. This 'Indianin', an Amerindian woman whose name Merian never recorded, had made the return journey perhaps preparing medicines and helping with the care of her feverish mistress along the way, and assisting in the reporting of her body of research. Because when she finally published her study, Merian's works had retained 'the names of the plants as they are given in America by the inhabitants and the Indians'. The Indianin had been brought along with Dorothea, and along with Merian's paintboxes and drawings, her magnifying lens and scientific notes and preserved plants. Other creatures of Suriname also made the journey back to Holland: the 'lovely and rare' coiled snake she had caught at the foot of a jasmine bush and a cobalt-blue lizard whose eggs she found in a nest under the floor of her house and 'took on the ship on my journey to Holland', from which young had 'emerged at sea . . . but for lack of their mother and of food, they died'. Also carried home was a female frog with 'its womb along its back, in which it receives and nurses its eggs [that] wriggled out of the skin, one after another', which Merian had preserved 'in brandy with its remaining young, of which some had their heads out, others half their body . . .'

But before Merian's studies on the metamorphosis of the insects of Suriname could finally be published as her most magnificent work; before she could prepare the copper plates to capture in print the wonder of any plant, any moth, or any cocoon of silk, she first had to overcome her illness, the trials and tribulations of a long and difficult journey, and the cyclical poverty of an artist who had invested everything she had on a labour of love that remained as yet incomplete. Before she could afford to finish her own *magnus opus*, she would have to work on the specimens of another naturalist. To earn money, Merian would colour the illustrations of the beautiful shells of Georg Eberhardt Rumpf, an ill-fated merchant-turned-botanist who had lost his sight in a different Dutch colony on the other side of the world.

6

IN AMBON

FOR SOME TIME BEFORE 1670, WHEN, AT THE AGE OF 42, GEORG Eberhardt Rumpf lost his sight completely, he looked hard at the blurred images around him. What little light still slipped into his eyes from a swollen Indonesian sun now lingered only feebly around shadowy shapes of plants and animals, fish and minerals. Living samples from the forests, seas and beaches of an island shaped like the claw of a lobster, where he lived like a prince, if one of strange humility. 'A terrible misfortune suddenly took away from me the entire world and all its creatures . . . compelling me to sit in sad darkness', one of his letters recorded. But 'with borrowed pen and eyes' he persevered with a work he had begun 'that describes in Latin such plants, field products, animals etcetera which I have seen during my residence in the Indies'. While his sight still permitted, Rumpf had 'sorted their proper names, compared them with, and differentiated them from one another, and drawn fitting pictures of them from life' – 'to the best of my artistic abilities', he wrote self-deprecatingly. It was the style of a man considered scrupulous, honest and good, who was neither covetous nor greedy, except for an ambition that had driven him to Latinize his name a decade before his eyes failed him, because that was how the names of great scholars were styled.

In this new incarnation Georgius Everhardus Rumphius filled his elegant house with natural specimens to study. He had a retinue of staff to serve its ample rooms and beautiful garden; a large armed vessel at his disposal, manned by forty rowers and a gunner; a 'wife' of native or mixed European blood and, therefore, known only by her Christian name; plus the clerks and draughtsmen who would later serve as his pen and his eyes. All were fruits of the distinguished career of a junior soldier-turned-spice merchant who made it known that his heart had really been set on accumulating the secrets of the natural world.

It had been the Dutch West India Company that had first ensnared the 18-year-old Georg onto a ship he believed was leaving Germany for Venice, but instead took him west along the same route Merian would travel, from the island of Texel past the torments of the Bay of Biscay, towards the failed dream of a Dutch-owned Brazil. From that came three lost years in Lisbon, where he was presumed to have been taken hostage by the Portuguese. It had been his recruitment to the armed forces of the Dutch United East India Company that had brought him to Indonesia. There, before he gained promotion to under-merchant, and then merchant, he had seen combat against Sultanate forces fighting to protect their sovereignty over Indonesia and the two 'noble fruit' that would be their ruin. For the sake of a monopoly on the clove and nutmeg tree that existed only on those islands, Georg and the Dutch United East India Company unleashed campaigns of brutal vengeance that saw the destruction of the very plants that produced the precious cargo.

If this was unfortunate for those who now fell under a new

and brutal foreign rule, for a man who sought the study of nature, and had the funds to do so, this remarkable place close to the meeting point of Asia and Australia came as a great gift. Thanks to the richness of species formed from the proximity of two continental ecosystems, Ambon Island was at the time home to spectacular, biodiverse life. Only thirty-two miles long and ten miles wide, Ambon is formed of two peninsulas fringed with lithe palm trees that so impressed Rumphius on the day his ship first approached the East Indieson islands. Across the narrow alluvial isthmus which connects the island's two parts, ships were hauled on rollers to ply new trade and furnish fresh terrors.

Under those waters were more than sixty species of mollusc; in the coral reefs not far under Ambon's southernmost shores alone swarmed almost six hundred species of magnificently coloured reef fish. Like its spice trees, much of the natural life Rumpf would collect could be found only in and around Ambon. It could be found either inland, away from the shores, where dense vegetation rose from its fertile soil and covered the island in a blanket of deepest green, or along its small rivers unnavigable by seafaring vessels, where the *embun* dewdrops after which the island had been named condensed during the night from water vapour that hung like a fog in the air and settled on plants upon which the caterpillars of gargantuan moths feasted.

. . .

On 17 February 1674, Rumpf's wife and their youngest daughter were dug out from under a house to which they had gone to celebrate Chinese New Year but whose walls had instead crushed them. Interrupted by one of the worst earthquakes ever to hit Ambon, Rumpf returned from his stroll that evening to sit, heartbroken, beside their bodies.

Portrait of Georg Eberhardt Rumpf aged 68, made by his son Paulus.

In 1682 came something that smelled of betrayal when an embittered Rumpf was coerced 'by the insistence of several friends, to whom I was obliged' into selling a most precious set of nearly four hundred shells that he had collected over nearly thirty years on Ambon. Each was, to him, irreplaceable. 'A treasure', as he wrote to the collection's buyer, Cosimo III de' Medici, Grand Duke of Tuscany, '. . . which I gathered over many years with much cost and labour, and which, in the future it will be impossible to acquire again, especially since I am now old and blind . . .'

And then, on 11 January 1687, the ageing naturalist's unpublished manuscripts, illustrations he had made or commissioned of his collections, his remaining botanical and zoological specimens themselves and his entire library were reduced to ashes in a fire that ravaged the European quarter of the town of Ambon.

But still Rumpf persisted. He was a man of humour, it was said, which would help him carry on in the face of many tragedies. His writings would resume. Some parts of his lost collections – crustaceans, shellfish, minerals from the seas around Ambon, of plants and insects – would begin to be rebuilt. And so it was, in April 1699, among the mangrove swamps of the island, that Rumpf located a plant upon which crawled a caterpillar whose adult form bore a remarkable resemblance to the large wild moth Merian had observed twenty thousand kilometres away in the dense forests of Suriname. Like hers, Rumpf's caterpillar was large, pale green in colour, with a back covered in fine hairs. His was marked with two warts from which longer hairs sprouted, and yellow circles lining the sides of the body, marking the place of each limb. 'This worm is found so abundantly there', he noted, much as she had, 'that it picks off all the leaves of the branches.'

Like Merian's, its metamorphosis took place inside a great cocoon formed of silk, except this one was first encased in two or three leaves of the same tree, hanging from a stalk like a curious fruit tightly wrapped in a mass of dull white silk. The moth that emerged was a dull yellow, 'two fingers long', with 'large wings . . . about a finger long, of an orange colour', Rumpf noted. 'A purple transversal streak runs through them, and each wing in the middle of it bears a window like that, which is drawn around a purple circle and translucent as glass.' The threads that bound its pupa into a cocoon appeared to be a mass of one continuous filament that unravelled to some twenty-five metres in length. Like Merian, he took particular care over these cocoons, taking pains to ensure that they were meticulously sketched. For, just as it had to Merian, so it occurred to Rumpf that if his people on Ambon could acquire the skill of expertly drawing out the fine threads of these great cocoons, the plentiful caterpillars that crafted them would generate a great deal of usable silk.

Creating fabrics of silk from their cocoons was not simply a possibility. From across the Java and Andaman seas, along the northern coasts of the Bay of Bengal, where the Dutch and British East India Companies rubbed belligerent shoulders, Rumpf had heard it could indeed be done. Still, after forty-six years on Ambon Island, the naturalist dictated to his scribes that he had not encountered anyone who had attempted the reeling or spinning of the threads of that silkworm for the creation of any textile. By then, the long-suffering Rumpf would have only two more years to live. On 19 May 1702, the Governor of Ambon declared that 'nothing more was to be expected of Georgius Rumphius, having lived his years'. Less than a month later, in a beautiful house restocked with manuscripts and wondrous specimens he could no longer see, the aged naturalist was dead.

. . .

At the same time, in the summer of 1702, Merian – still very much alive, if not fully recovered from her travels – was some eight months into colouring illustrations of Rumpf's treasured shells. On 23 September 1701 she had unloaded her precious Surinamese cargo, her daughter and 'her' Indianin from *De Vreede*. Their efforts to record in words and in astonishing life-size drawings of her most treasured specimens had also begun. It was work that 'absorbed her almost completely'. If her travels had been an expensive endeavour, so would the production of her great *Metamorphosis*

Insectorum Surinamensium, the funds for which were yet to be found. But no one doubted Merian's artistic abilities. And so, as Rumpf's mortal remains lay in a humble grave just outside of the town of Ambon, in Amsterdam a saddlemaker-turned-deputy sheriff of the city – a man most keen on metamorphosis – asked Merian to work on a publication that would become known as *The Ambonese Curiosity Cabinet*. Published three years after Rumpf's death, it contained recreations of sixty beautiful illustrations, including those Rumpf had lost either by theft, fire because of his eye disease, or through misadventure. In glorious detail, here, finally, were row upon row of the spectacular crustaceans, shellfish and minerals he had collected from the seas around Ambon. Three years later both *The Ambonese Curiosity Cabinet*, illustrated in Rumpf's name, and Merian's own masterpiece, wrestled from the thick forests that flanked the Suriname River, were complete.

On 17 January 1717, while fourteen pallbearers carried Merian to her grave, Rumpf's botanical studies were still being written up from beyond his. The Dutch East India Company's *de Heren Zeventien* comprised seventeen gentlemen whose interests in the economic value that could be squeezed from Rumpf's studies meant that his works were kept strictly confidential until their publication could no longer be delayed. And so the book which would finally describe his coconut palms and mangroves and that lovely silk moth was not to emerge for another twenty-four years. Merian was never to meet the man, nor see his moth that was so similar to hers, from the other side of the world. In 1775, a wool and linen merchant from Amsterdam would name Merian's wild silk moth *Phalœna aurota*, later changed to *Rothschildia aurota*. In 1834 a Paris physician and lepidopterist called Rumpf's silk moth *Saturnia rumphii mylitta*, before an Austrian lawyer renamed it *Antheraea rumphii rumphii*. Both moths would come to fall under a moth family proposed in 1841 as the Saturniidae by a librarian at Harvard University, and then the two would be separated into two 'tribes' within that family: Merian's was placed with the *Attacini*, Rumpf's with the *Saturniini*. Though these had once been cabinet curiosities, they would become part of a new science, one that placed into hierarchies living and inert objects taken from far-off places. But in the places in which they were found, silk moths of these 'tribes' were neither new nor discoveries. Both shared something in common with the Chinese *Bombyx mori* that was by then universally known, and long sought after. Because the fabrics made from the giant cocoons of the Saturniidae – wonderful cloths of wild silks – had been in use in very ancient times, too.

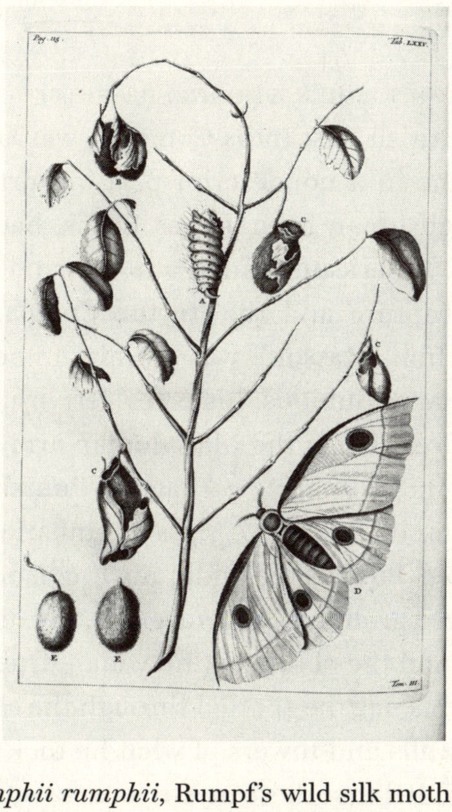

Antheraea rumphii rumphii, Rumpf's wild silk moth from Ambon.

7

INDUS

IN 1853, A COMMON SOLDIER WHO HAD DESERTED FROM THE BENGAL Artillery of the British East India Company was laid to rest under an assumed name in a nondescript part of north London. The deserter, an Englishman born James Lewis, had styled himself Charles Masson, American, scholar and spy, and in that way had largely evaded capture and the ire the Company reserved for absconders like him. Masson's was a brain immersed in ancient writings: vivid and dubious histories left by companions of Alexander the Great when the Macedonian army steered vessels down the River Indus to bring carnage to Punjab. In the pursuit of these interests, in July 1827 Masson embarked on a journey across India from Punjab to Sindh, an Englishman in disguise among an assorted group of local travellers, administrators, musicians, falconers and the obligatory holy man. One day, as Masson paused to graze his nag, he spotted through the close jungle ruins of baked-brick walls and towers of what he took to be a fortress. He quicky concluded that these mysterious, monumental mounds had belonged to 'a city, so considerable . . . bespeaking a great antiquity'. But not just any city. To Masson, those 'remains of buildings, fragments of walls with niches, after the eastern manner' were surely what was left of the stronghold of Purushottam – called Porus by the Greeks – a great king who ruled in eastern Punjab until he was brought to his knees by Alexander, two thousand years earlier.

Masson had not been the only English traveller to document the place, nor to speculate about its significance. The site Masson named as Haripah was called Harappa in records made two years later by Alexander Burnes, a multilingual military officer who had taken with him five horses with the intention of presenting them as gifts to enable him to gather clandestine political information in the name of the British East India Company. And then, in the year of Masson's death, a British general and engineer called Alexander Cunningham surveyed what was left of these astonishing ruins. Cunningham had read the accounts of both his predecessors and yet, by the time he was able to set to work excavating it, many hands had helped themselves to the materials of which its massive walls had been built. The city's ancient brick had been carted away by British railway engineers, as Cunningham noted sadly: 'Perhaps the best idea of the extent of the ruin brick mounds . . . may be formed by the fact that they have more than sufficed to furnish a brick ballast for about 100 miles of Lahore and Multan railway.' After that, what was left lay on a site he found to have a circumference of four kilometres, with mounds that stood up to eighteen metres in height.

While Masson's imagination had been inspired by the exploits of Alexander the Great, leading him to date the ruins to 326 BCE, Cunningham was influenced by the writings of a seventh-century

Buddhist monk. 'In describing the ancient geography of India', he announced, 'the Elder Pliny, for the sake of clearness, follows the footsteps of Alexander the Great. For a similar reason I would follow the footsteps of the Chinese pilgrim Hwen-Thsang.' Also known as Xuanzang, this monk left an epic travelogue from the seventh century, born of his quest for copies of Buddhist manuscripts that he might take back with him to China. From reading Xuanzang, Cunningham believed the same ruins, from which he had also by now 'traced the remains of flights of stairs on both the eastern and western faces of the high mound to the northwest, as well as the basement of a large square building', to be the remnants of buildings erected under a Buddhist reign dating back to 322 BCE.

Under Cunningham, exploration by the Archaeological Survey of India would commence, because what emerged there could show the world the forgotten grandeur of new territory of which the Company had become the ultimate conqueror. Because he had concluded the site of Harappa was Buddhist, and not Hindu, Cunningham hoped to loosen British purse strings by proposing that the finds might also 'prove that the establishment of the Christian religion in India must ultimately succeed'. Except that in their calculations, both men had estimated dates for the settlement's age that were spectacularly wide of the mark.

Cunningham retired in 1885 and would not be replaced as the head of the Archaeological Survey of India for another seventeen years. In Calcutta in February 1902, a shy but quietly confident 26-year-old archaeologist named John Marshall was appointed in Cunningham's place. Marshall was fresh from recent excavations at Knossos, a city built by a sophisticated Bronze Age culture whose people had been imaginatively dubbed the Minoans, after the legendary King Minos, and which was located just a few miles inland from the northern coast of Crete.

Nothing much was known of India when Marshall took up his post. Westerners versed in biblical and classical accounts assumed the country had no equivalent pre-history similar to that of the great Near Eastern civilizations: Assyria, Babylon, Persia and Egypt. But nor were there any hints of such a place in the earliest Sanskrit texts, India's ancient oral compositions, which were finally recorded in writing around 1500 BCE. That places of such antiquity or cultural importance could exist in India was inconceivable to its colonizers. And in any case, after the abolition of slavery in Britain and most of its colonies nearly seventy years before, in 1833, Indians had been transported as free labour by the British to their colonies in the East and West Indies, since these were people Calcutta traders Gillanders Arbuthnot & Co. referred to as 'more akin to the monkey than the man' who had 'no religion, no education, and, in their present state, no wants, beyond eating, drinking and sleeping; and to procure which, they are willing to labour'. It was an attitude that persisted a hundred years later, even after the system of Indian indentured labour ended in 1917, as pressure applied by Indian nationalists built, along the way to its independence from Britain. Even in 1937, when intriguing finds hinting at the sophistication of ancient India were still emerging, Winston Churchill would say of its colonies that he would 'not admit that a wrong has been done to those people by the fact that a stronger race, a higher grade race or at any rate a more worldly-wise race, to put it that way, has come in and taken their place'. How far back *could* their civilization have gone?

But then, in 1920, Marshall instructed the man who was soon to become his successor to excavate the site once again. Daya Ram Sahni's finds from that dig – a number of mysterious seals with unintelligible markings – would push back the age of that place to *before* Alexander. Seals just like those were also recovered from Ur, Babylon and Kish, in Mesopotamia. And still neither man suspected that the very ancient city they were uncovering was not just an isolated find. That same year, another of Marshall's superintendent archaeologists went south, this time towards the western coast not far from what was then the border between India and Iran. The site had previously been dismissed, because its bricks, like those taken as ballast from Harappa, simply looked too modern. But when Rakal Das Banerjee, one of the superintendent archaeologists, bent down and stood back up holding a flint scraper, he concluded that the site should be excavated, too. Mohenjo-daro turned out to be the most impressive, and best-preserved, Bronze Age city in the world.

On 20 September 1924, the front page of the *Illustrated London News* bore six images of the 'startling remains' finally unearthed by Marshall, Daya Ram Sahni, Banerjee and his assistant Madho Sarup Vats. They had found not one, but two cities, six hundred kilometres apart, both at least one hundred hectares in area. Their report likened them to other Bronze Age sites being discovered at around the same time. To the cities of the Mycenaeans: the people of Menelaus and Agamemnon and Helen of Troy. To Troy itself; to Mesopotamia, and to the majestic city of Persepolis. Coming not long after a period of discovery of the remains of these other monumental ancient civilizations of the Old World, Marshall's excavations in Punjab and in Sindh '. . . put back by several centuries the date of the earliest known remains of Indian civilization', which, by then 'must have been in existence for many hundreds of years'.

But even that reckoning was to prove an underestimation. The civilization that spread across what is now Pakistan and the northwest of India was older by millennia with roots in a culture dating back to 7000 BCE, and contemporary with the earliest civilizations of the Old World. The two cities reported by John Marshall were among the largest of their time; Masson's had stood in various guises for nearly six thousand years.

They were among the largest cities of what had been the most geographically extensive of all the early civilizations, extending from the Arabian Sea in the west to the Ganges in the east and to the banks of the Amu Darya in northern Afghanistan. At its height, this civilization boasted over a thousand settlements including four or five particularly large cities that in all covered well over a million square kilometres.

In these cities could be found large buildings and otherwise ordinary houses built of incredibly uniform fire-baked brick, mud, mud-brick or stone, many laid out on such a large scale and level of planning that they were not just unprecedented for their time – it would not be seen in other cities long, long after theirs had disappeared.

There were flood defences and reservoirs to mitigate the vicissitudes of their great, powerful, violent rivers. Under houses ran elaborate civic drainage, sewage and water supply systems with outlets for each house; inside were wells, bathing platforms and paved bathrooms. There were houses with toilets built of baked brick and perhaps wood. The people of that civilization made, first by hand and then on potters' wheels, painted pottery with origins dating back to about 5000 BCE, charming figurines of clay and metal and delightful toys. While its mysterious symbols, some form of writing, perhaps, seemed reluctant to give up their meaning, Mesopotamian inscriptions and texts instead revealed that these were a people that sailed the seas and crossed vast areas overland to trade their tin, copper, unworked lapis lazuli, raw and finely crafted beads of carnelian, stones the colour of agate, jasper, chalcedony, as well as pearls and silver and gold. From them, in Mesopotamia and along the Arabian coast, would be found imported timber: ebony, rosewood, mangrove wood and mulberry. From 3300 BCE many different sizes of spindle whorls were made from terracotta for both heavy and the finest of threads; tools made from cattle ribs, highly polished, perhaps to use with looms; and rectangular bone plaques with perforations, like simple tablets, for the weaving of small items. By 2800 BCE, this Indus civilization, for that was what it came to be called, had also become remarkable for textiles thought to have been dyed with indigo and woven with elaborate designs and tiny sequins crafted from pure gold. In this civilization skirts and shawls and turbans were made of many types of fibres, spun and woven in a variety of ways. Cotton was ubiquitous, there were wools of different kinds, and probably also jute and hemp.

And then, in the winter of 1935–6, the first American Archaeological Expedition to India led an excavation of the Indus civilization site of Chanhu-daro from which tiny beads of steatite were uncovered, lying inside a metal bowl. The beads had become fused together, but running through them were the intact remains of forty or fifty strands of silk that some fine-fingered artisan had, sometime between 2450 and 2000 BCE, twisted together in order to string them. Later, from the debris of buildings in Masson's Harappa was found a fragment of a hollow bangle fashioned from copper or a copper alloy; and a necklace made up of two strands of coiled wire made of the same. The first dated to 2200–1900 BCE; the second, even earlier, to 2450 BCE. Inside both were silk threads. The first was made of sixty to seventy-five spun strands of two thicknesses, presumably to hold the additional weight that the fine beads from Chanhu-daro did not have, but the copper ornaments required.

Although they were ancient, dating back to nearly 4,500 years ago, these silks were not those of the famed domestic silkworm from across India's eastern border. Instead, they had been extracted from different cocoons entirely. Rather than the *Bombyx*, all had come from proteins assembled into strings inside the larvae of the large, wonderfully coloured wild Saturniidae family of moths. What is more, their threads had been extracted from the cocoons of moths of two or three distinct types, and from distant locations across the subcontinent. One type may have originated from the tropical west coast of India, with the other two certainly from Assam – one thousand kilometres away from the ancient Indus cities of Sindh and two thousand kilometres away from Punjab. Here, out of the Indus, was another ancient silk road, forged from the great cocoons of moths that would come to be scientifically classified as the *Antheraea paphia*, *Antheraea assamensis*, and also probably the *Samia ricini*.

The last was of the same tribe as Merian's Suriname silk moth, called the *Attacini*; the first of the same tribe as Rumpf's specimen from Ambon Island, the *Antheraea*. Of all the Saturniidae, these, of the gigantic *Attacini* and the *Antheraea paphia*, have the largest cocoons of silk threads. This fact had not escaped the attention of the ancient peoples in the north of India, who appear, as the Chinese had, to have also begun a process of selection and breeding, and a sort of domestication, too. The long strands of silk from these cocoons were found to have been reeled as one thread, just like those of *Bombyx mori*, meaning that the larvae inside must have been stifled, to stop them from breaking the precious strand of their own making. What was more, from 1757 – three thousand years after the end of the Indus civilization – the British East India Company began their effective rule of India. With their busy merchants, magistrates and men of science they would find that the silks from all of these insects were being used still, woven on looms into curious, yet wonderful, cloths. Those threads of Indian silk moths unearthed from around the same time as the earliest Chinese evidence for silk, and that were still in local use, suggested that silk had never been an exclusively Chinese invention. That there had been other silk industries – peoples with the skill and technology who were also adept at producing silks that, though different, were no less special.

8

ANTHERAEA

AT SOME POINT IN THE YEAR 1777 SHAIKH ZAIN AL-DIN SAT DOWN IN front of a branch of a bair tree whose fruit looked like small plums but smelled of apples. At his side European watercolours replaced the powdered pigments with which he usually mixed water and gum arabic powder and burnished with gemstones. In the place of closely woven Indian cotton fibre on which he executed his usual masterpieces was paper made in English papermills from cotton and linen rags. Around Zain al-Din and his new materials was an expansive Calcutta estate that had belonged to a gifted divider and conqueror who entered the service of the British East India Company at the age of 13 and rose to the rank of Governor of Bengal just fifteen years later. Its house and gardens were now in the hands of Mary Readc, the eldest daughter of a baronet, and her husband Elijah Impey, the son of a gentleman soap manufacturer who became a barrister, was knighted, and sent to Bengal as the first Chief Justice of a Court the British deemed Supreme, in a fort they had named William. While Sir Elijah learned the languages of his new home and was impeached for the first judicial hanging of a stoical Indian revenue collector under the British Parliament Forgery Act, Lady Impey also learned languages, bought exquisite paintings and created an expansive menagerie of birds and animals in the grounds of her new home. Zain al-Din would be one of the artists the Impeys commissioned to capture 326 natural history images for posterity.

Upon the lithe, thorny branches of his bair tree, Zain al-Din prepared to paint a resident of Mary's aviary, a bird partial to both fruit and insects. Here it would stand at the centre of the composition, regal, immobile, tranquil alongside the mealy, floral flesh of ripe bair fruit. A single, light green caterpillar dotted with yellow spiracles feasted on a leaf. Stout and smooth, it must have been appealing to the bird as much as it was to hungry bats and beetles, except that this tempting caterpillar was half the size of the bird and sported warts from which clumps of unpalatable, bristle-like hairs sprouted along its back. A female moth, almost the size of the bird and coloured a soft yellow or fawn, was painted above its caterpillar, right in the bird's eyeline.

Below it, another moth, this one a male, somewhat smaller, spreads its reddish wings. On each wing are eye spots, as clear as glass. These moths Zain al-Din watched with great attention. They are beautifully observed, delicately coloured, with the texture of dusty scales on perfectly positioned lepidopterous wings. Zain's detail of these scales is important. For they are structures that became specialized by evolution to absorb sound energy from predatory bats that would attempt to echolocate such insects, so that these moths simply seem to disappear from the night sky. Each scale, on each wing, vibrates to the bat's sound waves, all with different frequencies, creating a cloak against every soundscape its predator might use for hunting. Those frequencies span some two hundred kilohertz of sound that the moths transform instead into energy and heat. Under these astonishing fore and hind wings, a furry thorax covered in setae, tiny hairs so wondrously light and porous absorb almost half their sound – averting again any attempts by predators to hunt them.

And then there were the cocoons. Above Zain al-Din's male moth is a finely crafted structure the fleshy caterpillar would have built, hanging like a light-brown egg from a strong, silken stalk. Its off-white silk is covered in a network of threads of a darker colour. The complex branching and swirling of this net-like layer Zain al-Din executed to near-perfection. It must have stood out to him, and to Mary Impey. His inscription, written in a Persian-stylized Urdu text on the bottom of the painting, reads 'the cuckoo is on the bair tree, and the ruby-like berries look like silkworm eggs . . .' In English, written in Mary's hand next to that, Zain's words were translated as 'The Bair Tree', 'Egg of the Eye Breaker'. In either language, what had been described as the eggs of this moth were very clearly not. Cocoons are one of the places in which these insects gestate. And an egg, after all, is where a new animal develops and transforms; except that these Lepidoptera evolved to change in more complex ways than that, through a complete metamorphosis, a profound altering of an embryo into an adult – wingless to gloriously winged.

It is hard to know exactly what Zain al-Din had in front of him as he drew this, or indeed at what time of year the composition was conceived. Perhaps it was towards the winter months as the bair fruit were on their way to becoming fully reddened and ripe, just as the caterpillars were about to begin their transformations, wrapping themselves into their threads of silk.

This precious painting was not a study in metamorphosis, and yet it was the earliest image the British would have of a silk moth new to Mary, and to the natural historians in the employment of the empire who were about to follow her across the seas. This was a moth of the same type as the Saturniidae that Rumpf had found in the mangroves of Ambon Island. It had been from cocoons so like Zain al-Din's that Rumpf had also proposed silk fabrics should be made.

That Rumpf knew it was even possible to extract silk from such a curious cocoon was because he had heard as much from a surgeon in Bengal, where Mary's menagerie was located. There, Rumpf knew, was a particularly fine thread he referred to as *tessero*, made from a cocoon not unlike his, though the Indian variety was of 'an earthy colour', rather than the dull white threads secreted by his Ambonese caterpillars. In India, these moths had long been known as *Tassar*, a word derived it seems from the Sanskrit *Trasara* – a weaver's shuttle, or reel or spool of thread. Indeed, from their cocoons was still being made a silk of the same name, much as it had been in the hands of the craftspeople of the ancient Indus, though what they might have called it is unknown: no one has deciphered their script. From the shape and size the cocoons looked like hen's eggs and as they hung from branches like fruit, Rumpf, too, had made the same assumption that had led Zain al-Din to label them eggs. It was also one popularized in the writings of ancient Romans, whose sources claimed not just that silk grew on trees, but that its origin was India. 'From this it is evident', Rumpf wrote, 'for what reason it has been widely known that the manufacture of Bengali silk is from the bark of a tree, for these cocoons hang so artfully on the branches of a tree, connected with a stalk, to swear that it is the very fruit of the tree . . . As one surgeon from Bengal came to assert, he assured me that this was the fruit which he himself plucked off from a tree, in which opinion I have been with many others for so long . . .'

This moth that Zain al-Din had so beautifully observed was to be named *Antheraea paphia* by European naturalists in India. It was also called *Phalœna attacus* by Carl Linnaeus, renamed *Bombyx mylitta* by his Danish student Fabricius and designated *Phalœna mylitta* or *Antheraea mylitta* by Dru Drury, a London goldsmith who went bankrupt, was bailed out and then gave it all up in the name of entomology. The specimens Drury used to name this moth were somewhat dubious, but if he did not have the correct samples it was not for want of trying. In the years preceding his career change Drury had specimens sent to him from across the world. He was sent beetles via traders in Antigua; water insects from settlers in New York; anything he could get his hands on from the Falkland Islands that had just been appropriated by the British; locusts and grasshoppers from Africa and Jamaica from an English slaver whose ship all too frequently plied that route. He acquired what he could wherever he could, and however possible. But it did not have to be that way. In 1768, Drury bemoaned the fact that the British had never 'sent out any Botanist or other Naturalist with a settled salary' to India. 'It is ye curse of this Country for public Bodies seldom to reward ingenuity unless compelled to it by a sense or fear of shame', he complained, with a hope that they would 'send out some Gentlemen to India with handsome salaries to make inquiries in Natural History'. He was still discontent in 1773, writing long begging letters to Calcutta. 'Mankind may be improved by committing your observations to paper', Drury said, 'for we in Europe are ignorant of the Nat. Hist of thousands of animals that live between the Tropics, particularly those of India.'

Ten years later, in 1783, and with the Impeys now recalled to England, a Scottish doctor who became a surgeon's mate with the East India Company at the age of 16 was endowed with the long-winded title of Superintendent of the Honourable East India Company's Botanical Garden at Calcutta. It was a role with a settled if unremarkable salary of 1,500 rupees a month. To the Botanical Garden, Dr William Roxburgh, who had worked in India alongside a pupil of Linnaeus, brought plants from as far and wide as the lands the British traded with or had occupied: North America, the West Indies, South America, Europe, Arabia, India, Bhutan, Nepal, the East Indies, China, Japan and New South Wales. He led a very full life which included marrying three women all called Mary, siring twelve legitimate children, and at least one illegitimate son: an 'Anglo-Indian orphan', with an Indian bibi, an additional local wife of an unofficial variety. He undertook the immense task of cataloguing the botany of India that was, or could be, of economic value to Britain: fabric plants like flax and hemp; coffee and cinnamon; mahogany and mulberry; black pepper, teak and indigo.

By 1794, Roxburgh had sent around five hundred drawings he had commissioned from Indian artists to Joseph Banks, the English naturalist who cut his teeth on the flora of Canada – or, as Dru Drury called him, 'a splendid man and one of the most useful citizens of England who was not adapted to scientific research, with its continued attention to minute details. His position in relation to natural history was that of a patron and promoter, rather than a student . . .' Banks did indeed do the job of promoting Roxburgh's most economically important products as subjects for engraving and publishing. Towards the final decade of Roxburgh's life, these subjects in which he had become so keenly interested now included the cultivation of sugar cane.

Roxburgh also began in earnest the study of silkworms for the manufacture of silk, a project in which the second Mary Roxburgh was at his right hand. This study, it was anticipated, would be highly profitable. She had sent a skein of tasar silk from Calcutta to another Scottish surgeon in Madras who hoped to create – by means of planting mulberry trees – a profitable *Bombyx mori* silk industry there. One of her husband's correspondents, who delivered this silk at her behest, wrote, 'Mrs Roxburgh has much merit in producing such as samples . . . Mrs Roxburgh will make more money than will be required for the Education of all the Children that she has already brought you & may still bring.' It was a fact that had not gone unnoticed, that Roxburgh had a family so large that he had struggled to find a house big enough for all of them. But the second Mary was not to be mother to many more. Between her demise and his marriage to the third Mary, who gave birth to a new daughter while still en route from Britain to Calcutta, Roxburgh travelled to the Cape of Good Hope on a botanical mission to Britain's newest acquisition.

By April 1798, and already a sick man, Roxburgh sailed 'on the passage from Bengal' to South Africa, and penned a letter to Joseph Banks to let him know that he had finally 'completed an account of the *Tasseh* silk worm'. It was an account which included some rudimentary drawings made by his own hand, showing the eggs of the same silk moth Zain al-Din had so perfectly captured, that Roxburgh would call *Phalæna paphia*. In Roxburgh's version, four small eggs floated off to the side of the bair tree, while two robust caterpillars clung to its branches. Much like Zain al-Din's, the plant bore leaves, a few blossoms and young fruit.

In his drawing Roxburgh suspended a ripe bair fruit opposite the moth's eggs, neither of which would have been present, but both were included simply to show naturalists or would-be wild silk producers the silkworm and its food plant at different stages. Roxburgh's caterpillars were neither as soft and expressive as those painted by the Indian artist, nor as real. But the main elements by which they could be identified were very much there. Though not so perfectly observed in their outer structure or colour, two cocoons still hung like pale hen's eggs from the branches, the larger, he noted, from which a female moth would emerge.

In the notes accompanying these illustrations were fuller details of his observations not captured by his images: 'Eggs white, round, compressed, with a depression or pit in the centre on each side . . . which hatch in from two to four weeks, according to the state of the weather. The larvae acquire their full size, which is about four inches in length, and three in circumference, in about six weeks. When the larvae approach their full size, they are too heavy to crawl in search of their food with their back up, as is usual with most caterpillars, but traverse the branch suspended by the feet. When the larvae are ready to spin the cases in which they are to pass this state of their existence, each of them connects, by means of the . . . filament of which the case is made, two or three leaves into an exterior envelope, which serves as a basis to spin the complete . . . cocoon in; besides, the case is suspended from a branch of the tree in a wonderful manner by a thick strong consolidated cord, spun of the same materials from the bowels of the animal.'

Roxburgh left the moths for another image, in which he drew a smaller male and larger female, awkwardly executed, but clearly tasar silk moths, or, as he referred to them, 'these most beautiful as well as most useful animals . . .'

'The wings of the male expand to five or six inches, and those of the female from six to eight . . . horizontal, expanded, slightly striped in the direction of the tendons . . . First pair, a cream or orange buff, or brownish colour, or a mixture of these . . . the margin rather concave, beyond that much curved, and bounded with a beautiful light blueish grey coloured belt. Posterior (fan) edges somewhat concave, scalloped, and ornamented with a pretty broad circumscribed scalloped border of sometimes a darker, sometimes a lighter colour than the rest of the wings . . . In the centre of each wing there is a remarkable eye, with the large pupil of micaceous transparency, and a beautiful party-coloured iris.'

Roxburgh's own eye had been drawn to these moths, their caterpillars and cocoons for a number of reasons, including because of information sent via correspondence with other British naturalists. It is not clear whether he even knew of Mary Impey's commissioned drawing, because by then she had long been gone from Calcutta. But he had seen the substantive studies of Georg Rumpf, made among the forests and the seas of Ambon, some seven thousand kilometres to the east. Rumpf's intriguing descriptions and drawings of the metamorphosis of a wild silk moth presented – where Roxburgh found it, 'on the 75th table of the third volume of Rumpf's *Herbarium Amboinense*', the blind scientist's magnum opus – was one Roxburgh began to suspect was the same as India's tasar silk moth, 'though they are represented feeding on the leaves of the *Rhizophora caseolaris* of Linnaeus' – a different food plant, a detail noted by the keen eye of Roxburgh, the botanist who would come to be known as 'the father of Indian botany'.

While Rumpf had only heard from his contacts in Bengal that silk was being made of cocoons such as Roxburgh had reported, Roxburgh had the advantage of actually observing them in Calcutta. And in that place, as Rumpf suspected, silk was being drawn and woven from the cocoons of his Ambon moth's Indian relation. This was a 'native of Bengal, B[i]har, Assam', Roxburgh noted, which 'feeds upon the leaves of the *Rhamnus jujube* (Byer of the Hindoos); and of *Terminalia alata glabra* (*Aseen* of the Hindoos)', of which 'the silk . . . is manufactured . . . They are found in such abundance over many parts of Bengal and the adjoining provinces as to have afforded to the natives, from time immemorial, an abundant supply of a most durable, coarse, dark-coloured silk, commonly called Tusseh silk.' The opportunity this source of a new silk afforded evidently made Roxburgh think that here was a substance that 'would, no doubt, be highly useful to the inhabitants of many parts of America and the south of Europe, where a cheap, light, cool, durable dress, such as this silk makes, is much wanted'.

It was not to be the only silk moth that would be rediscovered by the new wave of naturalists from the West who made India their laboratory. For Europe's was not an imperialism that could take global shape independently of animals nor plants, of local people, or of the knowledge of the nature of their land. But what will not have been evident to Roxburgh and those naturalists with whom he then worked, and those who would follow him not long after, was that this moth, recorded on paper by the hands of Zain al-Din and Roxburgh, may well have been one that was created in ancient times by a similar artificial means – selective breeding – by which *Bombyx mandarina* was transformed into the domesticated *Bombyx mori*.

If this giant silk moth, the *Antheraea paphia*, had come about through breeding by human hands, then the method that was used in India had not led to its losing its beautiful colours, nor its impressive flight, nor its ability to travel long distances to find mates with which to breed, as *Bombyx mandarina* had in becoming the pale and flightless *Bombyx mori*. As Roxburgh would have seen, and as Rumpf had heard from across the sea in Ambon, this was not a moth bred to be kept away from its natural habitat. Instead, eggs and caterpillars would continue to be reared outside, on trees, their cocoons harvested like fruit from their branches. The moths that Zain al-Din, the second Mary Roxburgh and

Roxburgh himself saw alive – and that Drury had sent to him in London already dead would not have looked so different from those the people who carried the silk of this moth westwards to the makers and traders of the Indus civilization had held in their hands.

And, just like the strands of silk recovered from the ruins of South Asia's greatest ancient cities, the silken threads being drawn from the cocoons of this moth were not being fragmented by a wild moth's escape. They were unreeled from cocoons harvested from branches from which they were plucked just a few days after the caterpillars ensconced themselves. Just as had been done in China with *Bombyx mori*, apart from a few male and female adults which would be kept alive for breeding, the developing pupae inside the great tasar cocoons were destroyed before these most beautiful adult moths were ready to emerge, so that they could not break the strands of their own cocoons and fly free.

Managed by the human hand, here was a process that could have created not just continuous threads, but more of them. Like those of *Bombyx mori*, these *Antheraea paphia* cocoons became larger than they needed to be, the third largest of all the cocoons of the silk moths of their Saturniidae family. If the *Antheraea paphia* had come about because they had been bred to do so for millennia, expressly for their silk, this moth would have arisen from a progenitor that also made tasar silk, though less of it, at a time reckoned to have been some three thousand years before. This ancestor was a moth whose cocoons are less than half the size of cocoons of *A. paphia*. A moth that, less than sixty years after Roxburgh had made his drawings, would come to be catalogued as *Antheraea frithi* Moore at the India Museum, that 'Oriental Repository' established in 1798 to exhibit the returns of the East India Company's commerce at a palatial house on London's Leadenhall Street. This was the building from which, for almost a century, British India was ruled. While Company servants in India sent preserved specimens, encouraged as they were to expand Britain's knowledge for her commercial and territorial ambitions, in the Museum of Natural History at East India House sat studious lepidopterists, working in wonderment at the theatre of life which had crossed the seas and landed upon their desks.

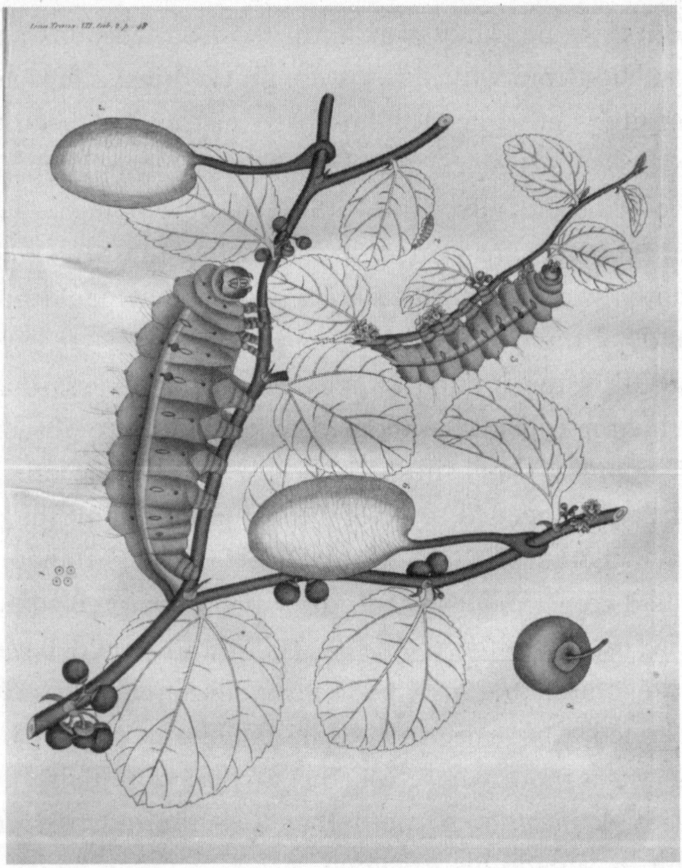

The tasar silkworm by William Roxburgh, 1802.

9

MUGA

BARONESS MATHILDE PAULINE DES GRANGES FIRST SAW THE YOUNG man who would become her husband in 1830 in the waiting room of a German stagecoach station not far from the Czech border. He was an Austrian born in Prague, a recondite intellectual, and still, at 19, almost girlish in appearance. But Johann Wilhelm Helfer was also both attractive and charmingly enthusiastic. He gave up his comfortable front seat in the coach for Pauline, while still remaining close enough to engage her in a breathless conversation centring on his plans to travel to foreign lands, and of his dreams, once there, of embarking on botanical and entomological expeditions. He spoke of how he had studied medicine for four monotonous years during which he skipped lectures but also developed an aversion to practising as a physician. Instead, his obsession with learning languages, and collecting butterflies and minute beetles, was strengthened, and his greatest joy had been in arranging them systematically. That for years he had yielded to the delight of dreaming of travelling in India as a naturalist. How in his imagination he was already revelling in his love of research and exploration of the area around Calcutta.

Pauline was 'greatly interested in his conversation, so different from that of most young men his age'. And perhaps, more than that, she, too, had wanted to see the world. He could acquire the means for 'so costly an undertaking as a journey in the East . . . by turning his medical knowledge to account', she would say. 'According to European notions, this was a singular idea, but a plan by no means impracticable in the East, where a hakim enjoys the greatest respect and is welcomed everywhere.' 'The staff of Aesculapius', she declared, 'is a better weapon for a European traveller, a greater protection, and a more effectual aid in difficulties, than the best revolver, or the most ample means.' Helfer was flattered by the attention with which she had listened to him. Those conversations began a correspondence that resulted in a marriage of affection and adventure four years later, in which they set out collecting specimens, pinning insects, pressing plants, sorting, examining and writing copious scientific studies that ceased only at midnight and were repeated almost daily. They would eventually accumulate some 48,000 beetles, 609 bird skins, 14 mammal skins, 508 Lepidoptera, 6,086 herbarium specimens; and a death that would be as remarkable as Helfer's life.

But before all that there would be journeys through Italy, Greece and Turkey. Attempts at treating people in quarantine from a plague that had begun in Alexandria but would greet them in the Turkish Gulf of Smyrna. Disguising themselves as brothers – Pauline taking a knife to her hair, donning men's robes and a broad sash in which she sheathed a dagger and two pistols – they explored the ruins of a recently destroyed Aleppo. Breathing in Indian spices through the city's surviving bazaars; handling silks, Indian shawls embroidered with silver and gold, Persian carpets, precious stones and pearls and bargaining customers. Helfer placing Persian and Hindi books under his pillow, absorbing the languages as he dreamed. Pauline falling asleep, her mind crowded with a jumble of Arabian fairy tales and German memories. Travelling to Mesopotamia driven by hot, dry winds which cracked their lips and cheeks until they bled. And Helfer finally securing a role as the natural historian of an expedition that set off on a large steamer called *Euphrates*, destined to navigate the river of the same name.

It would be seven peripatetic years before Helfer finally secured an invitation to stand in front of a room full of scientists in Calcutta and lecture on his research of the natural things he loved in the country he had dreamed of since he was a boy. The couple's final leg into Bengal had involved a six-week voyage during a monsoon in which storms, thunder and lightning competed to remove Pauline's sea legs entirely. Meanwhile, Helfer amused himself watching happily sporting dolphins and the drama of towering waves topped with crests of foam from which fish fell as if from heaven onto the decks and into the ship's kitchens. As their craft sailed up the Hoogly River to Calcutta, with the end in sight, Helfer led his wife – still dressed in Turkic men's robes, topped with a fez and turban – to the prow of the vessel, announcing with all the drama he could muster, 'the palms of India bend their crowns to greet us'.

After the Syrian deserts, the burning shores of the Persian Gulf, and the bare, dark cliffs of Arabia, they inhaled the fragrant, humid air, and the greenery they glimpsed whispered of wonderful things. That in this place was their great opportunity. As the shores of the Hoogly gradually closed in, palms appeared, their crowns bending not towards the couple but to local women who sat with their babies, and small children who frolicked around huts of bamboo and latticework with porches supported by slender poles, half hidden by gigantic banana leaves and gardens of mangoes and fragrant fruit. It was just past William Roxburgh's Botanical Garden on the right shore that they had their first glimpse of Calcutta. Approaching soon would be the palatial buildings constructed in a European style for trade and governance, and the masts of numberless ships tossing in the broad stream.

But on that steaming day towards the end of August, Helfer and Pauline ignored the advice of the ship's captain to disembark only in the European quarter, and Helfer beamed as he got into a local boat and set foot for the first time on Indian soil. Pauline watched as 'his eye glanced over the exotic vegetation, among which he hoped soon to search for hidden treasures'. It was as if he longed to take it in all at once, Pauline thought, certain 'he would have bent his knees and given vent to his excitement in words of thankfulness'. But the locals became curious about the strangely clothed couple, and, anyway, their ship's captain thought their disobedience imprudent and they were made to retrace their steps and return to his vessel. From there the river became so busy that boatmen 'steered dexterously through the crowd of ships of all nations . . . large ships, men-of-war, light brigs and bulky merchantmen; Arabian and Japanese vessels, clumsy Chinese junks and swift Indian clippers. All were engrossed in their own affairs without troubling themselves about those of their neighbours, as if the world existed for the sake of their particular interests alone . . . we were in the empire of the Ganges, the largest river of Asia, which pours every instant 500,000 cubic feet of sweet, wholesome water to the sea, spreads more blessings than any other, and is held sacred by the inhabitants of its shores . . . This is very appropriate to the teeming animal life of the Ganges territory; the shores of the river are inhabited by millions of living things, from the insect, almost invisible to the naked eye, to the huge elephant . . . it swarms with monkeys, buffaloes, wild boars, gazelles . . . reptiles crawl in the long grass . . . the woods are enlivened by flocks of birds with brilliant plumage, and luminous insects, in the water and on the tops of trees light up the darkness of night. Thousands of glittering glow worms cling in rows to the slender stems of the palm, which, swayed to and fro by the faintest breeze, look like diamond bouquets, more brilliant than any that ever adorned crowned head . . .'

Her first impressions were not wrong, for the pair had found themselves close to one of the two areas of the most profound diversity of natural life in India, one of only twenty-five in the world. Not far from Assam, from which some of Helfer's most precious specimens would later be gathered, they were on the margins of the region around the Eastern Himalayas within which lived over three thousand species of flowering plants; three hundred species of birds; nearly two hundred species of reptiles and amphibians; over eight hundred species and subspecies of birds; and almost two hundred species of mammals, large and small, among which were the highest number of primate species in all of India. There were more than four hundred species of Lepidoptera: butterflies and moths. That was also why it was the place from which several varieties of the Indus Valley civilization's ancient wild silks had been sourced. Better known to local naturalists by then was the *Antheraea paphia* of William Roxburgh. But Helfer's interest was caught by another moth, whose threads had also lain in the ruins of ancient Indus cities and would become known as the *Antheraea assamensis* Helfer. On 4 December 1836, the day on which Helfer stood before European scholars and amateur natural historians gathered in Calcutta, he would be the person who put this silk moth on the scientific record for the natural historians who would follow him.

Helfer secured a role as the natural historian of an expedition travelling on the *Euphrates*.

That gathering at which he had been invited to speak was convened by the Asiatic Society of Bengal, a society established just over half a century earlier, in January 1784, by Sir William Jones, a Fellow of London's Royal Society and distinguished orientalist, who, like Elijah Impey before him, had been a judge in the Supreme Court of Calcutta. During the same period the British East India Company began to assume greater administrative responsibilities, leading to the abolition of its trade monopoly with India in 1813 and a more sustained relationship with Bengal. Governing the country called for actions, for better or for worse, that went far beyond the commercial role the Company had been playing since 1600.

The style of new scientific endeavour in India would, therefore, mirror the needs of a new colonial administration. Indeed, from the beginning, Jones' scientific society 'resolved to follow as nearly as possible, the plan of the Royal Society at London, of which the King is Patron'.

Jones was not averse to devouring any advanced knowledge the Indians had in mathematics, astronomy and medicine, but was also firm in his belief in European superiority, and in the manifest destiny of England's commercial enterprise. The question of whether Indians would be granted membership to an Asiatic learned society headquartered in India took Jones a year to resolve, after which he suggested that prizes and medals be offered for the best communications from Indians 'with a view . . . to bring their latent science under our inspection . . .'

To be sure, European science had had a slow start in India. From the last decade of the fifteenth century the Portuguese had sought the knowledge of Indian doctors who might help them treat diseases Europe had not even known existed. In the sixteenth century the erudite Mughal emperor Akbar the Great, a man with a mind that eagerly sought all kinds of philosophies and cultural wonders, and who ruled at the zenith of his dynasty's power, showed no apparent interest in developments in European science. Granted, the missions that had approached his court were men of the cloth rather than science. Moreover, they had appeared some thirty years before Galileo – a man who had reconsidered his own priesthood for science – published his first telescopic discoveries. In Akbar's time Europe may well have had nothing of great value to offer his empire. Even in the eighteenth century, when the Indian ruler Raja Sawai Jai Singh II, founder of the fortified city of Jaipur and builder of elegant observatories, was actively seeking scientific discussion, this mathematician and astronomer king failed to be impressed by contemporary European advances in theoretical and observational astronomy.

And so there was undoubtedly value in the kind of scientific society that might convene these two bodies of knowledge. More might have been accomplished if, as other members of Jones' society had hoped, exchanges of mutual respect and equality had been encouraged. One of these members was James Prinsep, assay master for the British East India Company mint at Calcutta who not just tested coins but deciphered Brahmi texts of Ashoka, an emperor born in 304 BCE. Very soon after his arrival in Calcutta, Helfer would be heartily welcomed by Prinsep, a man he knew had not long before founded the *Journal of the Asiatic Society of Bengal*, which he also edited, and in which Helfer might, too, publish the longed-for scientific studies he wished to do in India. On paper, the Society was exactly the sort of vertiginous intellectual home Helfer could have revelled in. Except he was not in Bengal to enjoy an intellectual life with like-minded scholars, because to travel, to live, to work – to be free to do the research he had always planned – he would need some sort of income.

By then, Pauline had learned to question her earlier premise that a doctor's income would be assured in the East. They had arrived in a country administered by the British, where Helfer would repeatedly encounter 'the prejudice of the English against any doctors but their own'. Despite talking to Calcutta's men of influence to try to work out how he might make money from his scientific interests at the expense of the British Empire, the young doctor could not shake the feeling that the people in that vast empire were, in reality, simply too busy with more important – ultimately economic – affairs to trouble themselves with the joys of natural history.

But Jones' society *was* meant to promote the knowledge of natural history, even though its members also brought all manner of discussion, conceived, as it was, with the idea of broad inquiry into history and antiquities, the arts, sciences and literature of Asia. Over time, in the *Journal of the Asiatic Society of Bengal*, there would be papers on many subjects. Folklore and language;

local rituals and Roman coins; medicinal plants, music and laws; the dissection of a pangolin, cures for snakebite, the Indian game of chess; meteorology and astronomy, a register of the tides of Singapore; studies of the complex ridges and escarpments of the great Vindhya mountains; descriptions of hooded snakes and fossilized crocodiles and hippopotamus; analyses of ruins and inscriptions and the peoples and places of the region: Persians, Afghans, Arabs, Hindus; population censuses; surveys of Assam.

As such, some topics wore only the thinnest veils of intellectual concern, because there was always the potential for profit in the gathering of knowledge around foreign peoples, places and things. And so Helfer's best plan was this: to direct attention to various branches of natural history, which, as he communicated to Pauline, 'deserved the attention of Europeans and the government, not only from a scientific, but from a mercantile point of view'. To that end, Helfer set about giving his course of lectures. Hosted in Calcutta's town hall, they covered, as promised, various topics that might induce the Company to fund his interests. But among them was one of which Pauline made particular note. It was to be a long and fascinating discussion he entitled 'On the Indigenous Silkworms of India'. As he took the lectern, Helfer was introduced to his audience as a medical doctor, member of the medical faculties at the universities in Prague and Pavia, member of the Entomological Society in Paris, and so it went on – for, despite his youth, Helfer's achievements had been considerable.

And then he began: 'Silk was in all times an article of the greatest importance throughout the ancient world . . . in our days the introduction and manufacture of silkworms is a source of unlimited riches to the countries of Europe, where it is cultivated on a large scale. To elucidate this it may be observed, that France alone exported in the year 1820 wrought silk to the value of more than

123 millions of francs. The importation of raw and worked silk into England amounted to 4,547,812 pounds in the year 1828, of which about 1,500,000 pounds were brought from Bengal, 3,047,000 pounds were, therefore, brought from foreign countries, chiefly Italy and Turkey. The northern parts of Europe and chiefly, England are less suited for its cultivation on account of climate . . .'

But more than climatic difficulties, Helfer was aware that the European silk industry had met with crisis in recent years, partly because by then their strains of *Bombyx mori* had become increasingly inbred and disease-prone. The once highly lucrative silk industry in Italy, where Helfer had lived and studied, and from which England sourced the bulk of her silks, was one based squarely upon *Bombyx mori* silkworms, that had, from 1805 onwards, been threatened with collapse from a lethal disease which long-domesticated moths had become unable to fend off. 'For many years', wrote one nineteenth century naturalist, 'the utmost anxiety has prevailed on the European Continent . . . in regard to the common silkworm . . . which were centuries ago imported into Europe from the northern provinces of China, where for many centuries previously they had likewise been kept in a state of domestication . . . the constitution of the worm appearing to be so thoroughly weakened and undermined, by diseases arising from a long and uniform course of domestication . . . as to excite the most lively apprehensions lest the insect should suddenly become extinct.' It was true that multiple microorganisms had had a taste for these caterpillars: viruses, bacteria and fungi, against which the millennia of inbreeding had rendered the *Bombyx* weak at fending off. Added to this, solutions to such infections had not been easy to find, given that in Helfer's time the idea of 'microbes' had not even been defined.

Italian silk farmers called the disease that covered their

caterpillars in a white fungi-sprouting powder *un mal del segno*, which translated as 'a bad sign', and adopted silkworm-rearing practices to avert such omens by burning incense. It was as good an approach as any, because at that time scientists were little better informed. Then, bad air was a bona fide hypothesis. No one yet thought of infections as coming from germs, that is not until a twenty-five-year-long study of diseased silkworm cocoons begun in 1807 led an Italian entomologist to develop the germ theory of disease. His experiments on silkworms had shown that infection could be transmitted from a sick caterpillar to a healthy one; that such infection might be prevented by the use of disinfectant on infected silkworms; and that removing worms before they became contagious, and quarantining them, could prevent transmission.

If that were the case for silkworms, this Italian entomologist, Agostino Bassi, would also propose that human disease could also originate from germs. Those were the studies which would later end up on the desk of the French chemist Louis Pasteur, when, around sixty years later, a new disease hit France's silkworms, which he, too, was able to demonstrate was caused by an infection: this time, one not just contagious, but hereditary. Those silkworm studies would give Pasteur the robust body of evidence for contagion from which the study of human diseases would also benefit. Not long after, he developed a rabies vaccine that saved the life of a small boy bitten by a dog and whose death seemed certain. He followed this with a vaccine to stem an anthrax epidemic affecting French sheep and people. He then presented an 1880 lecture entitled 'Of Infectious Diseases, Especially the Disease of Chicken Cholera', in which he detailed some of the precedents for his work, in which he stated that 'the practices of vaccination and variolization have been known in India for the longest time'.

Back in India, at a society less welcoming of Indians and their science, Helfer explained that such catastrophic infection of Europe's Chinese silkworms was proving a thorn in the silk industry's side in the lands to its west. Then, he set out in some detail attempts made in Europe over time that used other animals from which silken threads could also be extracted. Notably, these were a wild moth known as *Saturnia pyri* which had spread across Austria, northern Italy and Switzerland, and a curious Mediterranean mollusc of gigantic proportions. Also included was a spider whose potential for the industrial manufacture of silk the French government had recognized and commissioned a mathematician, natural historian and experimental physicist called René-Antoine Ferchault de Réaumur to investigate. And still, all of these, to Helfer's mind at least, were unlikely to enter general use: the first were too fussy, the second, a matter of curiosity, and the third, too fond of cannibalism to really dedicate themselves to the French cause.

All that was a preamble to what Helfer had really hoped would excite his audience that day: his research on the potential of two Indian silk moths to succeed where other creatures had failed. 'A discovery . . . which promises to prove not so abortive as those . . .', he said, and that, should England wish to exceed the efforts and income of other silk-trading nations, these moths 'therefore, must be of the greatest importance'.

'Vast provinces of India are rivalled in variety, preciousness and perfection of their productions, only by the celestial empire', by which Helfer was referring to the competition that had been set by China, home of the finest silks of *Bombyx mori*, for millennia. But, he indicated, with all the erudition, charm and flattery characteristic of the man, plus a little sycophancy, that as these vast provinces of India were 'now in the hands of an enlightened, benevolent government, they will probably surpass it in a short time, when its natural resources, daily more conspicuous, shall be discovered, examined, and brought into general use . . .'

Helfer reflected William Roxburgh's words in his earlier study of the tasar moth, acknowledging, as the old botanist had, that 'as in China, so in India, silk has been produced since time immemorial', though this was 'not the silk of the later introduced mulberry caterpillar, but the silk from various indigenous cocoons, which are found only, and exclusively here . . .' For that reason, Helfer thought Roxburgh's studies cursory and insufficient. Roxburgh, Helfer said, had only mentioned two species, one of which had been the tasar moth, *Antheraea paphia*. 'Since that time', Helfer said, with very little exception, 'no further attention has been paid to the subject . . .'

His own studies, by contrast, had been more rigorous, because Helfer 'had ample opportunity of studying the tasar silkworm'. In September 1836, more than three thousand of their cocoons had been sent to him. He had been told by another naturalist that these were silk moths that 'cannot be domesticated, because the moths take flight before the females are fecundated'. This, Helfer announced, was 'against my experience: I kept them under a mosquito curtain to prevent their evasion, there they were impregnated readily by the males, and deposited everywhere many thousand eggs, and the young caterpillars issued the tenth day.' His point was a fair one. Other naturalists noted that 'no doubt, both male and female, will fly away if not confined in any manner to prevent them, particularly the males, for the sole purpose of seeking females'.

It was not the habit of male tasar silk moths to mate so closely with females which had hatched with them, and it was this that prevented the kind of inbreeding that had been so destructive to *Bombyx mori*, as Helfer already suspected. Left to their own devices, male tasar moths would in fact fly long distances in search of females, across the seven to ten nights of their adult lifespan. After mating, females, too, flew away from their mating sites to lay their eggs on the branches of trees further afield, spreading their eggs so that their caterpillars had ample food and need not compete for nourishment. Still, these strategies for the survival and diversity of their kind could be subverted in the name of an industry which might be more productive if they were artificially bred in captivity instead, Helfer thought, '. . . therefore the fear entertained of the difficulty in this respect seems to be easily overcome . . .'

But that was not all. From the moment of his arrival in India, he said, he 'had paid an unremitted zealous attention to the productions of botany and zoology, and had been so happy to identify in the course of two months, two other species of the Saturnia which yield silk . . .' Helfer went on to describe to those gathered in Calcutta's town hall numerous different moth species of India, 'which actually produce silk of which seven kinds have never been mentioned before'. There was no doubt, he believed, 'that in India exist some more insects which furnish this precious material. The repeated and so often frustrated endeavours of ingenious men in Europe would certainly find in India an ample, and highly remunerating field in this branch of speculation.'

No doubt in a bid to offer his own, hopefully highly remunerated services, Helfer offered a proposal. 'It would be very interesting to collect all moths which form cocoons, amounting, to judge by analogy, probably upward of 150 species, to watch their natural economy, and to send specimens of each cocoon to Europe, to be there attentively examined . . .'

The discoveries that emerged in Helfer's hands merited particular attention, not least because he responded to criticism levelled by some English manufacturers regarding the use of Indian wild silks. Helfer had heard that they, like their science, were considered inferior. 'This is yet an undecided question', Helfer said, thinking this an unequal comparison. Different silks bore their own unique characteristics, and, therefore, offered a variety of uses that *Bombyx* silk did not. But he also proposed that these moths might have, as had *Bombyx mori*, the potential to be studiously cultivated – strategically bred – in order to increase the natural qualities of the silks they produced; to raise them to a level that would make them competitive with the mulberry silkworm, that, as Bassi and Pasteur well knew, 'degenerates if not properly attended to'.

If Helfer proposed such an idea it was because by then he firmly believed that 'India has thus the internal means of providing the whole of Europe with a material which would rival cotton and woollen cloth, and would be preferred in many cases to both, if brought within the reach of every one by a lower price: and an unlimited resource of riches and revenue might be opened under proper management'. Because, he added, 'all silk produced in Hindustan has hitherto found a ready and profitable market in Calcutta, and the demand is always greater than the supply . . .'

In this, Helfer was not mistaken. Silk from the *Antheraea assama* moths he would go on to describe had indeed been produced since time immemorial – or at least for far longer than his contemporary orientalists could even have dreamed at that point. He had trawled through the studies of European naturalists, and there, although 'this species has never been mentioned before . . . the fabrication of silk from it seems to be very common amongst the Assamese'. But there were plenty of amateur naturalists and not long after Helfer began his silk moth studies in Calcutta, a report on that same moth would be sent to James Prinsep by a collector in Assam.

This 'remarkable province', due north of the British stronghold of Bengal, was, as Helfer noted, one that had only recently been acquired after an East India Company military intervention in 1825. Annexed from the Ahom kings, it was acquired following a war waged to safeguard adjoining British Bengal possessions, but culminated in the takeover of virtually the entire frontier region of northeast India. Assam's valleys and plains north and east of the snaking blue mercury of the Brahmaputra River system, and its hill tracts rising in the direction of the Himalayas, quickly became a region in which a number of amateur natural historians, some of them army officers, began accumulating collections. That was to be expected. Assam was located in a region created by tectonic plates, raised from terrain crumpled and buckled by the force of the Indian and Eurasian landmasses colliding. Assam was home to forests with great natural resources, and contained within them rich natural diversity including nearly four hundred species of Lepidoptera, with forty-one belonging to the Bombycidae or Saturniidae families. Among those was an astonishing, delicate cocoon of bright yellow silk, whose strands were worked into an open, oval net of golden filigree by the caterpillars of *Cricula trifenestrata*.

These *Cricula* silkworms lived on some of the same trees as Helfer's wild *Antheraea assama*; but it would be the cocoons of the *Antheraea assama* silk moths in particular that were among those found to have been reeled into a silk in the Indus cities of pre-history. Coarse and straw-like, these were created by caterpillars with yellow and brown stripes covered in copious spikes, that hatched out of clusters of eggs the colour of chestnut mushrooms and grew into soft and succulent pale-green caterpillars growing to some ten centimetres in length. Helfer had himself seen neither eggs nor caterpillars of the *Antheraea assama*, except

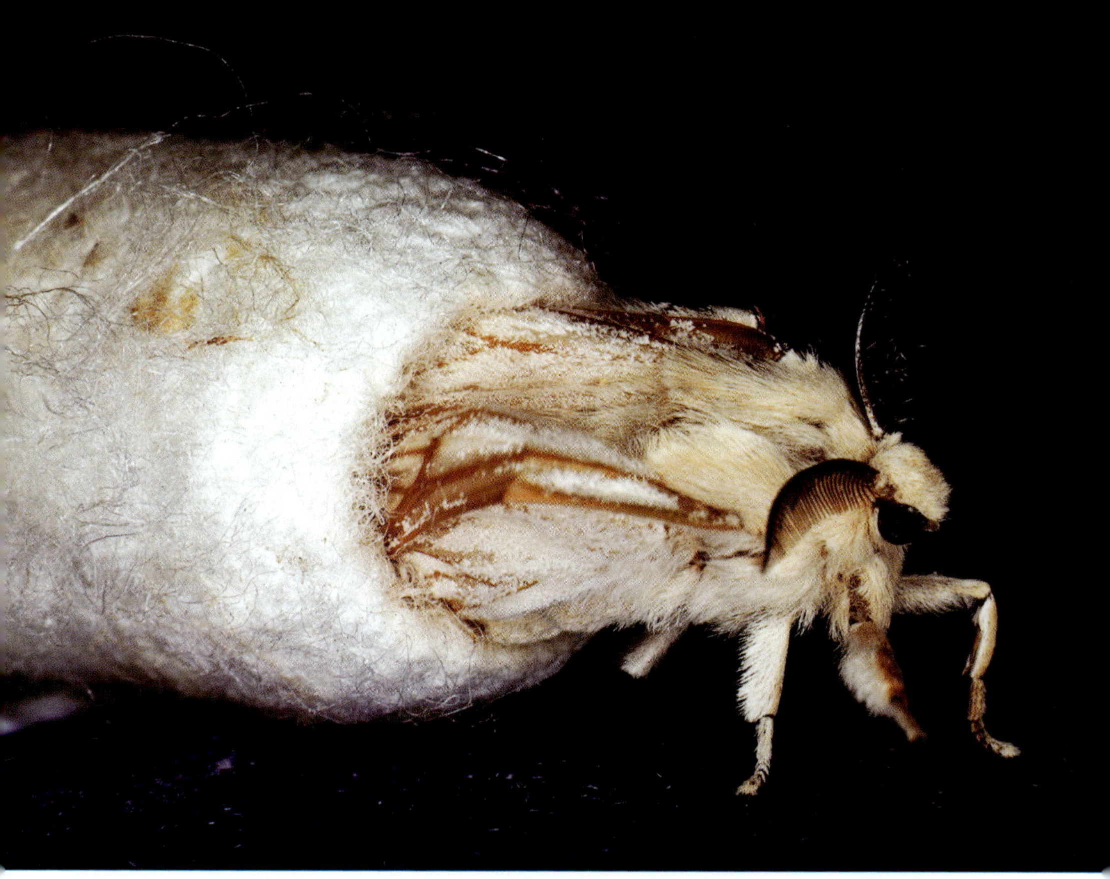

Domesticated silk moth (*Bombyx mori*) emerging from its cocoon. Once metamorphosis is complete, after around ten days inside the cocoon, the silk moth vomits a fluid containing an enzyme called cocoonase, which specifically breaks down the sericin protein in silk, making the cocoon soft enough for the moth to escape.

From 'The European Insects' by Maria Sibylla Merian, published posthumously as an expanded version in 1730, under the title *Caterpillars, Their Wondrous Transformation and Peculiar Nourishment from Flowers.*

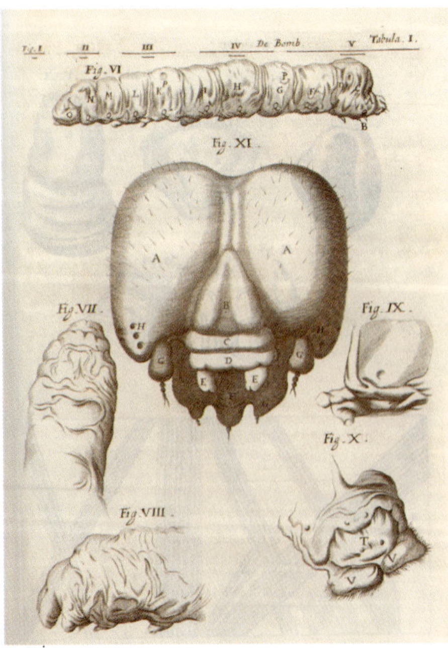

Head of the domesticated silk moth, (*Bombyx mori*) larva, showing its simple eyes (dark spots, left and right); mouthparts (centre); and of the adult form after metamorphosis, with compound eyes and large feathery antennae, but no mouth parts.

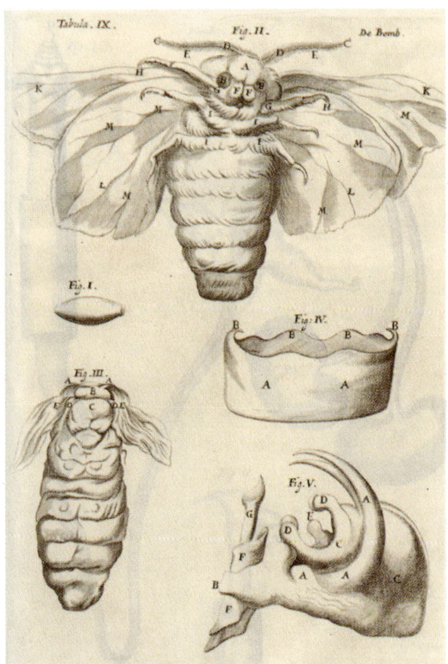

Insect anatomy. Seventeenth-century drawings of the anatomy of a silk worm and silkmoth as observed under the microscope by the Italian physician and microscopist Marcello Malpighi (1628–1694). These plates are from a volume of Malpighi's *Opera omnia* (1686).

These golden-coloured filigree cocoons of Jan Helfer's *Cricula trifenestrata* were collected in the 1880s and excited much attention in Wardle's exhibits. The filigree effect occurs because multiple larvae often spin their cocoons in close proximity, creating a silken network. At first silvery, the colour changes to metallic yellow gold in the space of a few days.

'The Manner of Feeding Silkworms', 1753. A silkworm farm, showing the interior of the rearing house or Magnangerie and the collection of mulberry leaves on which the silkworms were fed.

Zain al-Din's illustration of the *Antheraea paphia*, or tasar silk moth, including a male and female, alongside a tasar silkworm, and a cocoon that hangs from its food tree like a fruit. Calcutta, 1777.

In the seventeenth century, Queen Anne of Denmark commissioned the building of a silkworm house at Oatlands Palace. She is portrayed wearing a dress made of mulberry silk embroidered with *Bombyx mori* larvae and mulberry leaf patterns.

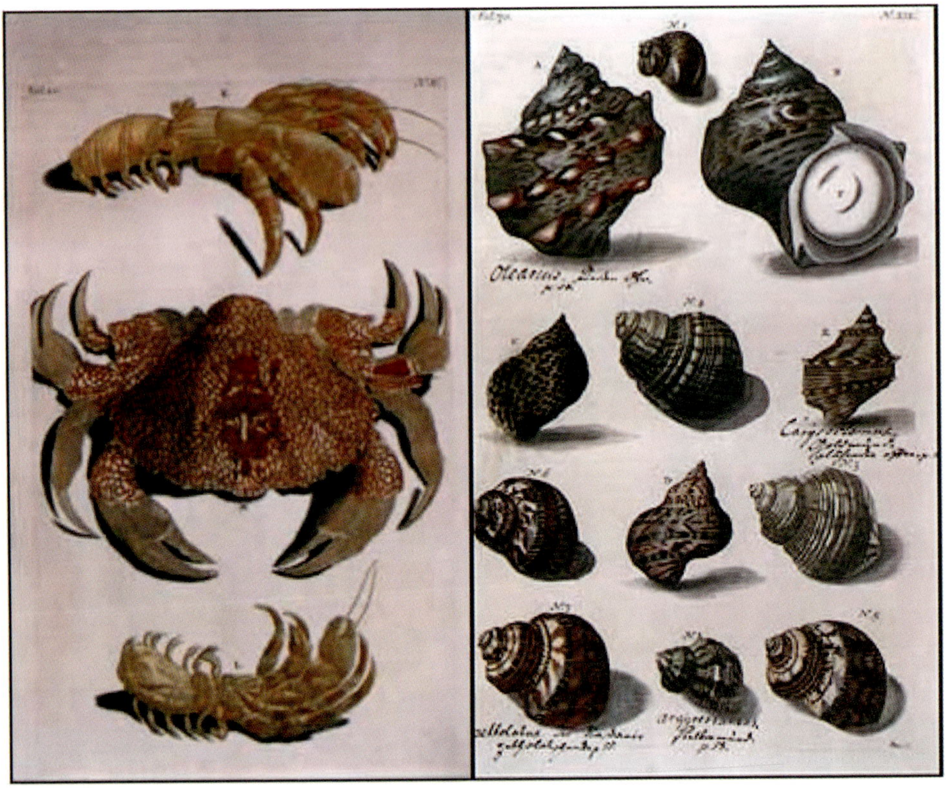

Maria Sybilla Merian coloured the illustrations of the beautiful shells Georg Eberhardt Rumpf had collected in Ambon, in order to fund the publication of her 1705 magnum opus, *Metamorphosis insectorum Surinamensium*.

George Emory Goodfellow's medical office was on the second floor of the Crystal Palace Saloon in Tombstone: a town referred to as 'the condensation of wickedness', where shootouts were all too common.

The weaving of a Banarasi Sari which are most frequently made from mulberry silk, but are also woven from tasar and other wild silk threads. Varanasi, India.

A woman weighs a batch of silk moth cocoons in order to determine their sex, circa 1955.

A string of diseased silkworm cocoons used by Louis Pasteur, 1865-1870. Pasteur demonstrated the cause of the silkworms' illness to be a contagious infection. It helped him build a robust body of evidence for contagion from which the study of human diseases benefited.

Silkworm cocoons arranged on trays to be dried in the sun in a Tamil Nadu village, India, 1980.

in a drawing that accompanied the specimen of the male moth that had been sent to Prinsep. If Helfer had been able to watch them undergo their metamorphosis, he would have seen this take place inside a large cocoon of a naturally golden-hued silk that could also look white, depending on what food plants the caterpillars had access to. These cocoons, more perishable than those of the tasar moth, were reeled into a silk that, like its moths, was known as muga.

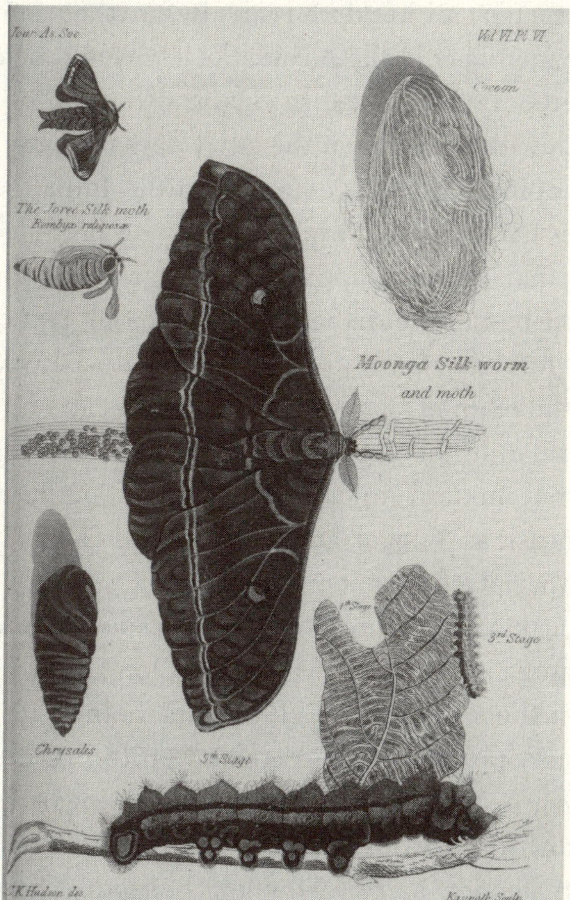

Muga silkworm and moth.

Though Helfer would not have known it, the earliest specific account of the use of muga in Assam dated from 1662, from the records of a general of the Mughal emperor Aurangzeb, who invaded the Ahom kingdom some 160 years before the Company. Those Ahoms supported Assam's silk industry, particularly during the reign of their dynasty's second ruler, late in the thirteenth century, and the silk of the muga silkworm seems to have been reserved for the exclusive use of the descendants of those royal families for the next six hundred years. Before that time, the attention of some members of the Asiatic Society would be drawn once again to references from Western classical sources, 'of the ancient trade of India with the west, in the latter days of Rome', with some being of the opinion that silk commerce from India to the west in Roman times had consisted exclusively of the products of Assam.

Far earlier than Roman trade records, muga would appear among the silks described in the Arthaśāstra, a Sanskrit text on domestic politics and foreign affairs probably dating to between 321 and 297 BCE, in the reign of Chandragupta. He was an emperor whose dynasty would rule for the next five hundred years, his domain extending from modern Afghanistan down to southern India, and as far northeast as Bengal and Assam, with all of the natural wonders of that place, and its wild silks.

Strictly speaking, the enormous moth responsible for the large cocoons of muga silk was not wild. It had long been reared inside houses, or in the trees around cultivators' homes, in which state they were most productive, and created up to five broods a year. Muga moths are striking, with males whose wings appear in hues from a reddish-orange to a deep blood-red, and females a rich orange; with slender, hairy yellow legs beneath. The antennae of the males, Helfer noted, were broader than usual in the Saturniidae, and their abdomens were more than two-thirds the breadth of both their wings. The thorax of the male specimen he studied was 'clothed near the head in a silverish-grey colour', with white lines the shape of half a crescent moon on their upper wings. Two further specks were also present upon the wings, this time semi-circular in shape, though these, unlike the wild silk moths Merian and Roxburgh had described, did not have the astonishing glass-like transparency. More similar to the *Bombyx mori* triangular strands, the silk strands of muga cocoons are round in shape, rather than the flattened ribbons of the tasar.

Because of their cocoons' structure, which is less regular than that of the fully domesticated silk moth, no more than half of the muga silk from any cocoon might ever really be spun, and sometimes a little less. Much waste silk is produced, but this too could be used in other ways, if not in the manufacture of fabrics. Like the tasar silkworm, muga caterpillars also produce a cementing fluid as they build those cocoons that protect them until they are transformed into splendid moths. That substance, however, made any bleaching of their natural colours laborious, but it also meant that cloth woven from it would quite naturally resist staining. And so, where some saw inferiority, Helfer saw their potential, because while it may have been coarser, and more difficult to work with than the smooth silk of *Bombyx mori*, the beautiful glossy, golden-fawn hue of the muga was not one that faded with time, for the molecules that built its particular fibroin proteins would also give it its golden lustre and a remarkable tensile strength.

Helfer would also describe a variant of the *Attacus atlas* silk moth he had identified, an insect so large (around twenty-five centimetres across) that it could be mistaken for a small bird, and whose brown and beige hued cocoons produced a silk known as fagara, which was woven undyed for its natural shades. That was related to another *Attacus* moth, whose silk had been so long in use that, like Helfer's *Antheraea assama* and Roxburgh's *Antheraea paphia*, it would also be uncovered from the ruins of ancient Indus Valley cities, sourced, millennia ago, from the region around Assam, and Darjeeling, in the northeast of Bengal.

To the traditional silk workers of Assam, these threads – like the moths that were responsible for them – were known as eri, or arrindy, which were bred and reared 'in a domesticated state, as they do the common silkworm,' as Roxburgh had noted some years before. The Victorian naturalists called moths like this *Phalaena cynthia*, *Samia cynthia* or *Samia ricini*. Housed indoors away from natural predators, their voracious young were fed copious quantities of the leaves of the castor oil plant, known by Roxburgh as the *Palma Christi*, or *Ricinus communis*, but which in Bengal was called, much as the worms were, arrindy.

There would, in fact, be four species of the genus *Samia* to be found in India: Roxburgh's *ricini*, which had been domesticated; the *canningi*, the wild progenitor from which the *ricini* had been derived; as well as the *kohlli* from a state that would be known as Mizoram, also in India's northeast; and the *Samia fulva*, whose natural home was to the southeast, in the islands of the Andaman Sea, which perhaps Helfer might have found there if he had survived long enough.

Their cocoons, like those of the domesticated *Bombyx mori*, were remarkable for their softness and coloured 'white, or yellowish'. As Helfer would note, this silkworm, too, 'is so productive . . . The worm grows rapidly, and offers no difficulty whatever for an extensive speculation.' Except, unlike the *mori*, the large number of soft and white cocoons produced by the eri were made of a 'filament so exceedingly delicate, as to render it impracticable to wind off the silk'. But there was also another reason for this impracticality that Helfer would not be privy to. Unlike tasar and muga cocoons, which their moths break out of by softening the silk with a strong fluid that softens and digests it, eri cocoons needed only a weaker chemical concoction because their caterpillars ingeniously incorporated an escape valve into their cocoons for when the time came for their adults to emerge.

That meant that the threads of its cocoons could never be entirely unbroken, nor, therefore, simply reeled into a long, seamless strand as *Bombyx mori*'s were. In any case, this would not be an impediment to Roxburgh or Helfer. Nor had it been for the people of Bengal who had long made their own fabrics from it. But though '. . . the people were obliged to spin it like cotton', and though it was coarser than mulberry, the silk of the eri was evidently not just finer than muga and tasar, but was the softest and warmest of all silks. As Helfer had found in an old letter written to Roxburgh, the qualities of this silk were intriguing: 'it gives a cloth of seemingly loose, coarse texture, but of incredible durability; the life of one person being seldom sufficient to wear out a garment made of it, so that the same piece descends from mother to daughter.'

'On account of the double profit which would be derived', Helfer would therefore suggest, 'from the same area of land cultivating it with the castor-oil plant, which produces oil and feeds the worm, and extensive cultivation of this species would be highly recommendable . . .' Because Helfer knew that 'the silk of this species has hitherto never been wound off' their cocoons, he had offered up an alternative suggestion, posing the question of whether it might 'not be particularly well adapted to mix it in certain textures with cotton?' To the people of Assam who had known it long before the Asiatic Society gathered before Helfer that December day in 1836, the cloths made from the silks of all of these moths were valued not just for their beauty, but because their colours did not fade, but improved with use and with age.

And that was what Helfer sought to persuade the men who attended his lectures. It wasn't that his persuasions did not gain traction; on the contrary, they so excited attention that the *Friend of India* took notice. This was a newspaper published every Thursday morning, covering topics almost as diverse as the Society's, with articles ranging from 'Steam Engines and Railroads' to 'The Landed Aristocracy' to 'The Toleration of the British Government of India'. The paper picked up on Helfer's fixation on India's silk moths, and urged the government to profit by his suggestions.

But 'still they did not produce the desired effect among the influential classes', Pauline would later write; 'in spite of the politeness with which he was treated, it seemed as if something inexplicable frustrated his wishes'. After those repeated disappointments, Helfer gave up on his Calcutta dream and instead looked north to Lahore, seeking the patronage of the one-eyed Ranjit Singh, the Lion of Punjab, whose 11-year-old son would, in a few short years, be exiled to England, forced to renounce all claims of sovereignty in exchange for a British government pension.

But while Ranjit Singh was still on the throne, as far as Helfer had been given to understand the Maharaja quite liked Europeans, and was not averse to employing their knowledge to the advantage of his vast territories. But, before Helfer had even considered seeking his patronage, he was advised against going to Lahore by a general who had started life in St Tropez, served in Napoleon's army and was now in the service of Ranjit Singh himself. This Frenchman, Jean-François Allard, had made Pauline's acquaintance at the house of Elizabeth Jane, Lady d'Oyly, a woman with a large and elegant mind who had become one of her best friends in Calcutta. Pauline had accepted drawing lessons from Eliza's husband, Sir Charles d'Oyly, a Company official and former opium agent who spent so much time painting Indian landscapes that he had become, like his wife, an accomplished artist. In return, Pauline acted as translator when Allard called upon the d'Oylys.

Allard told Pauline that he believed Ranjit Singh to be 'a clever but capricious and arbitrary man' with whom Helfer's future would continue to be insecure. And in any case, he added, 'there may soon be a change in government, the consequences of which, under Asiatic despotisms, are incalculable'. After that, Helfer also decided against an offer from Dwarakanath Tagore, an entrepreneur who had partnered with British industrialists, and who lived in a country seat so splendid that English newlyweds would honeymoon there. Helfer and Pauline had first encountered Tagore in the music room of his grand house, dressed in rich Indian costume, sitting at his piano and singing an Italian aria. A series of long and fascinating conversations about soil culture ensued between the two men, but in the end Helfer turned down a very gratifying proposal to work, at Tagore's expense and across his extensive territories, fearing that it would turn him from a man of scientific research into a mere agriculturalist.

But he determined to try one last time to persuade the government in Calcutta to accept the offer of his services as a naturalist. On the last day of 1836 his efforts paid off and he received an official notice of his appointment. That commission, however, was to draw him away from India. Now, Helfer was to undertake an expedition of exploration in the Malay Peninsula, a region the British had not long before occupied at the expense of Burma. There, 'he was not only to collect specimens in every department of natural history, but to investigate the nature of the soil, with a view to discover for what it was best adapted, to send in seeds, plants, and specimens of wood for the botanical gardens, to take meteorological observations, and make mercantile and statistical returns. Further he was to visit the vast teak forests, which furnish the best timber for ship building, and the old tin mines; the search for coal-fields also, which was of great importance for the intended steam navigation to China, was a point specially insisted on . . .'

And so, on 21 January 1837, the couple embarked on the schooner *Elizabeth* and left as they had arrived, along the Hoogly River. Four years later, almost to the day, with Pauline settled on the Burmese plantation that became their home, Helfer set out on a new adventure to the archipelago surrounding the Malay Peninsula. 'His special destination this time was the Andaman Isles, although they were not among British possessions, and it was therefore not part of his mission to explore them', Pauline wrote. 'Very little was known of the formation or products of the islands, and still less of the natives, of whom fabulous stories were told – some asserting that they were not men but anthropomorphic apes, others that they were men but very much like monkeys. All this inspired Helfer with a desire to go and see for himself . . .'

It was a decision Pauline begged him not to take, and one that she would live to regret.

The last notes in Helfer's diary make for compelling reading: of how he 'gave orders to steer for the Andamans'. That 'the first object that met his eyes was a black, naked, Andamanese negro . . . they did not appear to me to be less than the ordinary height, walked very upright, and were, so far as I could see, unarmed . . . I was very sorry that prudence forbade landing. I should have so much liked to see these specimens of humanity near.'

Instead, Helfer studied a peculiar species of tree that looked like a fine oak and produced a fruit he found inedible. He thought about how the flatness of these islands would be admirably adapted for the importing and planting of the coconut palms he so loved. He looked at the nests of swallows and walked along sandy shores, botanizing. He sat with his sailors and drank water for the rest of that fearfully hot day. Helfer's head felt like it was burning in the heat of the day. Bearing firearms, he rowed out to offer coconuts to a young Andaman islander who 'chattered a great deal, grinned with white teeth, and laughed aloud. I laughed too', Helfer said, 'when he broke out into roars of laughter.'

The next day Helfer rowed out to a sandy bank with his captain and eight soldiers and a pilot who enjoyed looking for periwinkles. He was not armed. He offered coconuts to the islanders. They had no particular wish to be friends. Moments later, a group of them reappeared, all carrying bows. Helfer's boat capsized under a shower of poisoned arrows. One of them pierced his already burning head. Pauline would never again set eyes on her husband, dead or alive, because as his sailors scattered for safety in the ensuing chaos, Helfer's body sank slowly below the gentle turquoise waves. And although he was never to see it, just a few years after his death, experiments in the seamless reeling, and in the generation of a new variety of fabrics from India's wild silk threads would finally begin.

10

ATTACUS

ALTHOUGH ELIZABETH D'OYLY WAS BORN IN SCOTLAND, THE VISIT TO INDIA during which she had met and married Sir Charles was not her first. She had travelled to the subcontinent twenty years before, aged about 4, with her mother and a father who was then in the service of the East India Company at its fort in the Madras Presidency, for that place was closer to Calcutta than the precious clove and nutmeg islands due east of the Malay Peninsula. It was in Madras that her younger sister Isabella was born in 1794.

The girls' father was Major Thomas Ross, a Royal Artillery officer who was posted to India after distinguished service in Martinique, Havana, Florida and Grenada, including commanding a detachment in St Vincent 'with which he happily suppressed the black Charibbee Indians', descendants of Caribbean Amerindians and Africans who had come from other islands in a bid to escape slavery. Orphaned at an early age, the sisters were placed in the care of the husband of a close cousin of their mother's, the sixth Countess of Loudoun, Flora Mure-Campbell. Flora's husband, Francis Rawdon-Hastings, was a Company administrator and a Fellow of the Royal Society of London and had fought in the American Revolutionary War, and was ennobled for his efforts. As Lord Hastings, he would later become Governor-General of India, and then of Malta, and would die at sea on board HMS *Revenge*. In life, he was a dedicated guardian to the Ross sisters; though he initially disapproved of Elizabeth's choice of Sir Charles d'Oyly due to the interest of far wealthier suitors, he had already given his blessing to the marriage of Isabella, by then, aged 19, to Sir Walter Raleigh Gilbert, an army officer with the East India Company descended from the celebrated sixteenth-century Elizabethan legal pirate of the same name, and so praised for his roles in the Anglo-Sikh Wars that he was made a baronet.

While Isabella's husband battled for territory in India, she followed the aesthetic inclinations of her artistic sister and brother-in-law, also taking up watercolour painting, with the assistance of an Indian artist. Her albums would be filled with natural history images 'drawn . . . some by myself and some by a native painter', as well as her copious scientific observations. There would be at least three such albums, in which were ninety-one drawings of butterflies and moths, caterpillars, other insects, and flora, and ninety-six pages of natural history notes made between 1825 and 1828, eight years before Helfer's arrival and the blossoming of Pauline's great friendship with her sister. It is not clear whether Helfer counted Isabella among his scientific peers, or if he conversed with her about her studies; his lectures made no mention of her. But by the time Helfer communicated his studies of the wild silk moths of India to the members of the Asiatic Society of Bengal, the pages of her manuscripts already contained, in fine detail, observations of some of the same moths as Helfer had described, and many more.

These observations did not just match the detail of the two moths Roxburgh had identified as candidates for a new source of silk for

Britain, but exceeded them in the elegance of their descriptions and the finesse of their images. Isabella had sat with these insects over many months, capturing their transformations. She watched those of the *Antheraea paphia* with attention as her 'Tusseh moths are hatched twice in the year, in May and August: the larvae go into the chrysalis state in September, remaining so til the May following; whilst those that enter the chrysalis state in July come out in three weeks . . . The caterpillar . . . spins a strong cord, composed of many threads, altogether about the thickness of a crow quill, at the end of which it weaves the cocoon. The cocoon is so transparent for the first six and thirty hours that the larva may be distinctly perceived at working the interior; after that time the cocoon gradually acquired consistency by the continual industry of the caterpillar, and becomes quite opaque from the addition of a glutinous liquid with which it moistens the whole. When that dries the cocoon appears as if covered with white powder, and in the course of a couple of days becomes perfectly hard.'

Except that, unlike Roxburgh and Helfer, and though she knew that silks were made from those cocoons, silk would not be the focus of Isabella's interests. Her eye was not on the industry or economic uses of these insects, but on their metamorphoses. Her studies were independent of income or application, rich in detail and exquisitely observed.

The tasar moth was not the only moth with silken cocoons that Isabella had observed or drawn. There were others, even more peculiar, like the Indian moon moth, *Actias selene*, with its almost luminescent pale parrot-green and pink hues. These were moths that dissolved their cocoons with a colourless fluid, and separated their own threads of silk with a remarkable wing spur, so that they could break free as adults to fly at night in the skies that Isabella knew well, over Calcutta, and across four districts of West Bengal.

There was *Hypsa ficus*, with its dark, red-speckled caterpillar with menacing spikes, and *Chalcosia pectinicornis*, whose larvae were reminiscent of orange-toned sea cucumbers, which built large, oval cocoons with dense outer coverings and interiors of soft silken fabric half hidden inside the folds of leaves, from which Isabella watched 'perfect moths' emerge twelve days later. The *Psalis securis* caterpillar with its tufts of silken hairs that protruded like long brushes and metamorphosed inside soft, irregular looking cocoons both silky and hairy in texture. *Enome ampla*, whose larva she found one August in a hollow bamboo, from which it ventured out for food only at night, and fifteen days later wove a transparent web out of which its moth emerged a week after that, though strangely, as Isabella noted, 'the female is apterous' – meaning that it was entirely without wings.

There were the *Trisula variegata* larvae that covered their cocoons in earth; a cocoon 'covered with small short stiff hairs, which adhered so closely to the hand, that pincers were necessary to extract them', that had been crafted by a *Trabala Vishnu* caterpillar brought to Isabella on 20 June 1825, and that 'when touched, left a sensation on the skin similar to that of the sting of the nettle . . .' She also studied the curious and interesting *Parasa laleana*, whose moth 'cut a perfectly circular hole in the top of the [cocoon] case', leaving 'a kind of hinge' on the porthole from which the insect emerged; and *Parasa Isabella* (Moore), a dainty, delightful moth with green and yellow wings that she had collected in Bengal and which would later be named after her by a London entomologist named Frederic Moore. Of all the moths Isabella described, there was one group which, in Bengal, had long been nurtured for its silk in particular. This was the *Attacus* group, and the specimen that had come to Isabella's attention was the largest among their type. These were not from the *Saturniini* tribe as were the *Antheraea* moths like the tasar and the muga, of even the Indian moon moth, *Actias selene*, but from a different tribe – the *Attacini*.

In 1767, Carl Linnaeus had given a moth like this the name *Attacus atlas*. On 4 September 1825 Isabella had had 'a specimen (female) of this magnificent moth . . . caught . . .' Ten days later, the young caterpillars, 'black with numerous white spines', that a few days after they hatched 'had become a light green . . . ate their skins after casting them', and '. . . day and night devoured leaves' and '. . . grew to an enormous size'. 'On the 12th of October, one of these began preparing for its transformation by bending back a large leaf, and inclosing itself in a web, which it completed on the 13th . . .'

Less grand, but bearing wings a reddish-brown, with triangular, translucent patches much like Merian's glass-winged *Attacus* from the forests of Suriname, there was one other, highly significant Indian silk moth that would soon be placed into the same *Attacus* genus.

Although Roxburgh had described his *Phalæna cynthia* scientifically twenty-one years before Isabella's enormous *Attacus atlas*, a close genetic relative, his attempts at illustrating the metamorphosis of the eri had been problematic.

It would not escape the notice of one naturalist captain in the Bengal army that 'Dr Roxburgh's figure of the caterpillar is . . . so thoroughly unlike those occurring here, that, notwithstanding the identity of the [adult moth], I am unwilling to pronounce decisively as to the species . . .' It may be that he had wrongly identified another caterpillar from Bengal which had ended up in his sketches. Even so, what he recorded of the use of this eri did capture something remarkable that would be of particular interest to those searching for a new silkworm with the potential to support an alternative silk industry.

In the meantime, British naturalists in Bengal would note that eri silkworms emerge nearly black ten to fifteen days after their pure white eggs are laid. That, as they grow, the head and legs remain black, while the body of the larva changes to an orange colour, bearing six black spots, one on each of its segments; and as they increase again, turn to green, or else white. They are soft and rubbery, without formidable protective spines or hairs. 'On attaining its full size, the worm is about three and a half inches long; its colours uniform and dull; the breathing holes are marked by a black mark; the moles have become the colour of the body, and have increased to long fleshy points, without the sharp prickles the *Muga* worm has; the body has a few sharp hairs, hardly perceptible.' It made sense that they should be so.

11

THE WORKS OF INDUSTRY OF ALL NATIONS

OF THE MANY PROBLEMS THAT HAD EXERCISED DR FREDERIC MOORE DURING his life, it may have been the abandonment of his fourth, and greatest, work that brought the deepest sorrow. *Lepidoptera Indica* was to be a study of ten volumes on the moths and butterflies of South Asia, and it had already absorbed seventeen years of his life.

In the decades approaching the 1890s, there was still much to be studied, even for a man whose life had been dedicated to specimens of butterflies and moths, captured from the East, that were flooding British collections. By 1867, Moore had completed another comprehensive publication, *On the Lepidopterous insects of Bengal*; in 1864, his *Descriptions of New Species of Bombyces from North Eastern India* appeared. And in 1858, he had already published an illustrated study focused entirely on a few fascinating varieties of *The Silkworm moths of India*. It had also been Moore who, in 1872, had named *Bombyx mandarina*, the most likely ancient ancestor of the Chinese domesticated silkworm. But through all these works, this illustrator-turned-lepidopterist had himself never boarded a ship to venture east. Instead, he had worked his way up to become curator of the Indian Museum, in London's South Kensington. Moore's was a role in which he enjoyed the good fortune of having held in his hands innumerable as yet, at least to European natural historians, unknown, unnamed specimens. Those had been sent from personal collections made by civil servants, doctors and military men posted to India in the service of the Company, informed by the notes of other naturalists born in India, in the continued pursuit of enriching their minds with the type of knowledge that might also engorge the distending treasury of their home country.

But the insects Moore had occasion to study would not just be those that held scientific value, nor were they simply objects of curiosity from foreign lands. Some had come to him via a new type of Victorian circus that had opened in the summer of 1851 in London's Hyde Park, inside a 'crystal palace' of plate glass and cast iron, the brainchild of Prince Albert, designed by Joseph Paxton. Among its exhibits, separated into classes and subclasses of 'raw materials', 'machinery', 'manufacture' and 'sculpture and the fine arts' were delicate carpets, polished iron wares, wallpapers, furniture, firearms and fabrics, printing presses and textile machines, Assam tea and Indian vulcanized rubber, and a tropical water-lily pond. But there were also particular curiosities: the 186-carat Koh-i-Noor diamond that had been surrendered by the 11-year-old Maharaja of Lahore to the Queen of England on the occasion of the Kingdom of Punjab being formally annexed by the East India Company just two years earlier; a 'noctograph, or instrument for writing in the dark' at stall 805 in the section given to France and Algiers; and the human bones of native peoples of Nova Scotia.

Some of the exhibits sourced from different nations would be unique, but others showed a common ambition in particular industries, not least those engaged with the production of textiles.

Of these, there were 499 stalls dedicated to wool, some of it sourced locally, some of it imported; and sixty-two stalls dedicated to cotton products, made of a fibre then sourced by English mills only from India and Egypt, and since the 1790s from the plantations of the southern United States, where they had been grown and harvested by slave labour.

Under the vast glass panels of the Crystal Palace's south-transept galleries was also a space filled with products categorized as 'Class 13', containing eighty-one stalls laden with silks and velvet. The manufacturers of these materials hailed from the industrial areas of London, including Spitalfields, Bethnal Green and Cheapside; but also from Coventry, Macclesfield, Halifax, Manchester and Leek, mill towns in England's industrial North and Midlands. In order to make high-quality silk textiles on such a scale in England, as Helfer had noted, the raw silk itself had to be imported. There was some mention of fishing line made from imperfect silkworms, and waste silk and cocoons sourced from Hampshire. But apart from small-scale local production of silk of a mediocre quality, much of the raw silk needed for the larger manufacturers was being brought to England from Italy. That there were other, and substantive, sources of raw silk, silk textiles and silken articles of clothing was evident from the exhibits of other nations, especially Egypt.

These foreign exhibits were notable not just for what they had been able to make from silks. Many had also included silk cocoons themselves: white and yellow, from different varieties cultivated in France and Algeria, Spain, Italy and Malta. Cocoons had also been sent from Russia, Switzerland and Belgium. They had also been sent from mulberry plantations created across three hundred acres of the cooler regions of Mauritius by a company formed by a French barrister and planter, that was eventually expected to form an important source of silk for the Victorian market. In the year of the Great Exhibition, 1,148,841 pounds of this variety of raw mulberry silk had been also exported from India, or, in a strange circular cycle of re-exportation, from Malaysia and Singapore, China, Persia, Egypt and Japan via India, and thence to England, Egypt, Aden, Arabia and France. That alone was valued at £707,706, the equivalent today of well over £18 million sterling.

But from no country, nor in the varieties exhibited, was there any sign of a silk other than that of the ubiquitous *Bombyx mori*. Paradoxically, although the East India Company had many naturalists in and around India who had been reporting back for some time – William Roxburgh had, after all, written about India's wild silk moths nearly fifty years before – the tasar moth from India was not mentioned at all in the exhibition catalogue. The fact that even more detailed information had been collected on a greater variety of India's wild silkworms by then made it more curious still that no such wild silk, nor their striking moths with expansive, colourful wings, nor their egg-like cocoons, made an appearance in Hyde Park that summer. There had been murmurings that Indian silks were of an inferior quality. But then, in a nine-volume publication, A *Dictionary of the Economic Products of India*, a substantial section that covered 'Silk to Tea' devoted 237 pages to 'Silk and Silkworms of India', where 'Silver' managed only five and 'Spices' only seven and a half pages. The dictionary's Scottish author, George Watt, a doctor and botanist, much like Roxburgh, had not failed to notice that 'in perhaps no other country of the world does the necessity exist so pressingly as in India to treat the subject of its silk industries under two important and distinct sections . . . the domesticated, and the wild . . . the term "wild" may at the outset be explained as here used in a commercial more than a literal sense, for, of the insects so designated, some have for centuries been completely domesticated both in India and in China . . .'

There may have been little evidence of that inside the glass walls of the Crystal Palace, but outside England these wild cocoons were attracting new interest.

. . .

Four years later, in 1855, after the hugely profitable and popular success of London's Great Exhibition at the Crystal Palace, another spectacular exhibition was held in Paris at the Palais de l'Industrie, sited between the River Seine and the Champs-Élysées.

It was at the Paris exposition that cocoons and various silkworm products were to be displayed in three different classes, including under a section designated 'Forestry, art, hunting, fishing; harvesting products obtained without cultivation'. The 'Indian Collection' from that exposition would be the origin of the Saturniidae silk moth specimen of the *Antheraea frithi* that, four years later, ended up in London and under the inquisitive eye of Frederic Moore. It had come from Darjeeling, in the northernmost reaches of West Bengal, from the collections of a naturalist named R W G Frith. He was a self-funded naturalist with an interesting sideline on the managing committee of the Bengal-Australian Association, under whose auspices the first vessel had sailed conveying 'Indian hill coolies' as a new class of labour to the colony, and which was set to augment their numbers by the dispatch of yet other ships.

Frith's silk moth samples, or at least how he had procured them, had been a matter of some discussion by the growing number of naturalists who passed pleasant days pursuing Lepidoptera in the northeast of India. 'The Tusseh moth which Mr Frith says he has procured from Mussoorie and Kussowlee', one pointed out, was 'a statement doubted . . . The practice . . . is this: - a person wishing to make a collection either takes a native Collector into service, or purchases the specimens singly from independent Collectors who hawk about insects for sale . . . collectors are in the habit of jumbling species from various localities into the same box, and calling them a collection of Himalayan species . . .' Specifically included in those doubts about Frith's acquisitions was a note on the moth he also believed to be tasar. It differed from Roxburgh's in some respects, including its size, and did, at least by serendipity if not through any particularly meticulous practice of Frith's, turn out to be a new specimen altogether. 'We have here at Mussooree', the record continued, 'and also at Simla, a species of Saturnia . . . bearing a resemblance to the Tusseh moth, though much smaller, and quite distinct; - can this be Mr Frith's Kussowlee species?'

And, indeed, the moth that Moore would study via the Indian Collection from the Paris exposition and name *frithi* was smaller than the *paphia*. The specimen he worked with had been a male, for their larger antennae with which to sense mates was of interest. And it had been a striking one, according to Moore's observations: 'yellow-ferruginous' in colour, with a forewing of grey, marked with a dark, evenly undulated line that ran parallel with the 'ocellus' – those wonderful glass-like eye spots, with inner spaces between 'suffused with yellow'. The eye spots on its hind wings were small, Moore noted, 'similar to those in *Antheraea paphia*' – the better-known tasar silk moth – or, though the moth itself, in expanse, was smaller, spreading to five and a half inches, not quite the full size of a person's open palm.

Here was the potential ancestor of Roxburgh's *Antheraea paphia*, both insect and cocoon made larger so as to produce a greater amount of silk, through a sort of domestication in India, many millennia before. But it was not to be the only moth whose raw and worked silk was about to be put on display in Europe, some eight thousand kilometres from the Asian lands in which those insects were being placed into collections to be bought and sold. Frederic Moore's *Silkworm moths of India* had featured five silkworms, moths and cocoons other than the tasar; his *Catalogue of the Lepidopterous Insects in the Museum of Natural History at East India House* also borrowed observations from Helfer's silkworm lectures to describe the remarkable golden-cocooned *Cricula trifenestrata* and muga moths. He also drew on Isabella Gilbert's detailed records of many insects, including *Actias selene*, the moon moth, and the enormous *Attacus atlas*. Moore also based his scientific illustrations on the drawings that either Isabella or her Indian artist had made of their metamorphoses.

Back at the 1851 Great Exhibition at the Crystal Palace in Hyde Park, at stand number forty-one of the eighty-one that formed the silk and velvet exhibits, were laid out the wares of 'Wardle, H & T + Co, manufacturers of Macclesfield', from the industrial North of England. Among their items were ladies' silk handkerchiefs, plain and checked, figured and chine cravats and small silk shawls, all made from the industrious *Bombyx mori*. But, like Frederic Moore, the proprietor of these goods, Thomas Wardle, was about to become intimately involved with the silks of Indian *Antheraea* and *Attacus* wild moths. His work would create a new demand and encourage a trade for these other silks, one that would see India's global exports of wild silk overtake its shipments of silk of *Bombyx mori*, and spectacularly so.

12

WARDLE

THOMAS WARDLE HAD LINGERED FAR TOO LONG ON HIS LAST DAY IN a village called Phukhuria, some twenty kilometres east of the Ganges at a place where the great river snaked southeast through Bengal. By then it was late in the day, and so he was compelled to travel through the night in a roadless jungle on the back of a squat pony, with no light other than a lantern and the stars overhead, and occasional colonies of fireflies slowly sailing about him. As for the roars of tigers, howls of leopards, diabolical yells of packs of jackals, the unearthly cries of hyenas, and, in all probability, a few silently lurking panthers, Wardle had come prepared, riding with a loaded rifle in hand. He was also accompanied by twelve men escorting him through the wilds to the safety of the night mail at the nearest railway station. Those twelve were Santals, a tribe he had found to be kind and considerate: their young women sang to him, their old men showed him how to use their bows and arrows and their young men had carried him across rivers on their bare shoulders. This time they bore Wardle's luggage on poles but had for themselves only the clothes that they wore; and as he perspired inside his three-piece suit and pith helmet he admired their minimalism – for garments, in such a hot country, had struck him as little more than an encumbrance.

It had been precisely their clothing that Thomas Wardle had been invited to India to inspect. Santal villages spread across Bengal's verdant silk districts; in them Wardle had seen sacred groves of a tree known as the sal, whose Latin name was *Shorea robusta*. Like the bair tree, its leaves were a favourite of the caterpillar known to European scientists as *Antheraea paphia* or *Antheraea mylitta*. To the Santal people who worshipped among those trees, it was called tasar; their tribes were known for their cultivation of its silkworms and for the production of fabrics made of their cocoons. Thomas Wardle had found himself in Santal territory at the instigation of an India Office Under-Secretary of State, Sir George Birdwood. Like Isabella Gilbert, Birdwood was a child of the British army in India, born to a military father in the south of the country. Like Roxburgh, he had trained in medicine and botany in Edinburgh; and like Roxburgh and Gilbert, Birdwood would develop an all-encompassing passion for the natural history of India.

In 1885, the year of Thomas Wardle's visit to Bengal, Birdwood had charged him with the mission of collecting typical silk textiles and traditional Indian embroideries for the Silk Culture Court of a new Colonial and Indian Exhibition to be held in London the following year. It was an exhibition that was to showcase the techniques used in making the 'beautiful manufactures' of India; and so Wardle's was a commission that had come with a specific request that he should, in particular, visit these silk districts of Bengal, and report on the cultivation of India's wild silkworms and how their silks were produced by local peoples.

By this time Wardle had already made a name for himself at

home, in the textile town of Leek, in the heart of the English Midlands dominated by silk industries. The name Wardle had associations with silk that preceded any personal fame. Born in Macclesfield, a market town just south of Manchester, on 26 January 1831, Thomas was barely a year old when his father founded the family's silk dye works in Leek, naming it, with some optimism, 'Joshua Wardle and Son'. Joshua was not to be disappointed with his firstborn: Thomas entered the business as a young man, made a success of it and, soon after his father's death, created a new incarnation of that business. His enterprise would be called Wardle and Co., and it would focus on the block printing of silk and cotton. It made sense that Thomas Wardle should indulge in colour. He was a keen student not just of chemistry, but of geology and archaeology. He would experiment with naturally occurring products, turning to museum collections and traditions of the past to identify dyes and patterns to create fabrics in colours in which they had never before been seen.

In the breadth of his knowledge, Wardle was polymathic. And yet his experience had not then extended to natural history, for he was quite unaware of the women and men in India who, with nets and magnifying glasses and Indian staff bearing paintbrushes, had been obsessing over capturing and describing silk moths for science, for an income, or simply for the sheer pleasure of it. Neither metamorphosis nor sericulture – the farming of silk from the animals that produced it and the study of these insects – had yet seized Wardle's imagination. The last time Birdwood had enlisted his help, it had been with a request concerned only with the cloth, and one of a purely commercial nature: to make tasar silk a suitable commodity for the British market.

Birdwood had written extensively, and very influentially, in *The Industrial Arts of India* on the value of Indian craftsmanship. He bemoaned the new Victorian style of industrial manufacture: 'The very word has in Europe come at last to lose well nigh all trace of its true etymological meaning, and is now generally used for the process of the conversion of raw materials into articles suitable for the use of man by machinery'. He praised Indian artistry: 'In India everything is hand wrought, and everything, down to the cheapest toy or earthen vessel, is therefore more or less a work of art'; and he had been the one individual who would focus Wardle's attention on the silk of the tasar moth. Not only was this a silk gathered from the wild, as it had always been, but one that was still being woven into textiles by hand.

In the months of October and November especially, but sometimes up to six times a year, Santal people gathered the tasar cocoons of *Antheraea paphia*. Once these cocoons had been collected, they were softened by steaming. The coarse tasar cocoons would be placed in a chemical bath, and then left in the sun to dry, spread out upon enormous plaited palm-leaf trays, striking for their circular shape filled with row upon row of bright canary and pale amber ovals propped up against the burned-red walls of silk workers' buildings that rested under the cloudless deep-blue Bengal sky. From there, the cocoons would have been treated in much the same way as those of the *Bombyx*. More than four thousand cocoons would become just one pound of silken yarn – all set into production within five days from harvesting, first soaked and steamed to loosen and unravel the cocoons, the impossibly fine stands from several drawn together at once to form thread of a workable size. Then that raw silk wound or spun, with some of those sold in thread form, and others strung vertically in warp and horizontally in weft directions onto wood-framed looms, to be woven by expert hands into plain or intricately patterned fabrics.

Outside India, out of the hands of botanical and entomological enthusiasts and the local peoples who had long made textiles from the cocoons of wild Indian silk, tasar threads and their artisan production had long been seen as inferior, too different from the fine white *Bombyx mori*: too coarse, too brown, too impossible to manipulate. Some forty years before Wardle's visit to the Santals, his own father had tried working with tasar silk brought from India, which he hoped to process in the family workshops. At the time, Joshua Wardle was one of the best English dyers, but, because of the irregular way in which naturally brown tasar took up dyes, his and others' attempts were ultimately abandoned. That meant that little tasar silk even passed through the dye houses of England's industrial North, and the result of accumulated failures had meant that little or none of that wild silk had been used since.

But Thomas Wardle was a persistent man. Patient, even.

After all, his great commitment to, and passion for, colour was not just well known, but so admired that he had been especially sought out by fashionable designers of the day. Arthur Lazenby Liberty had come to him for the designs he would sell at his eponymous department store in London's Regent Street, whose doors had just opened in 1875. Around the same time, William Morris, leading light of the Arts and Crafts movement, would become intimately associated with Wardle. These two shared a concern about the colour blue, specifically Prussian blue, a synthetic colour made one hundred years earlier from a lemon-yellow chemical compound. That compound was called a 'ferrous ferro cyanide salt', from which was created a hue so lavish, a blue so heavenly, it had dared to approach indigo, but in so doing had given rise to a powerful by-product. Within sixty years, in the hands of the Nazis, that prussic acid – hydrogen cyanide – would prove a devastatingly murderous poison.

But for their textiles both Wardle and Morris found only 'coldness' in the hue of Prussian blue. And in any case Morris' emerging Arts and Crafts ideals bemoaned, just as Birdwood's had, the increasing automation of industry. Wardle was not averse to mechanization for the improvement in the quality of textiles, but, perhaps surprisingly for one with a chemist's mind, he seemed to like his dyes natural. The source of blue Wardle preferred was indigo, a colour extracted from the leaves of certain *Indigofera* plants, named from the Greek *indikón* – because India had been the ancient world's major supplier. The great problem the would-be producers had was that the process of perfectly colouring silks with the striking blue of indigo was difficult, lengthy, expensive, and furthermore, required phenomenal timing and expertise.

William Morris had his products dyed at Leek; from 1875 he even moved into the Wardle family home and worked 'in Wardle's dye house pretty much all day long', producing yellows with ease, reds with some difficulty, lovely greens. And then, one very exciting morning, he assisted in the dyeing of twenty pounds of his own silks in the blue vat. But Morris complained that getting that colour right at Wardle's works was unreliable. That could have been the case anywhere in Europe, where dyeing with indigo was notoriously difficult. Morris must have expected better of Wardle. He implored him to 'do something' to get the indigo dyeing done for his orders coming in for silk, to have a chance of 'putting that business on its legs'. As frustration mounted, he complained bitterly about Wardle's head dyer, a respected man whom Morris called 'hippopotamus thumb', because in his opinion he did 'not seem to be able to do anything'. Wardle printed fourteen designs for Morris at Leek. Eight of those used patterns or colour schemes sourced from India and were exhibited at the Paris exhibition in 1878. After that, Morris finally set up his own printworks at Merton Abbey, and when he left Leek, no one shed a tear.

Wardle's struggle with blue continued. For inspiration, he looked to the results of local dyers in India, whose mastery of colour he firmly believed was the best in the world. He knew that they had

had thousands of years of experience of using indigo. His breakthrough came not in dyeing silks blue, but in printing indigo onto wild silk cloth, the first time anyone had been able to do so. Having set a precedent, Wardle would repeatedly urge the government of India to support the work in which he brought together his knowledge of chemical engineering and his love of natural Indian dyes. 'The Hindoo and Mahomedan dyers still remain untaught in the application of chemical science to their art', he argued, 'and the European dyers remain unaware of the excellencies of scores of, to them, unknown Indian dyes.' It was a matter of some frustration to him that it would have been more economical *never* to have published his substantial study undertaken for just such instruction. That work, *The Dyes and Tans of India*, had been no small effort: in it were contained 3,500 dyed samples, including those of tasar silks 'illustrating the tinctorial results of 181 kinds of Indian dye stuffs commonly used in India'. Not one of them aroused any interest. He had found that using metallic salts instead of the mordants traditionally used in India brought out the most spectacular hues in Indian natural dyes. But it was his dead letter, he said. His love's labour lost. 'That work of so laborious and valuable a nature has, as far as my experience goes, never had such scant treatment at the hands of the government of any country.'

Still, Wardle and his own dyers continued with their own trials, and in the end would succeed in what many believed was impossible. There had been many local attempts to dye the wild silk, and over many decades. Wardle had even heard of an intriguing alternative to bleaching tasar silk from Major George Coussmaker, another titled military Englishman who had become entirely absorbed in cocoon collecting in the forests of Bengal. Coussmaker had sent to Wardle's factory in Leek two hundred pounds of cleaned tasar cocoons he had acquired over two years. Most of these he purchased from villagers or collected mainly from bair trees across Bengal's silk districts. But he would also carry a few empty cocoons around in his pockets, showing them to little village boys as they tended their cattle, and telling them to bring him as many as they could find, and that he would pay them for doing so. 'The consequence was', he reported, 'that every day when I returned to my tent, I used to find three or four children sitting down, waiting for me.' Coussmaker never refused even the smallest collection from them, giving them a third of a paisa for every two cocoons they handed over, 'and they went away exulting in the possession of two or three coins . . .' But he had something else up his sleeve: his own experiments with tasar sericulture. He kept a thriving plantation of trees that tasar silkworms loved. He had simple cages made in which to keep his succulent caterpillars safe from rats, lizards, birds and wasps, though they did little to prevent the entry of spiders and 'other equally minute enemies' which he 'did not perceive'.

From his experiments, Coussmaker reported to Wardle that he had succeeded in obtaining perfectly white tasar silk simply by altering 'the conditions under which the caterpillar spins its cocoons'. He claimed he could cause the caterpillar to void all its 'cement' – sericin – before allowing it to spin its cocoon, a fascinating observation, as the natural colour of any cocoon depends on the surface of the sericin layer of the silk its caterpillar produces. Indeed, removing the sericin, a process called 'de-gumming', can strip silk strands of its colour, at least in the silk of *Bombyx mori*. Perhaps Coussmaker had found a food plant among those in his plantation that had the effect of turning the brown sericin of tasar white, because what silkworms eat can have that effect. But, in the end, Coussmaker never revealed to Wardle the particulars of his method, and in any case, before he travelled to India, Wardle knew little if anything about the rearing of these silkworms.

Still, Wardle found Coussmaker's experiments 'very remarkable'. As proof of his work, Coussmaker had sent to Leek one such 'cocoon which is free from all brownness'. '. . . [I]f this result is attainable', Wardle thought, 'the difficult and costly bleaching process will be rendered unnecessary. It would be curious and useful to know if so desirable a result is practicable.' Ultimately nothing came of this exchange, and so Wardle's employees in Leek carried on with their own experiments in bleaching; and, in the end, his was the team that would succeed in whitening the formerly intractable silk of the tasar caterpillar – and to such a level at which they could colour it to perfection. Now it would no longer just be the undyed fawn-coloured tasar threads, which Wardle considered its pleasing natural shade, that could make seaside dresses for women and girls promenading in Brighton or Bognor Regis, where the salty air tended to leach the starch out of clothes made of cotton and linen. Nor were tasar colours limited to what had been possible up to that time, what Wardle thought of as any middle or dark shade of drab that could be placed on top of that silk's natural shade: slate, brown, green, violet, or dark red. But all that was to change. Wardle and Co. had now created fourteen 'gem colours' which could be applied to this wild silk: wonderfully named sapphire, emerald, topaz, pink topaz, spinel-ruby, beryl, jacinth, chrysoprase, amethyst, coral, gold-quartz, turquoise, ruby and peridot, all laid out like jewels in a glass case in the great exhibition hall in the heart of Paris. By that time, he was also able to produce yarns in almost any shade that any manufacturer or designer might desire. Birdwood will have known that this innovation was of such significance that it could make the manufacture of this wild silk serviceable – even profitable.

But there was still more that Wardle might do.

Before tasar silk would excite the British industry, it had been the French who were quick to see its potential from Wardle's displays. It was the French who had exhibited Wardle's tasar textiles in Lyons, already at the epicentre of Europe's silk industry; the French who appointed Wardle a judge at their International Exhibition; they who made him a Chevalier of the Légion d'honneur, France's highest honour. Wardle and his workers deserved such recognition. Thanks to their efforts, tasar went from being an almost unknown silk in 1876 to an import amounting to almost 7,500 pounds in weight, some 3,500 kilograms, just a year after the Paris exhibition. Indeed only a few years later, the French would inform Wardle of vast quantities of 'Indian raw silk which we are making ourselves in our Bengal factories in large quantities, 40,000 to 50,000 kilogrammes yearly . . .' In 1874 and 1875, in contrast, no tasar silk at all had been imported into the London silk market. But things were changing there, too. What Wardle had done in Paris was being noticed in his own country. A year after he exhibited his textiles in France, some 73,000 kilograms of tasar silk – Indian-woven cloth, reeled threads and leftover waste materials – would all be consumed in his domestic market.

Although Wardle had never intended to replace the silk of *Bombyx mori*, the influx of imported tasar silk had come about because he had seen a material that might just compare with the silk of *Bombyx*, where others had seen something they considered quite useless. Textile firms he had approached had told him as much. 'Each one I appealed to turned a deaf or derisive ear to me', Wardle complained, 'some laughed at me; others said it was quite impracticable to make anything of that rubbish . . . but there is little difference in lustre between them, and there are some cases in which tusser silk is made to possess the greater lustre . . .'

It was true that a strand of tasar was coarser than one of *Bombyx mori* silk – 750th of an inch of diameter, according to Wardle's notes, compared to 2,000th of an inch for *Bombyx*. But that difference made it just as valuable, because that thickness contributed to its remarkable strength and durability: tasar, after all, was three times the strength of cultivated silk. To the English manufacturers who had sarcastically dismissed Wardle as a 'visionary', Wardle's retort was to say that 'the idea of the measuring of the diameter of a fibre had never entered into a manufacturer's head; the furthest his practice would carry him was to discriminate between the various sizes and thicknesses of "raw silk," which, as you know, consists of a bundle of many ultimate fibres . . .' While his critics laughed, Wardle studied both silks closely through a microscope. The fibre of *Bombyx mori*, as he saw it, looked, '. . . round, homogenous, and resembles a glass rod', a shape representing 'the characteristic and structureless form of all of the *Bombycidae* I have examined. But the family *Saturnidae* produce silk of another structure. In all the species of *Saturnidae* known to me, the fibre is always more or less flat, especially in tussur silk . . . and in its narrow width there are about 20 smaller fibres or fibrillae lying longitudinally, and connected with each other by a hardened fluid seriposited at the time the worm forms this silken thread.' Wardle had also succeeded in 'isolating these fibres by dissolving the hardened medium . . .' That, though, had taken some persistence. In Wardle's experiments, he placed both silks in a solution of chloride of zinc. So immersed, *Bombyx*, which Wardle called 'ordinary', or 'the silk of commerce', could be entirely dissolved in three days. But the tasar had not budged in a fortnight.

The struggles with the use of tasar in Europe, Wardle had found, had resulted from the structure of its threads to which others who worked silk had paid no attention. And what he found was that, while *Bombyx* 'is easily dyed, owing to the homogenous structure of its fibre, which absorbs the tinctured matter with regularity, and, moreover, has a chemical affinity for many kinds of dyes, tans and mordants . . . in Tussur silk the opposite of this is the case'.

There were two reasons why dyeing had proved impossible. The first, 'the well-nigh impervious nature of the fibrillae, and their consequent impenetrability to . . . absorption; secondly, the flatness of the fibre, which causes light to be reflected at different angles to that of the silk of commerce. This difference in structure causes the natural brilliance of tussur silk to be seen in scintillations instead of being evenly diffused over its surface.'

As a chemist, to Wardle the unique challenges and unique beauty of tasar were more a result of the structure of the silk extruded by the caterpillars that made it and less due to any differences that existed in their chemical make-up. He had read the reports of chemical analyses done on both silks by two chemists at Bradford Technical College in Yorkshire, about fifty miles from where his printing works were based. He knew that there were minimal differences in their balance of carbon and nitrogen, of which tasar had less; hydrogen, about the same in both; and oxygen, of which tasar had more. He had taken it upon himself to understand how they reacted when heated and when placed under pressure; and the composition of their respective sericins, the substance silkworms secreted to bind the strands of silk to build their cocoons. His patient observations of the structure and the chemistry of tasar was what helped him to do what no one else had yet done: to break tasar's resistance to dyes and create his gem-coloured wild silks.

As for the other major problem tasar faced, that it could not be reeled, he would also eventually analyse and subvert that. He had watched silkworms as they moved their heads from side to side, depositing a double thread in loops. As the cocoon took shape, it occurred to him that the sericin gum might adhere more firmly at the points at which these threads made contact. That meant that reeling the threads off from cocoons – normally done by pulling a thread from each of four cocoons together, in order to create one strand of silk thread thick enough for human weavers – also created an aggravated knot of loops, layers that created tangles and led to an uneven, slub-like finish in a textile. That effect some found charming: this was, after all, a wild silk, artisanal, handloomed. Perhaps because he was so concerned with dyeing and printing, Wardle's personal preference was to keep his silks smooth. To his mind, smoothness was something that was down to the skill of the reeler, and in which perfection could be aspired to, particularly in the new world of automated cocoon-reeling machines that were being made in Lyons. In Piedmont, northern Italy, Wardle himself had 'unwound an Indian tasar silk cocoon in an unbroken thread nearly three-quarters of a mile long', and supervised the reeling of tasar silk into a strand 'of such fineness as to surprise the managers, who said they had no idea that tussur silk could be made of so fine a thread, and that they should think seriously about sending a person to India, to collect tussur cocoons, that their people might wind them after their mulberry crops had finished'.

If, like mulberry silk, tasar could now be dyed and reeled, the only question that remained was whether it stood any chance against the legendary sheen of *Bombyx mori* silk. Wardle had claimed it could compete, because he had seen tasar made so lustrous it could not just hold its own, but even become 'of greater lustre' than *Bombyx* silk. If he knew this could be done it was because of how closely hc had observed their microscopic structures; because of his understanding that both silks refracted light in different ways:

'The natural lustre of brilliancy of tussur silk is quite as great as that of ordinary silk, if not greater; but, owing to its peculiar structure, the effect of an equal diffusion of reflection is not possible . . . its peculiar scintillations . . . at the points of reflection – that is, where they are at an angle of incidence with the eye, from the source of light – a white point or surface appears, which, in contrast with blackness or a depth of colour, becomes a more noticeable feature. Manufacturers have yet to learn that the peculiar effect caused by this structural difference is really part and parcel of the natural property of the silk, and it ought to be considered, even welcomed . . . There is this charm in it, that monotony of structural regularity is broken up and varied.'

In short, what all Wardle's studies had been telling him was that the strange characteristics of wild silk threads brought with them immense new possibilities for novel materials, innovative formats that could not be so easily dismissed. One of his triumphs would be a tasar replacement for sealskin, which was a popular material for overgarments. A plush, velvety piled fabric, Wardle called his version, made of tasar threads, 'seal cloth', equally 'as soft as fur and quite durable; wonderfully rich, soft and glossy' as the real thing. The remarkable thing about seal cloth was that it was produced from waste tasar yarn, using a method Wardle had experimented with in Germany. The new technique he developed there involved weaving waste tasar yarn onto a cotton backing. Like genuine sealskin, it was waterproof – but, better, Wardle's version was washable and breathable, and didn't require any seals. Seal cloth boosted Wardle's standing and it was another nail in the coffin of those who had looked down on the wild silk of the Indian *Antheraea*. 'Take the case of seal-plush alone, and see what a charming product it is. Lighter, more lustrous, durable, and more healthy to wear than sealskin, it is a marvellous fabric', Wardle declared in a lecture chaired by Lady Alice Egerton of Tatton, a woman who would host the 'Egerton Exhibition' of silks at her home, but who was, at that time, leading a discussion on the ever-growing uses of tasar silk, at an esteemed crowd gathered at London's Royal Society of Arts.

Fig. 12.

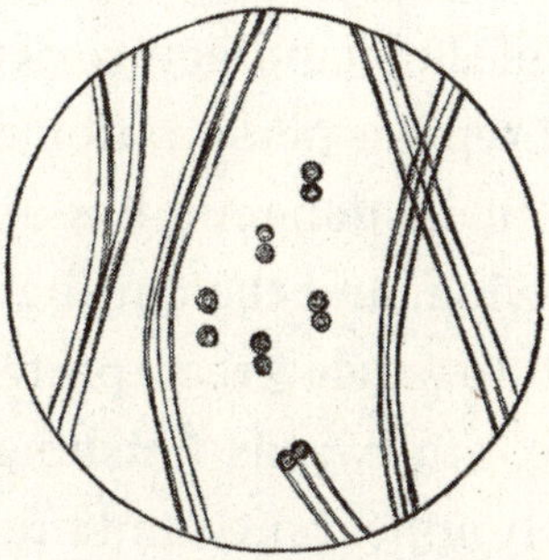

Silk of Bombyx Mori of Commerce, showing also Transverse Sections.

Fig. 14.

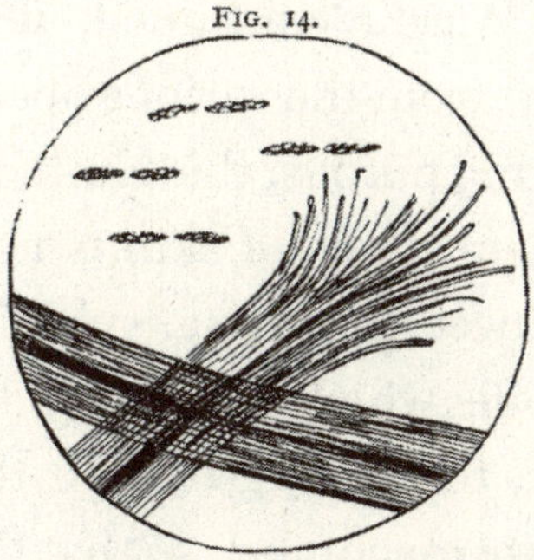

Silk of Antheræa Mylitta, or Tussur Silk-showing separated Fibrillæ and Trans, verse Sections.

Figs. 17 and 18.

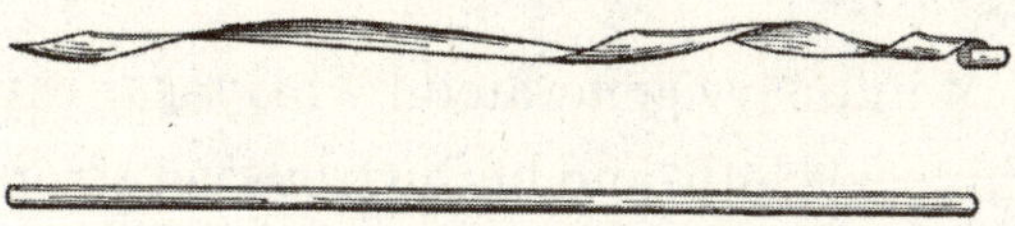

Fig. 23.

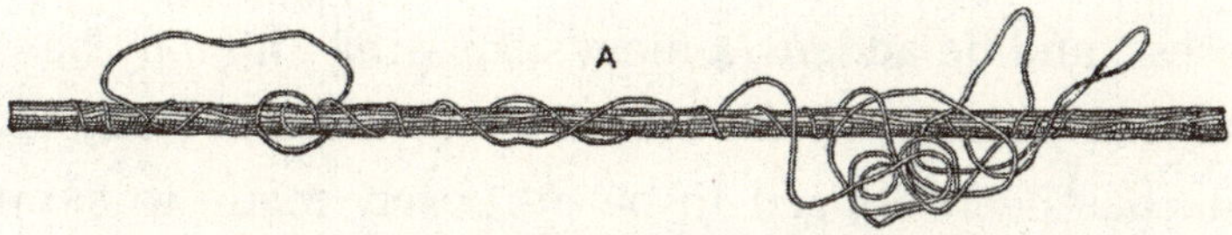

Reeled by a good French Reeler by Hand, System Chambon.

Fig. 24.

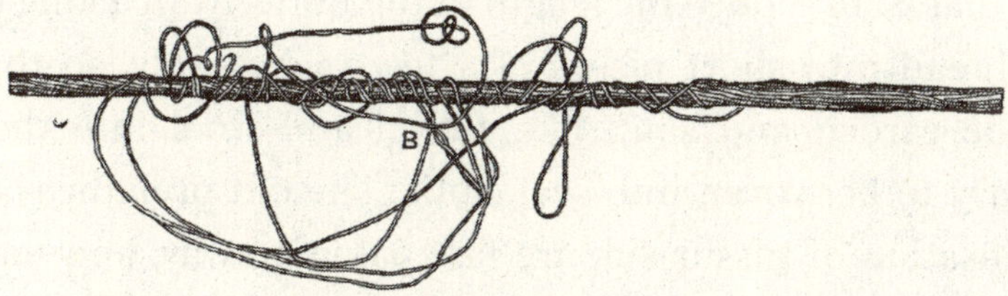

Reeled by an Apprentice by Hand, System Chambon.
(Magnified 50 diameters. A & B, duvet.)

Fig. 25.

Reeled Mechanically, New System. (Camel.)
(Magnified 70 diameters.)

'Yet', Wardle continued, 'it is made out of the waste, or short ends left from the various operations of the manufacture of tussar silk. Being porous, this cloth does not repress perspiration, whilst a garment made of skin is not without its dangers. Besides, the skill educed in reeling, spinning, weaving, and the cutting of the deep pile which has been brought to such great perfection: besides, the dyeing of it in the piece, afterwards finishing it by elaborate machinery, so that the velvety appearance and the erectness of the pile shall be so perfectly maintained, is most praise-worthy, and I consider it a marvel of manufacturing skill and cheapness.'

The branch of industry generated by his tasar experiments, and in particular this seal cloth, and his lustrous yet strong tasar carpets which were 'peculiarly suitable for embroidery', had become so extensive that sufficient waste tasar silk could not be procured for the process, and he added: 'a most surprising anomaly has for the first time in the history of silk-manufacture of any country occurred. Raw silk has been obliged to be purposely made to supply this demand, that is, that tussur cocoons which have been reeled into raw silk have had to be cut up in that state into short lengths like waste, that is, to reduce the length of the fibres from a long continuous thread into short pieces of a few inches only, so that they could be carded and spun like cotton and wool into the yarns necessary to be woven into seal cloth. The old prejudices against the utilisation of tussur silk are fast passing away, and manufacturers who looked upon it doubtfully, and even with strong prejudice, a few years ago, are now bound to admit that fabrics spun or woven from the waste of this silk, are products of such superiority and beauty as, to have utterly upset their ideas as to what could be produced from it.'

And then, Wardle made his trip to India.

There, around the Santal villages, he watched attentively as tasar cocoons were collected and boiled, as its silk was reeled, and woven into cloth; he bought wonderful samples of threads and textiles to take back home. He inspected reeling machines of which he was so fond, including one of a new design created by a man who collected opium taxes across another district a few miles south of the River Ganges, a place the British celebrated for the bravery of fifteen Englishmen who 'successfully and gallantly held their own for a week against two thousand mutinous' Indians.

In a town called Fatwah on the banks of the river he visited tasar-making houses no Europeans had ever entered, was followed by a crowd and pelted with stones, and only escaped injury because his guide asserted the authority of the British government. Unfazed, to Wardle everything in that 'great land of the tussur silk' teemed with interest. He drew images of these silk workers anyway, of their weaving equipment, their bows and arrows, their moths.

He watched those enormous moths as the males flew through the night over long distances. He marvelled as they alighted on tall trees; as their females deposited three or four eggs on the leaves of each, their wings perpetually in motion. He saw some females collected into baskets so that their eggs could be gathered for domestication. And he became extremely fond of the charming caterpillars that over his years spent in Leek had spun him so many cocoons. Spotting them suspended from branches in Bengal, Wardle took 'two, beautiful, full-grown tussur silkworms, feeding on a tree', put them in a bottle, and preserved them in spirit so that he might show them off back in England. By the time he returned they had 'lost somewhat their size, and also their beautiful colour', but he would never forget that first encounter, because he 'had never before seen such a beautiful living object', and particularly not one that had made him feel 'quite repaid of all the attention' he had devoted to their silks.

Processing silk cocoons in Bengal, 1895.

And so, Birdwood's mission to send Thomas Wardle on his travels – to collect wonders to be showcased at the 1886 Colonial and Indian Exhibition in London's South Kensington – had turned out to be a splendid success. It was one that added to his services to the silk industry, for which he would soon receive a knighthood. Wardle had returned from India with other trophies, one of which, a huge Bengal tiger, took pride of place at his country house in the Staffordshire dales. But in the other trunks he shipped home were the triumphant contents that would illustrate beyond doubt the Colonial and Indian Exhibition's aim, to show the 'solidarity of a world-wide Empire, its unity of interest, and its manifold resources', since 'our own small and comparatively insignificant island has little room for expansion, except in these broad lands across the sea we have made our own'.

Some of the Indian artisans brought to the Colonial and Indian Exhibition in London's South Kensington.

When the richly sculpted gateway to its Indian pavilion – the most spectacular in the exhibition – opened on 4 May, over the next six months five and a half million visitors would wander through its re-created palace, a bazaar, a leafy, humid jungle, alongside a chariot drawn daily by two oxen through upper Kensington Gardens. As they did so they saw not just artworks and crafts in fantastical showcases, but Indians crafting them; or as the Prince of Wales was overheard exclaiming, 'Why, you have India itself here!' As eagerly as they were observed by visitors as they worked, they were even more keenly scrutinized by a prison superintendent, because these were men who were both artisans and artifice. Most had not been brought from the villages or tribes Wardle had been welcomed into or infiltrated, but were men who had been imprisoned by British justices and held in the Central Jail of Agra, where they seem to have either trained or been trained in crafts within the penal system.

Among them were Muhammad Shaban, a silk and gold brocade weaver and lace maker from Banaras; Vilayat Hussain, a dyer, and Hemchand, a goldsmith, both from Agra; Mughal Jan, a silversmith, and Nazir Hussein, an ivory miniature painter, both from Delhi; Bhupla, an 18-year old *dhurri* or cotton carpet weaver, originally from Mathura, but who was now seated at a hand loom in South Kensington; and Bakshiram, 'the old potter of Agra . . . believed to be over 102 years of age'.

In among that very British circus of smoke and mirrors sat Wardle's own displays of silks and dyes, of moths and caterpillars and their magnificent cocoons.

There, he would not just show items made of tasar silk, but also collections made of the muga, the silk of the unfortunate Johann Helfer's *Antheraea assama* silkworm, 'even superior to tussur, and more amenable to dyeing', and the golden filigree cocoons of his *Cricula trifenestrata*, 'which excited so much attention'. Of eri silk cloth from William Roxburgh's *Attacus ricini*, woven in England and printed by Wardle; and the threads of Isabella Gilbert's *Attacus atlas*, 'the largest known moth'. The first two, Wardle had come to realize, had been 'long and extensively cultivated in Assam'. He had found the *atlas* silk being used in Nepal by the 'Mechi people, in the form of rudely made cloths, of which I have brought two extremely rare and almost unknown kinds'. None of these three were yet being used in Europe. With characteristic prescience, in the next two decades still left to him Wardle hoped to turn his attention to 'yet other wild silk worlds to conquer . . . which are capable of having an important future', if', he added, 'I am spared'.

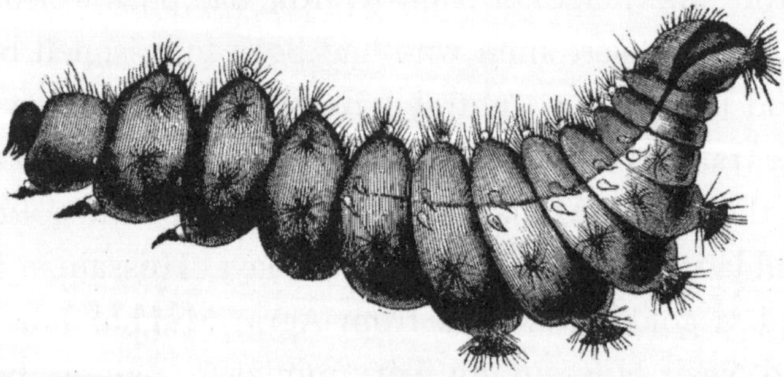

Larva of Antheræa Mylitta, or Tussur Silkworm.

SHOWS COCOON CUT OPEN, WITH CHRYSALIS INSIDE.

ANTHERÆA MYLITTA, OR TUSSUR MOTH, FEMALE.

ANTHERÆA MYLITTA, OR TUSSUR MOTH, MALE.

PART TWO

SILKEN SHELLS, GOLDEN ORBS

'So many examples ought to shew us of what Importance is to neglect nothing in the Study of Nature: What at first seems of no use, or almost impossible to be put in execution, oftentimes turns to the greatest advantage, and becomes easy by care and Industry. This is the Fate of all new Discoveries . . .'

– François Xavier Bon de Saint Hilaire, 1710

13

COQUILLAGES À SOIE

IN 1757, TWO MONTHS AFTER THE COFFIN OF THE ELDERLY entomologist René-Antoine Ferchault de Réaumur was lowered into the grave and sprinkled with holy water, in Paris the Académie des Sciences held its general assembly at the Louvre. There, France's most esteemed society of scientific researchers graciously accepted the legacy the encyclopaedic spirit of Réaumur had bequeathed. In it were curiosities of natural history. Minerals, collections of birds and insects. There were memoirs, which he wanted them to open up and examine. One hundred and thirty-eight portfolios filled with finished manuscripts and drawings, as well as near-complete ones that his will instructed should be finished. The inventory of his studies had been so extensive it had condemned a Paris notary to seventeen months' labour in the room of a hotel on rue de la Roquette in which Réaumur had lived.

In among those drawings of reptiles, polyps, insects and beetles, fossils, manuscripts on agriculture, research on the composition of porcelain and observations on auriferous rivers, turquoise mines and the thermometer was a singular manuscript. Comprising fourteen pages of descriptive text, two detailed drawings and three further pages written specifically to explain the fine structures, carefully numbered and lettered, the study was entitled *Observations on the shell called Pinna Marine*. This was not Réaumur's first study of shelled animals, but they were the first animals he had studied. Before 1711, the young Réaumur was a promising mathematician. One day he would become known as a founder of the study of animal behaviours. It was the lure of shells that had turned his head. This particular work on the biology of the Pinna Marine was published in 1717; fifty years later, as part of the grandiose project to give all living things a first and last Latin name, Carl Linnaeus would call the same shell *Pinna nobilis*, or the noble pen, the name by which it is known today.

Pinna nobilis, with its byssus.

The noble pen is an enormous marine mollusc, reaching over a metre at its zenith. It narrows to a sharp point at its base and fans out into a semi-oval above, like a gigantic quill pen. Outside, under the algae and small invertebrates that liberally attach to its surface, it is golden brown, covered with fine spikes that coalesce as they rise into crowded rows of delicate, razor-sharp frills. Inside, a smooth, reddish-brown fades downwards to an iridescent inner layer of nacre, the mother of pearl that sometimes gives birth to shining spheres of silver, orange, red, black or brown. It can live for up to fifty years anchored to the substratum of billowing meadows of Neptune grass up to sixty metres below the Mediterranean Sea. Its preference is for moderate temperatures, in the shallower waters of protected bays. It would not have been very difficult for a scientist of means to get hold of one.

Some of the shells Réaumur had acquired were well over half a metre long and perhaps a decade old. He heaved them out of the containers of saltwater and brandy in which they had arrived, and moved them to his dissection table. Then, he slit the long bands of ligament that hinged their halves together and set to work. Before they were bottled for transport they had been fished from the Mediterranean coast of France on the orders of the Intendant Général de la Marine of Toulon, who was instructed to do so by the Duke of Orléans, a generous patron of the natural sciences with agents who could acquire wondrous objects to order.

Toulon is a port city due west of Cannes. It is also close to Marseilles, which was founded Massalia in 600 BCE by Greeks who sailed there from the coast of Anatolia, and erected temples to Artemis and Poseidon north of the Lacydon cove, now in the Panier district of the modern city. The *Pinna* was well known in that ancient Mediterranean world, and it could not have escaped the notice of a seafaring people for it was the largest shelled animal in their seas. Fully grown, one shell alone could provide a kilogram of meat. But *Pinna* also produced something even more remarkable. At its sharp-pointed base is a shock of long, fine filaments disturbingly like auburn locks of human hair, but up to three times finer. They spill from its 'foot', a muscle a third of the way from the bottom of the shell, and anchor it firmly in the sea. If they were human hair, these filaments could grow long enough to reach almost to the chin. When Réaumur prised the *Pinna*'s halves apart, he noted this 'prodigious forest of threads' emerging from the flesh inside, from 'a viscous juice which takes on the consistency and shape of a thread'; and how the shell 'opens on one side . . . to let out the thread that it has shaped'. These astonishing threads form early in the life of the animal.

Many molluscs of the Pinnidae family are hermaphrodites, of which *Pinna nobilis* is a very particular sort. Over at least its first four years of growth, as it reaches up to more than a third of a metre in height, the immature reproductive systems, male and female both, ready themselves for procreation. From that point, each year, when the Mediterranean is at its warmest, one *Pinna* will rapidly and successively release male or female reproductive cells as it sees fit, that mingle in the water around them. Any that are fertilized develop into tiny larvae. This will be the only time in its life that the *Pinna* can ever swim freely. In a matter of days, the larvae develop a thin shell of calcium carbonate, sinking them towards the seafloor. It is then that the first liquid secretions fated to become threads form in glands inside the new binary shells of young *Pinna*. This liquid coalesces into its silk on contact with the waters around them. The silk itself is composed of many proteins that extend like tendons from muscle cells, and end in adhesive pads. Those pads attach it to where it lands, rendering it forever immobile. The pads are crucial to the *Pinna*'s security, and to the metamorphosis of the misshapen spheres of little larvae as they morph into their final, fan-like form.

Pinna nobilis is not unique among its relatives in having anchoring threads. There are many mussels that live in the sea, or in bodies of freshwater, that create hair-like strands of protein. Most of these animals, those with shells of two parts, possess such filaments only when they are young larvae, about to settle into the sand. Because of its great size, *Pinna nobilis* and its close relative, the rough and reddened *Pinna rudis*, are among the few that retain their lustrous threads for the rest of their lives. Different mussels use other fascinating strategies. In life, species of the *Mytilus*, the blue mussels so popular in kitchens all over the world, are exposed to waves in rocky intertidal zones, and so use a versatile underwater glue to hold them fast to rocks, wood pilings, or even the shells of other mussels. They do have threads, but they are sparse and short. They are also immensely tough, yet flexible, with semi-crystalline insides that dissipate the energy of the crashing waves. But *Pinna nobilis* live in calmer waters. Burying about a third of the length of their shells well beneath the sediment, tens of thousands of long, thin fibres moor them firmly in the seabed. *Pinna* threads are different from those of the *Mytilus*. They are elastic, but not made from collagen like the threads of other molluscs. Theirs are transparent, built of different proteins, with a structure that is quite distinct.

The differences between the threads of the *Pinna* and *Mytilus* suggest that although these animals are not such distant relations, the threads they strategically placed to resist the currents evolved independently of each other while developing in a similar way. It was prescient that in 1711, in one of the earliest scientific studies of such animals, Réaumur already suspected this to be the case. 'I put forward . . . that there was reason to believe that [the *Pinna*'s] threads were spun like those of the Mussels, because nature does not limit itself to a few examples, even of its most singular productions', he wrote. Until the Duke of Orléans sent his divers into the seas off Toulon for the sake of the scientist, however, Réaumur was not able to verify his hypothesis, 'not having been within reach of the Seas where Shell lives'. All that was about to change, despite the fact that Réaumur was working five hundred miles north of the Mediterranean coast of France. What the Duke's divers came up with enabled him to describe scientifically the twenty to thirty thousand threads of the *Pinna*. Formed from highly aligned helixes of globular proteins, they had the power to weaken the drag forces of subtidal currents beneath the calm surface of the Mediterranean Sea. These hairy anchors were crucial to the *Pinna*'s survival. They may have looked delicate, but they were both powerful and robust.

In the year Réaumur conducted his study, *Pinna nobilis* was still plentiful in underwater fields with its disordered rows of long, fan-shaped shells lined up like headstones in a cemetery. These spread through shallows from the South of France to the western Levant, skirting the Mediterranean coast of Spain, to Corsica and Sardinia, Calabria, then south towards Malta and Tunisia, and east to the coast of Greece, Dalmatia and Turkey. The waters around these parts were clear because the living shells filtered any detritus suspended there. Clear waters also made them more visible. Divers knew where to find them and could often reach them, with enough air in their lungs, in a single dive. Along some of those coasts, their shells could be uprooted if tugged repeatedly and forcefully. As they were hauled from the seabed, their infinite number of threads were still entangled with little shells, seaweed and pebbles, with sand trailing through the water behind them. On land, while the two parts of the *Pinna*'s shells were split and crafted into decorative objects, and their flesh cooked or consumed as a medicinal diuretic, their copious filaments were washed in the waves, dried and combed, immersed in an acidic liquid to turn their auburn colour to gold and spun into a shimmering textile fibre. It was known as sea silk. It shone like gold in the sun, faded and changed to colours of countless shades. It was as thin, bright and expensive and as coveted as the finest threads that *Bombyx mori* had been engineered over millennia to create.

Réaumur was aware of these uses of the *Pinna*, for this is how his study began: 'I have described in the memoirs of 1711 some of the ingenious means which nature gave to seashells and other sea animals to hold out against the waves . . . the mussels are fixed by a considerable number of threads that are for them like ropes which hold them at anchor. I showed that they were spinning them by an admirable and simple mechanism . . .

'I observed at the same time that if the earth has its silkworms the sea also has silk shells; that which is called Pinna . . . is attached like the mussels by fine threads which were used by the ancients, and of which we still make handiwork today.'

Réaumur was correct in his comparison. To the human eye, sea silk washed and combed can barely be distinguished from the mulberry silk of *Bombyx mori*. With a microscope even a scientist such as Réaumur would have access to, its golden, elliptically-shaped weft threads would have easily given its identity away. It is distinct from other fibres, and from the rounded triangular silk threads spun by the Chinese moth. Under a simple microscope it is flat, twisted, very fine and exquisitely smooth. It stretches easily, particularly when wet, but when woven into a textile it is weaker than moth silk, weaker than wool.

In strong light, it is translucent. It takes its colour from pheomelanin, a pigment related to the family of melanins. These are the most common pigments in the animal world, responsible for the colour of skin, hair, eyes and feathers. Depending on the light, its location, and perhaps on the age of the shell, Réaumur might have seen silk of the *Pinna* that looked bronze or copper, golden yellow to brown, olive-green to black.

But how ancient actually *were* these ancients Réaumur believed worked the threads that anchored the *Pinna* against the waves?

14

A TANGLE OF THREADS

THE TWELFTH OF JULY 1941 WAS A BUSY SATURDAY ON THE CAMPANIA plain, in the southwest of Italy. Just above the blue and flat Bay of Naples, the heat was intense. A silvery light emanated from bored summer clouds that hung about the darkened outline of the southern Apennines. Looming in the distance, these mountains framed one end of the Via dell'Abbondanza, a major public way stretching almost the full length of Pompeii.

On the street of that once buried city, a formerly grand house emerged from the layers of debris, pumice and ash under which it had remained sealed for almost two thousand years. According to an inscription attached to the right of its entrance, and the name etched on three amphorae inside, it had been the residence of Marci Epidius Primus. Whether in his last moments Primus had raised his hands to the gods or cursed them as Vesuvius blackened the afternoon sky on 24 October 79 CE, this man, it seemed, had lived a good life. His was a house of more than ten rooms surrounding a large atrium. It had its own kitchen and lavatory and space for a garden. Its walls were plastered and painted white and yellow and shades of red, decorated with winged cupids and birds, flowers and insects, panthers and lions. Perhaps he was a skilled physician for those who could afford him: buried within his walls on the day of the eruption were medical instruments and cauldrons made of bronze. There were also jugs, two-handled cups, small vessels and a mirror fashioned from pure silver. Among the other remains was also a soft object in shades of brown and green. Inventoried as find number 7652, it would later be listed with the treasures of that day as *fiocco di Fibre grezze*, a small flock of raw fibres, and labelled *vero bisso o seta marina* – true byssus or sea silk.

Sea silk is sometimes called byssus. And *Pinna nobilis* is not its only source. Still found attached to crevices and hollows in rocky fissures across the Mediterranean, through to the Azores and the Cape Verde archipelago live other *Pinna*, like the amber pen shell, *Pinna carnea*, and *Pinna rudis*. Reddish-brown with a rough shell, *Pinna rudis* only grows to a third of the size of *nobilis*, and on the gravelly floors of shallower waters, from below the low tide line down to just over thirty metres under the Mediterranean and the northern Atlantic coasts of Africa and Europe, from the Azores, St Helena and Morocco to the Strait of Gibraltar, Sicily and the Tyrrhenian, Ionian and Black seas. Byssus is the biological term for the filaments, the 'beards', of all of these mussels, whether woven or not. That fact has been a source of great consternation.

Because in the ancient world there was a textile also known as byssus. Delicate, diaphanous and expensive, this byssus was the Latin name for what the Greeks before them called Βύσσος – 'vyssos or byssos'.[1] On the icon of language decipherment itself, the

1 Robes of byssus were mentioned by Aeschylus and Euripides in the fourth and fifth centuries BCE, but long before, the word itself must have been

granitoid slab discovered in 1799 by Napoleon's troops as they passed through the village of Rosetta in Egypt's western Nile Delta, the Greek word 'byssos' was translated from Egyptian text as 'the king's linen'. This slab, the Rosetta Stone, was one of many produced in 196 BCE, but its texts, which were duplicated in Egyptian and Greek, were around a hundred years older than that. Some say this byssus may have been cotton, threads spun from the cloud-like seed cases of Gossypium plants; but *būṣu* may also have been fine linen, the fabric very expertly woven out of long fibres cut from the stems of *Linum usitatissimum*, the plant commonly known as flax, or linseed. In the second century CE Pausanias, the Greek geographer from the western coast of Asia Minor, wrote that byssus was different from common flax, that he called λίνον – 'linon'; and distinct from hemp, called καννάβις – 'kannabis'. But it was grown, and in a place he called Elis, in the western part of Greece's

---

adopted into the Greek language. Both Greek and Latin belong to an Indo-European family. But 'byssus' does not have an Indo-European origin. The words are relatives of earlier Semitic terms: of the Phoenician 'bṣ', 'būṣu' of Hebrew, and *būṣu* of the Assyrians, who were certainly very familiar with it by the ninth century BCE. The Assyrians themselves seem to have acquired *būṣu* as tribute from Sūḫi, which was an ancient geographic region around the middle course of the Euphrates River, that today would lie somewhere between modern-day Syria and Iraq. None of the few texts that quote the use or trade of *būṣu* appear to date from before the first millennium BCE. But it was never for common use: this was a textile that was precious, and difficult to get hold of. It was mentioned in missives between Egyptian and Hittite courts sent in 580 BCE, in which it was said to have been a cloth of kings. In the Old Testament of the Bible, *būṣu* is a fine quality of linen. It is mentioned over forty times. When the Bible spoke of ordinary linen, it was referred to as 'bäd'.

Peloponnese Peninsula, where it was made into headdresses by the women of the city of Patra by the sea to its north. So whatever byssus was, it seems to have been understood as a cloth made of something that was harvested from a plant.

Then, in the fourth century BCE, in a less sartorial and more biological frame of mind, Aristotle compiled his extraordinary *History of Animals*. It was voluminous, replete with rich descriptions of animal anatomy, development and behaviour. Among these animals was the *Pinna*. The book would be studied by natural historians and zoologists during subsequent millennia. What Aristotle wrote there, of how these mussels grew upright in the sand and mud, emerging from ὁ βυσσός, meaning 'the depth', would, in the fifteenth century CE, be read by a Byzantine humanist as ἡ βύσσος, which meant 'the byssus', that is, the fine cloth. The difference had a lasting effect, because the translation he then made, that 'Pinna-mussels grow upright from the byssus', is one that entered the vocabularies of zoologists, being that, at the *Pinna*'s foot are its silken threads. From then on, his writings would confound the fine linen fabric of 'byssus' with the thread-like secretions of marine mussels. With one flick of a pen, one change in the gender of an indefinite article, and one accent, the anchoring filaments of all two-shelled molluscs became known by the same name. If before there were arguments about whether the ancient cloth that started out as the *būṣu* of the Assyrians had been crafted from linen or from cotton, questions would also now be raised about whether the mysterious cloth the ancients wore was actually neither, but, rather, silk cropped from the foot of a mussel that lived in the depths of the Mediterranean Sea.

It is partly as a consequence of this confusion that no one knows for sure how long the threads of the *Pinna* have actually been woven. Hundreds of broken fragments of *Pinna* shells have been found that date back a very long time, to between 6500 and 3000 BCE, at locations including Thrace, Sardinia, Sicily, Mycenae, Corinth, the Cyclades and Cyprus. In Crete, such fragments were uncovered during excavations of Minoan sites in Chania, and in the Unexplored Mansion at Knossos, built of magnificent limestone inside a palace complex which fell into ruin in the Late Bronze Age somewhere between 1380 and 1100 BCE. A number of them have shown wear marks on certain edges, suggesting perhaps that the shells may have been used as some type of tool. Since there were many uses for the shells and their contents, the presence of its fragments suggests that this shell was exploited by the people of the Mediterranean. No one can be sure of how it was used. Fabrics of sea silk have not been found in any of these locations.

The lack of indisputable images, and the absence of any remnants of textiles of *Pinna* silk from the very ancient archaeological record, does not definitively rule out its use in those worlds, or at those times. But other ancient textiles have sometimes emerged. Wool and linen are the most common, including wool laced with gold and the imperial purple of another marine mollusc, the murex, from the fourth-century BCE tombs of the family of Alexander the Great. There has also been cotton from the Kerameikos cemetery in Athens that dates to the ninth century BCE; and from Crete, between 1500 and 1150 BCE. As the Minoan civilization drew to a close, a buried fabric was also found that had been made from linen mixed with what was probably goat hair and fibres of nettle. Perhaps sea silk has simply not been found. Or perhaps it was found, and labelled as something else.

By the time the soft, greenish-brown object uncovered in 1941 in a grand Pompeiian house on the Via dell'Abbondanza had been inventoried as '7652: true byssus, or sea silk', the word byssus had long been used liberally, frequently and indiscriminately, over different times and in different languages. The fine, luxurious and rare byssus textile had sometimes been called linen, sometimes cotton and sometimes silk. Among the textiles that had been preserved by the volcanic ash that destroyed Pompeii was evidence of all of these luxury textiles. Some had been imported items, but other materials were produced locally. From under the rubble emerged examples of cotton, Spanish broom, hemp, kapok and linen, all of which come from seeds, stems or leaves. There was also wool, and angora, as well as silk of the *Bombyx mori* moth whose source had for so long been such a mystery to the Romans. But the fibres that came from the house of Marci Epidius Primus were none of these.

When its identification was announced at a conference not far from Naples in 1996, the archaeologists had this to say: '7562 Pompei, was . . . a flock of fibres, brown-green coloured. We have identified this finding as Byssus (sea silk) obtained from the mollusc *Pinna nobilis* secretion. The presence of this fibre aligns with the possibility that the manufacture of byssus textiles was developed in ancient Pompei, in accordance with other evidence.'

But in the first decade of the 2000s, inventory number 7562 was examined once more, by different researchers, and under a very powerful microscope. If a standard, modern, light microscope can magnify by up to a thousand times, the type used to capture this object could enlarge an object by up to one million times. With that detail emerged superbly clear images in fine resolution. In greyscale shades they showed a mess of convoluted, branching, almost thorn-like filaments against a pitch-black background. Though fragmented and broken in places from the destruction wrought in Pompeii and by the passage of time, it was eminently clear that these were not the linguine-shaped threads of the *Pinna*, not so distinctly smooth or glassy, transparent or elliptical in section.

Instead, the fibres were actually remnants of an elastic, absorbent skeleton formed from collagen and laid out like an irregular mesh of polygons. They had come from another marine creature. This one did not produce silk of any sort, but it, too, had been recorded by Aristotle in his *History of Animals*. In the ancient Mediterranean world it was commonly used for cleaning, in medicine, art, and war. It held a particular importance in medical practice, and for the washing of the dead before their final journey. These were the remains of the sponge *Spongia officinalis*, an animal with no true organs or tissues, no nervous, digestive or circulatory systems. For most of the history of biology it was not classified as an animal at all, but as a plant.

When the first incontrovertible proof of silk made from the *Pinna* finally appeared, it was discovered in the burial tomb of a woman in another Roman colony in Hungary. On 12 August 1912 she was disinterred from a sealed grave built from raw, unworked limestone. Her grave was situated outside the walls of a city once called Aquincum, but which by then lay under the Szemlöhegy neighbourhood of Budapest. Bordered by the Danube, the Roman city held a legionary fortress, two amphitheatres, a town for the military and another for civilians. Surrounding it were farms and hilly ground on which stood exquisite villas. Aquincum had been the capital of the Roman province of Pannonia, the northeasternmost frontier of its empire. Politically, it was so important that almost every Roman emperor had visited it at least once during their reign. It was a cosmopolitan city and one of great wealth.

Coins found with the woman suggested that she died sometime between 326 CE and the destruction of Aquincum at the beginning of the fifth century CE. Whenever her end had come, she was placed in a wooden coffin finished with brass fittings and laid to rest with her personal possessions: a beautiful necklace of gold spheres and glass beads, two round glass bottles, a pair of cork sandals. Next to her were wooden boxes crafted from beech, ash, poplar and pine. They carried her cosmetics to the afterlife, mixtures of rice flour and the reddish-brown spores of a mushroom that made up a face powder to perfectly match her complexion. There was also a fragment of sponge for a powder puff. Her body was wrapped tightly in bandages of cotton and linen that had been twice impregnated with fragrant resins, which gave the cloth the texture of bark. Among the wefts of those bandages were violet-blue-coloured threads. All that remained of the silk of *Pinna nobilis* was a brownish fragment of fabric that lay between her legs.

This woman, it was said, was either an Egyptian, or that the method of mummification that had been performed upon her with such care was also intimately known to the Romans of Aquincum. Wherever she had come from, the trappings of her death suggest she may have been a woman of wealth; and of those trappings, perhaps none more so than the remnants of the very fine dress that lay under her luxurious wrapping. The cloth from which it was made was the only surviving piece of the sea silk ever to be recovered; a rectangle of only around five by seven inches. Its matted tangle of frayed and twisted woven threads were taken to the Aquincum Museum, to be studied and stored. It was last photographed in 1935, before the outbreak of war in Europe. In March 1938 Hitler annexed Austria, and the Third Reich became Hungary's immediate neighbour. The horrors of the Second World War swept through Hungary. When the war ended, as the Aquincum Museum was slowly rebuilt, the oldest known textile fragment of sea silk in the world was nowhere to be seen.

Both the excavation diary of the archaeological team and the original analysis of the textile had also vanished, and with them any hope of confirming its origin with the use of more advanced technology. All that was known was that the first person to have inspected the textile was Dr Francis Hollendonner, the same scientist who had examined under a microscope the fungal spores in the buried woman's face powder and identified them as the mushroom *Tolyposporium junceum*. He had also identified the types of wood from which the boxes among her grave goods were crafted. He wrote of the species that had infiltrated her wrappings over the passage of time. They were the sporangia and spores of Mucoraceae, fungi that in life can cause a sudden, severe infection of the central nervous system; and the very rare zygospores of the Phycomycetes, found in soil, in animal manure, on fruit, in fridges as bread mould and as infections in humans and other animals. In this Hollendonner was an expert. He had qualified in plant histology, and he would have known the studies that had, by then, used chemical and microscopic analysis to identify both natural and artificial fibres. He would not, in other words, have confused the byssus of the Assyrians with the secretions of a marine mollusc; or the parts of a plant or a fungus with that of an animal. Not even one as strange as the *Pinna*.

There are records of microscopic studies made in the very early years of the 1900s that have survived. Among these are publications that Hollendonner would have known, given his very considered identification of the cloth from the Aquincum mummy as sea silk. Scientists have staked their reputations on far less. When, in 1917, Hollendonner presented his results to the Royal Hungarian Society of Natural Sciences, he described the fabric as coarse, the fibres as brittle, degraded and easily broken. It looked, he said, like a fabric made of hair. The diameter of the fibres was 24–32 micrometres, around a third finer than a human hair. In cross section they were a compressed ellipse. Among natural fibres, this was a shape unique to the *Pinna*. By the time of the cemetery's excavation analysis of *Pinna* threads had already been published, in 1901 and 1905, and microscopic images were released in 1914. Hollendonner had compared these dimensions and that form with the threads of *Pinna nobilis*. He had found a perfect match.

Situated in the middle of landlocked Hungary, Budapest lies over three hundred miles from the nearest Mediterranean coast, the natural habitat for *Pinna nobilis*. But like its population, the treasures that Aquincum held were also brought from many parts of the Roman Empire. The epitaphs of its legions named their original homes: Egypt, Libya, the southwestern shores of Italy, and Syria. All of these were also places once rich in *Pinna nobilis* populations.

It seems remarkable that classical Greeks and Romans, from whose writings it appears were well acquainted with *Pinna nobilis* – as food, in medicine and probably also in religion – were not also using its threads in textiles. The possibility that they did must be considered. It is only after Aquincum was founded, in the early centuries of the first millennium CE, that the first explicit written records of textiles made from the *Pinna* appeared. When they did, it is not just from the pens of writers from the Mediterranean world. Its wonder had spread to far distant lands, too.

It is not clear why this should be the case, but from that time many descriptions appear. In the annals of the later Chinese Han Dynasty, dating between 25 and 220 CE, there is an account of the inflammable cloth of asbestos used by the Romans, fabric made from wild silkworm cocoons and '. . . further, they have a fine cloth said by some to originate from the down of a water-sheep . . .' Tertullian, who lived between 155 and 220 CE, and was an author and Christian theologian from Roman Carthage, situated on the Mediterranean coast of what is now Tunisia, was critical of the extravagance of the cloth: 'Nor was it enough to comb and sew the materials for a tunic', he wrote. 'It was necessary also to fish for one's dress. For fleeces are obtained from the sea, where shells of extraordinary size are furnished with tufts of mossy hair.' And in the *Weilüe*, written between 239 and 265, the author Yiu Huan described how 'they weave fine cloth, saying that they utilize for this purpose the down of the water-sheep, this product, hai si pu, cloth from the west of the sea'. Some Christian teachers also used the *Pinna* to show, through natural wonders, the great glory of God. 'Whence had the pinna its gold coloured wool', wrote St Basil the Great, Archbishop of Caesarea, in the third century, '. . . that colour which is inimitable!'

During the reign of the Byzantine emperor Justinian, until the year 565, Procopius of Caesarea, who also documented the first appearance of Chinese silk moths in Europe, also recounted a story about a place on the Euphrates River, north and west of the city of Amida, today Diyarbakır, not far from Turkey's border with Syria. There, Justinian had established a ruling group of five provincial governors and furnished them with symbols of their office. 'It is worthwhile to describe these insignia, for they will never again be seen by man', Procopius recorded. 'There is a cloak made of wool, not such as is produced by sheep, but gathered from the sea. Pinnos the creature is called on which this wool grows.' And then water-sheep appear again, in the annals of the T'ang Dynasty that ruled Imperial China for most of the years between 618 and 907. It included an account of a place that is either Constantinople or Syria. In any case, the records tell of how 'the wool of the water-sheep is woven into cloth'. Later, in twelfth-century writings from the Islamic world, Andalusian-Arab physician, botanist, pharmacist and scientist Ibn al-Baiṭār reported the use of suf el-bahr, 'wool of the sea'.

But from the eleventh century, a cloth of another name had also been written about, from Islamic Spain to Syria. Its description was more detailed. It joined the ranks of luxurious wools, linen cloth so fine it was weighted down with gold, so costly that its export might be forbidden. Used in saddlecloths and for covering royal palanquins, this cloth was called Abū Ḳalamūn. The origin of this is uncertain. It may have come from the Greek *hupokálamon*, a term used by the Byzantines for a precious, striped or brightly coloured textile, although Abū Ḳalamūn was said to have been of a colour that varied with the time of day and the intensity of the sun, and one that was manufactured exclusively in Egypt. Over time, the word would also come to mean other things in Arabic, including, strangely, a mollusc.

Around that time in the eleventh century, a book appeared that covered the countries of the western Islamic world between the fourth and the tenth centuries, in which the Palestinian geographer Muhammad ibn Ahmad al-Muqadisi left an account of the empire, up to the borders of the province of Damascus, Syria. In that place many curiosities were to be found, not least of which was the Abū Ḳalamūn. The garments crafted from these precious hairs, al-Muqadisi wrote, were forbidden for export, but were, nevertheless, 'passed along secretly'. Ruling between the years 661 and 750, Umayyad princes of Cordoba, it is said, reserved this 'wool' only for themselves. A garment made from these threads could fetch a price equivalent to between around half a kilogram to four kilograms of gold.

The origin of this material was, al-Muqadisi said, '. . . a beast that, on the edge of the sea, rubs itself on rocks and makes thus to come off hair that has the suppleness of silk and the colour of gold. People are careful not to lose any of it because it is rare and precious. One collects it and weaves it into cloth that, in the space of some hours, takes on various colours.'

So precious, so rare – this silk from the sea was perhaps really only ever a fabric fit for princes.

15

SLKY

THE ISLAND OF SANT'ANTIOCO IS CELEBRATED FOR ITS CAVERNOUS catacombs and Bronze Age nuraghes, towers built of enormous stone blocks; a Phoenician Tophet in which lie the burned bones of babies still interred on a hillside inside terracotta urns; a basilica that held the relics of the martyr for which the island was renamed; and its golden-handed weavers.

The island, with its main town of the same name, is reached by crossing a narrow strip of land from the southwest coast of Sardinia, formed by an artificial isthmus originally built by the Romans. This region, now called Sulcis, had been populated by a prehistoric people for twenty thousand years, and then by whoever had built its nuraghes for at least a thousand years, a group who may have gone on to mix with Mycenaean, Levantine and Cypriot traders. It had been named SLKY, or Sulki, by Phoenicians from present-day Lebanon and northern Palestine in the eighth century BCE; was occupied by Punics expanding from Carthage on the North African coast of present-day Tunisia two hundred years later; and was conquered by the Romans four hundred years after that.

No one knows the real name of the Phoenician people, but it was the Romans who first called them 'Phoenician', or 'Punic', from the Greek word φοῖνιξ – phoenix – which was also the name given to a highly prized deep purple dye tinged with red. These 'Phoenicians' had perfected the extraction of the colour, which would become the preserve of royalty and nobility, from the small, long-spined murex mollusc, and were responsible for the trade in this valuable commodity from the sea. Later, in honour of another commodity from deep below the earth, the Romans would change the name of their territory from SLKY to Plumbaria, with a rapacious eye on the island's lead deposits, which the Christian St Antioch would be made to mine after he was tortured in more traditional ways for inciting the locals to convert. After that the blood of the people of Sant'Antioco would be presented a fine opportunity to blend with sailors of all colours from naval frigates and pirate ships and luggers, Byzantines and Saracens, French and North Africans, Spaniards, Pisanos and the Genoese.

In the north of the island is the town of Calasetta, built by a people who had fled from the Tunisian islet of Tabarka, which was part of the Republic of Genoa until its capture in 1741 by the Bey of Tunis, Abu'l-Hasan Ali I. Calasetta is a name which claims a number of derivations, one of which is, some say, for the *cala*, or bay, which surrounds it, and *seta*, the Italian for silk. Among the shellfish of this island is the *Pinna nobilis*, called nacchera for the large quantity of the inner pearlescent nacre that lines its shell, and which in days gone by, put tough, unpalatable, but enormous steaks of mollusc meat fried in cheap oil on the plates of its most impoverished inhabitants. At that time the waters of Calasetta and surrounding Sant'Antioco were home to vast populations of the *Pinna*, which were brought ashore in fishing boats.

Within the living memory of its expert weavers and from historic records and collections, textiles spun from sea silk had been present for some time, though exactly how long is uncertain. Whatever the case, the making of sea silk would always have been possible because the *Pinna* was known and used there. But it was a curious art. It was practised by some, was produced in small quantities, and yet remained highly valued for the fabric that it made. And then, just after the turn of the nineteenth century, the weaving of sea silk began to be more widely taught there, though more to preserve it than to profit from it. What is truly remarkable is that the anchoring threads of *Pinna nobilis* are still used in Sulcis. It is the last place in the Mediterranean where the knowledge of weaving textiles from sea silk is being kept alive.

. . .

In 1914, a collection of travel notes called *In Sardegna* was published by the Florentine photographer Vittorio Alinari. It contained a description of the island's places and people, architecture and animals, traditions and history. It had been, Alinari wrote, his first visit, and the places he explored there were almost exclusively spread along its coastline. In the latter part of his visit Alinari travelled to Sant'Antioco through picturesque winding roads, past astonishingly beautiful scenery in the verdant lands around Iglesias in Sardinia's southwest. Two millennia after the Romans, the land was still being mined, not just for lead but for its rich deposits of iron and coal. When on 18 December 1938 Mussolini ordered the building of the new city of Carbonia, founded for the extraction of coal, and to the glory of Fascism, the Iglesias and Carbonia provinces were merged. It was from that region that Alinari crossed from Sardinia to Sant'Antioco.

Alinari wrote of a bridge through which boats with lowered masts sailed across to the smaller island. Passing that bridge, he saw the town of Sant'Antioco, which, as Sulcis, had extended to the south, but of which by then only ruins remained. At that time, the town had stood some way from the water. By Alinari's day, Sulcis had been invaded, abandoned and rebuilt for its own protection over the highest part of the Phoenician town, places in which it had been customary to build funeral grounds, leaving its future occupants to live over, and often within, what had originally been reserved for the dead. As he entered the town, Alinari faithfully photographed its original Roman bridge, its castle and the Phoenician burial caves beneath it, cut from soft, sedimentary tufa rock. He recounted stories he had heard of idolatrous locals who terrified proselytizing friars, and of poor settlers from Iglesias who made their homes in those cave tombs, which they converted from rooms for the dead into places for living, cooking, dining and sleeping.

Alinari routinely took portraits wherever he visited. When he published his travelogue in 1914, his images showed the men and women of Sant'Antioco in traditional dress. Here, he also photographed the island's oldest traditional musical instrument, a decorated flute of two reeds that was difficult and tiring to play, not unlike the aulos of the shepherds of ancient Greece. Alinari found the people to be particularly industrious in the creation of textiles. He described about two hundred looms, and that in a tranquil region of just over one hundred kilometres in area that seems deserted of people even today. Most of its looms were dedicated to the making of orbace, a rough, scratchy but robust water-resistant fabric made from felted wool. In a few short decades, Sant'Antioco's looms would be co-opted, and their orbace made compulsory for the uniforms of Fascist party officials. Before that, these looms also made other fabrics, for tablecloths, carpets and saddlebags.

'But', Alinari wrote, 'the most curious works are made from the *Pinna nobilis*, that come fished in great numbers from the gulf, and whose terminal appendix, the byssus, forms silken filaments . . .' What he went on to describe, how these filaments were first cleaned of the shells and concretions that had adhered to them in the deep, and how they were then separated into threads and woven into a textile, culminated in a description of a finished cloth that he found utterly remarkable. Alinari wrote of the beautiful effect produced by the *Pinna nobilis* silk. It was 'of a beautiful metallic colour that approaches copper', with which he saw petticoats being made, exquisitely finished with gilt buttons. Each of these petticoats was crafted from almost nine hundred 'tails', the byssus of the mollusc, costing around nine lire for the spinning of the silk. That included the complex process of cleaning, first in seawater, to remove the marine debris, and then further washing, the combing of the nine hundred silken 'tails' with a fine-toothed brush, the spooling and spinning of the indulgently soft, delicate floss produced through this process into threads, and then the looming of those threads into a fabric to be sewn into the luxurious undergarments. The copper colour might also have been lightened by immersion in lemon juice, or, more traditionally, cow's urine, and the gilded buttons, brought from the region around Cagliari, one hundred kilometres to the east on the larger island of Sardinia, would have added to the cost. The making of the complete garment could take up weeks of a skilled artisan's time. It was delicate, slow, difficult work. At that time, the cost of spinning that much unprocessed sea silk alone was equivalent to the entire day's salary of a skilled artisan. 'This cannot be considered an exaggerated price', Alinari commented, 'because only about a hundred a day can be worked, since the thread is very delicate and easy to tear.' Even though the *Pinna* was abundant and its meat cheap, there were probably few who could afford to wear its silk. This beautiful, fine copper cloth of sea silk, worn close to the skin by those Sant'Antiocans who could afford it, would have been quite beyond the means of those who fished or farmed, or indeed squatted in the former houses of the Phoenician dead, and so it would remain entirely absent from their wardrobes.

16

ITALO

THE LETTERS OF EFISIO DIANA TO HIS WIFE MARIETTA PASSARELLA DURING the illness that took her life are so heart-achingly sad that they are still difficult for their living descendants to read. Efisio had met and married the beautiful, clear-eyed Marietta after she was deported to Sant'Antioco, when her life in the northern Italian region of the Veneto was interrupted by political unrest. She had become a mother at a young age, but her death would precede the loss of two of her children in their teens, one to tuberculosis, the other probably to the malaria that plagued the lagoons of Sulcis. By the time of Alinari's visit, all that remained of Efisio's immediate family was their eldest daughter, Emma, and their youngest son, Italo, by then 24 years old, unusually tall, with the beautiful face and green eyes of his mother. Though young, Italo had long been deeply absorbed in his island's traditions. It was he who would introduce Alinari to the local customs and costumes he would record in images and words.

When Marietta died, Italo was just 8 years old. Thereafter he was raised by the women of the family – by his elder sister, Emma, by his aunts, by the ladies of the household staff – and learned from those women who cared for him. This was why, when he was not studying at home with tutors, he spent his days engaged in pastimes not expected of a boy. Every day, the women of his household would sit at the loom. They spun, wove and prepared threads of many types, all of which Alinari, when he later came to stay with the family, would note as being typical of Sulcis. Italo's childhood experiences would come together in an unusual ambition. He developed a particular passion for the arts, the traditions of his island, and a love for weaving above all else. As a young man he studied paintings, but preferred the practical to the scholarly. He joined local folklore groups, mastered the ancient flute of the shepherds, and had begun weaving in earnest before reaching his teens. Aged 12, he built his own loom on which he would weave just as the women of the household did. On it he first replicated traditional designs of the island, but later began using the old techniques to create new patterns. He had, by his own hand, made some of those textiles that would so impress Alinari.

Portrait of Italo Diana.

Although a small island, Sant'Antioco had long welcomed people of many cultures, and what might have been considered unusual in another place perhaps did not seem quite so implausible here. That was fortunate for Italo, as his choice of weaving, it seems, was not judged as harshly as it might otherwise have been. Perhaps because of all the loss he had suffered, his family left him to it, and was happy as long as he was. He had a father who was kind, an elder sister and aunts who adored him, and a substantial home, formerly a convent of twenty-five rooms. All this allowed him to dream of a life as an artisan, one led on his own terms. In Italo's gift was also a disdain for practicalities, or, indeed, an income, and that curious combination of the spirits of laissez-faire and altruism that has so often culminated in achieving that which could not or should not be done.

Still, to the wider world, women's work did remain a curious passion for a boy to pursue, and would be even harder to imagine in a young man. And so, from 1914 to 1915, as Alinari finalized his reports and departed Sant'Antioco for Florence, and the world fell into a turmoil on a scale never before seen, Italo was forced to leave his loom and take up arms, as all young men were, when the First World War began. When he eventually returned from the front, he was gaunt, sad, determinedly silent about his time in the army. But when he set foot once again in his home on Sant'Antioco's Via Regina Margherita, his mind was alight with a very singular purpose.

The bitterness of war must have deafened him to any criticism of making his official entrance into an exclusively female career, because, by the early 1920s, Italo finally followed his youthful dream and opened a weaving school. It was housed on the far side of the expansive ground floor of his home and was financed entirely from his own wealth. Italo wanted both tradition and innovation. He hired local women, talented weavers in their own right, and paid them to teach girls sent to the school by their families from the age of around 16. He provided them with materials to spin and the tools of the trade. When the girls married, and inevitably left to continue weaving at home, Italo gave each a wedding trousseau, complete with everything they would need to continue working textiles. As for the textiles, the materials he chose to weave and teach were cotton, wool, linen, orbace and sea silk.

No more than a ten-minute walk due east from the school was the port where Sant'Antioco's fishermen moored their boats and landed their catch. Italo was there when they did so, ready to pay for *Pinna* freshly wrenched from the seabed with a tool they called *manu de ferru*. It translates as 'iron hand', and it could reach places where fishermen could not. A number of different designs existed, but all were typically six or seven metres in length and had fixed at their base a sort of open saddle bracket that would be rotated to displace the shell from its anchored foot and lift it into the boats. It was a process that left the silk still attached to *Pinna* large and small, so Italo bought the entire mollusc, extracted the silken tails and returned the rest to the fishermen so that they could take the meat. It was worth the effort to Italo. It is said that of all his materials, these fine filaments of *Pinna nobilis* were the threads of greatest personal value to him, although no one knows exactly why that was so. It is also said, because his eye had always turned as much to antiquity as to posterity, that he had taken his inspiration for the spinning of sea silk from stories that he had read of the use of those threads in Pharaonic legend. That he was inspired by what he had studied of Egyptian textiles. That he reproduced the tools necessary to work the finest sea silk from drawings and texts from ancient Egypt. By Italo's time, records of the production of sea silk in Sant'Antioco were already being kept in archives which held remnants of fabrics contemporary with Italo's, but independent of his school. There is a tie made by the hands of another weaver, Mariannicca Serra, and collected histories of a few people who made their own items on domestic looms, fabrics made of all the yarns available on the island, including those of the *Pinna*.

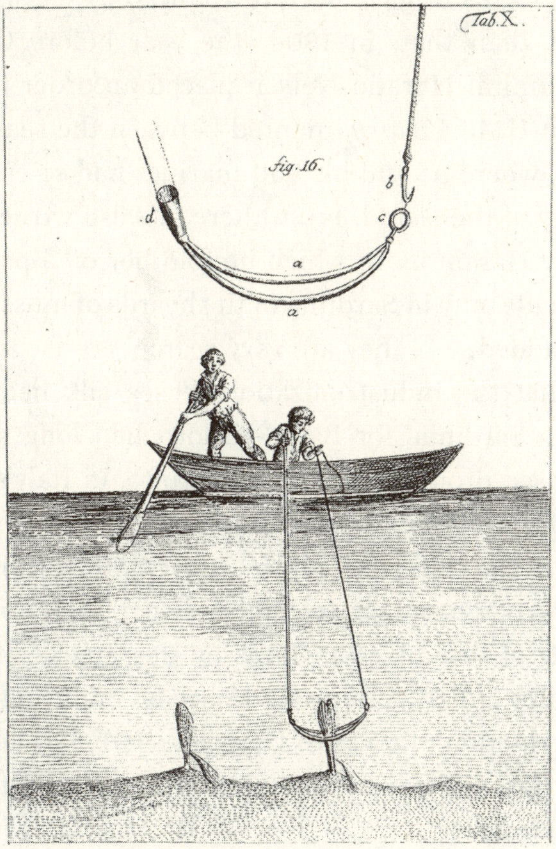

Fishing the *Pinna nobilis*, Taranto, 1793.

Before that, in 1908, a Cagliari doctor named Giuseppe Basso-Arnoux founded the pragmatically named 'Byssus Ichnusa Society for the promotion of sea-silk', which, oddly, was headquartered in London. In 1910, Basso-Arnoux sold several sea silk items to the new Musée océanographique in Monaco for a hundred French francs; in 1916 he produced a report that sought to promote the production of the silk of *Pinna nobilis* in Sardinia, although no physical traces of any of his silk remain. Basso-Arnoux was born in 1840 and seems to have been introduced to sea silk as a child. Even earlier than that, in 1804, the year before the Battle of Trafalgar, Admiral Horatio Nelson placed an order for a muff of sea silk from HMS *Victory*, moored between the seas of Sardinia and Corsica, where he and his 850 marines had so enjoyed taking in the beauty of the island. From there, he also wrote to his lover, Emma, Lady Hamilton, in which he told her of 'a pair of curious gloves . . . made only in Sardinia of the beards of mussels . . .' 'They tell me', he added, '. . . they are very scarce.'

It's not that the industrialization of sea silk had never been attempted in Sardinia, for Basso-Arnoux had long set his sights on its increased production; and in Taranto, in Italy's deep south, tapestries of sea silk had been shown at industrial and trade fairs as far back as the mid-nineteenth century. Some think that there was already a very ancient sea silk industry there, perhaps since the founding of that place as Taras by the Greeks. It is true that Taras, the later city of Taranto, did have an enduring relationship with the production of textiles. Dating to 540–530 BCE, the oldest known inscription from the town itself seems to refer to a prize for teasing wool.

Two and a half millennia later, Taranto's archaeological sites are still replete with the fragmented shells of that murex mollusc. The remnants of the textile dye industry were so plentiful there that there is even a hill that formed from their discarded shells over time; this is the Monte dei Coccioli, which for centuries characterized the coastal landscape of the city's inner sea. But Taras was also famous for its eponymous Tarantinon cloth, long, very light and delicate. It was typical of Taras, said to be particularly suitable for women, but was also worn by men who wanted to flaunt their wealth. This Tarantinon cloth may well have been the finest wool of the Tarentine rams that were used in breeding programmes around the expanding Greek empire. Because no such quantities of broken *Pinna nobilis* shells have been found as testament to any sea silk production there. In one sense, they should, or would, have been present. In 1928, a teacher of natural history called Beniamino Mastrocinque recorded how, in his time, twenty to thirty thousand *Pinna nobilis* were pulled from the sea every year for their meat. That quantity would produce only thirty to forty kilograms of sea silk a year, since only one and a half grams can ultimately be extracted from each *Pinna*. One kilogram of silk can produce around seven metres of fabric, enough perhaps for two ancient Greek dresses, which means that no more than fifteen to twenty pieces of substantive clothing made entirely of sea silk could ever be created each year, even with the destruction of so many *Pinna*.

Then, between March 1938 and January 1939, an anatomist who had started his academic life with the study of toads and ended up as the director of the state-run marine biology laboratories and technical inspector for shellfish farming in Taranto, attempted to grow the *Pinna* on managed farms, in much the same way as blue *Mytilus* mussels. It was Attilio Cerruti's best attempt to mitigate the large-scale fishing of wild *Pinna* that could not be avoided if production of the fabric was ever to become economically worthwhile.

Cerruti published his study under the title *First breeding experiments of the Pinna in the Mar Piccolo of Taranto*, and his most pressing concern was that the natural populations of these molluscs in the seas around that ancient city should not be destroyed. But Cerruti's experimental shells grew to only seven centimetres, when they might have grown to as much as twenty in that time. Farming them proved a difficult undertaking, and, though it is still unclear why, it was one that was ultimately doomed to failure.

But all of this suggests that even in 1804, when Nelson wrote to Lady Hamilton, he must have been right in saying that sea silk was something curious. Despite all attempts, despite the immense number of *Pinna* in the seas at that time, sea silk itself remained scarce. In 1837, in the lecture he delivered to the Asiatic Society of Bengal expounding the glories of the silks of India, Johann Helfer had also said much the same. He reported that the silk of this mollusc was always dearer than the silk of *Bombyx mori*, '. . . though to this day caps, gloves and stockings are woven from it in Calabria and Sicily'. Helfer added that he had himself seen a considerable number of these small items manufactured from it when he was in Palermo, but that it was his impression, too, that 'it will probably remain forever a matter of curiosity, rather than an article of general use'.

The fact is that Italo's school, in which he trained students in the weaving of all fibres and sent them out into the world to continue their work, could not have had any effect other than to preserve what would have been, at best, a small, local practice in whichever part of the Mediterranean it would have been carried out. There would not have been many buyers for something that took so much time and attention, and such trades that do not make a financial return tend to disappear. Working such a demanding and delicate material must always have been a labour of love. Because even for Italo's school that was dedicated to the art of all the various fibres they used, sea silk turned out to be the one material with which only he and a select few of his best weavers could ultimately work.

Still, by 2 September 1928 the school had such an impressive collection of Sardinian clothing made from sea silk that their application to exhibit at the 16th Venice Biennale that year was received with great interest. Each item had a price tag of between 140 and 180 lire . . . and alongside was a second tag indicating that all the clothing had already been sold. It would have been surprising if anyone had bought them: at today's prices, taking inflation into account, the items would have been valued at over 9,000 euros. Italo happily brought them all back with his team when they returned. They had not been sold. It was what he had wanted.

Among the grandest items the school created from sea silk but did release into the world was a habit for the statue of St Francis in the Church of Assisi, which was interwoven with linen, and a cape sent to Princess Mafalda of Savoy, daughter of King Victor Emmanuel III of Italy, made entirely from *Pinna* threads. Both were given freely, the first a donation to God, the second a gift to the royal family. And then there was a large tapestry designed to impress another higher power, woven so that the metallic threads of silk formed patterns on the loom on a base of linen, of birds and horses and traditional motifs of Sant'Antioco, geometric shapes and trees and tiny stick people perpetually dancing, hand in hand. Juxtaposing the harmony of that evocative idyll, under its powerfully built horses and above its peacock-like birds, was a stylized representation of the *fascio littorio*, the bundle of bound sticks, fasces, that gave Fascism its name. Mussolini was well known for adopting symbols from ancient Rome, including this insignia of power. In this instance, the *fascio* proved to be a poor choice, because, rather than being Roman, it was of Etruscan origin, a people considered racially inferior to the so-called 'Aryans', but after whom the Romans named Tuscany, and the Greeks had named the Tyrrhenian Sea. Still, when the tapestry was made by Italo and Assunta Cabras, one of his expert student weavers, that contentious bundle of power was woven in just beneath the title of Il Duce, 'The Leader'.

In 1938, Mussolini visited Sulcis to inaugurate the coal-mining town of Carbonia. Italo came up against the local Fascists, and decided against presenting the gift his workshop had so painstakingly created. In 1939, in a grand autarkic gesture, all of the looms of Sant'Antioco were requisitioned for the weaving of itchy orbace with which to clothe the Fascist armed forces. In 1940, Italy joined the war against Great Britain and France as one of the Axis powers. Once again Italo left Sant'Antioco, this time for Monte Cresia, just east of Cagliari. Sant'Antioco sat squarely within the Allies' theatre of bombing. Italo's bustling workshop in his house on Via Regina Margherita fell silent. Inside it lay abandoned silken beards packed into sacks, their threads of copper and gold and green still attached to the long-withered muscle of the *Pinna*'s foot. The doors of Italo's school were sealed shut, never to reopen again.

Across the Tyrrhenian Sea on the Gulf of Taranto, the only other remaining school that taught the weaving of sea silk would meet much the same fate. There, it had been started by a seamstress called Rita del Bene. In contrast to Italo's insistence on the traditional, artisanal, slow labour of love, and an ethic that distanced itself from the ruling regime, Rita experimented with industrializing the processing of sea silk using mechanical looms. Rita was said to have believed the *Pinna* could become an alternative to the domesticated silkworm. She also seemed to have been an ardent supporter of Fascism. To her, the industrial production of sea silk fitted beautifully with the 'autarky desired by the omniscient leader', she once wrote, '. . . not only to be sufficient for ourselves but also to impose our products on other nations.' And so, perhaps the demise of her school was ultimately for a different reason than that of Italo's. When Fascism collapsed with the end of the Second World War, so did her ambitions for the mass production of sea silk.

In Sulcis, however, Italo Diana's students carried on weaving with the remnants of the threads of *Pinna nobilis* that had been abandoned in the aftermath of the war. They passed these skills on to new artisans, so that four generations on there are women there who weave sea silk still.

17

PINNIDAE

AT THE END OF SEPTEMBER 2016, MARINE BIOLOGISTS BEGAN noticing more and more *Pinna nobilis* turning up dead across hundreds of kilometres of the southwestern Mediterranean Sea, from Spain to the coast of Morocco. By the third week of October, close to 90 per cent had been destroyed. In mid-November, their destruction had spread towards Mallorca; by March 2017 those around the rest of the Balearic Islands were also disappearing. By June, the scale of death approached 100 per cent. Some of their enormous shells would be found washed up on beaches.

Whatever was devastating *Pinna nobilis* was so catastrophic that in a short space of time it had destroyed almost the entire population along those central and southernmost coasts of the Iberian Peninsula, even as it continued moving steadily east towards Sardinia. This tragedy, referred to by biologists as a 'mass mortality event', followed a progressive decline in the *Pinna*'s numbers during the twentieth century. Then their deaths had been caused by fishing and ornamental harvesting for their shells and for their silk. Later, recreational and commercial fishing, accidental killing by anchoring, shipwrecks, bottom nets, trawlers began destroying their habitat, too. In 2016 they started to disappear from the Tyrrhenian Sea coast of Italy, and by the beginning of 2017, in Campania, Sicily and Sardinia almost all *Pinna nobilis* and some *Pinna rudis* had succumbed to the devastation.

Mass mortality events are described as catastrophes that affect all the life stages of an animal simultaneously, showing little mercy and leaving no time for the young of a species to breed or for the old to recover. Similar tragedies have also now been seen worldwide, affecting corals, sea urchins, sea turtles and marine mammals, as well as its molluscs. They are known to be the consequence of a variety of diseases, including those caused by virus-like parasites. One parasite that affected *Pinna nobilis* had already been noted in 1993. In that case, it attacked only its reproductive organs, effectively castrating the animals. Mostly, what is known of the diseases of the Pinnidae, the family to which *Pinna nobilis* belongs, has really only been recorded in the most general of senses. This time, however, the *Pinna* sickened. They became emaciated. They did not respond to stimuli, became slothful in the closing of their valves and could no longer shut tight the two halves of their shells when they were threatened by predators.

The first culprit identified seemed to have invaded the *Pinna*'s digestive system and was only found in dead or dying *Pinna*. But quite what it was remained undetermined. It would be identified in 2018, but only after it had already almost entirely decimated *Pinna* populations after two years of infection. Though it seemed to be some species of a protozoa, a haplosporidan-like parasite, it was one so different from most of its relatives that it was classified separately. And it was so unknown that, once it had been identified, scientists would refer to it by a combination of the name of the parasite and that of the *Pinna*. This so-called '*Haplosporidium pinnae*' was specifically 'a haplosporidan parasite associated with mass mortalities of the fan mussel, *Pinna nobilis*, in the Western Mediterranean Sea'. Various parasites of this type had already been known to infect fish, oysters and cockroaches. They have tough spores which transmit the contagion quickly through a population, and cell structures that rapidly divide into a growth that fills the digestive glands of the *Pinna*.

Effectively, the parasite had starved them to death. But such massive numbers of deaths could not be easily explained by just one type of infection, and what exactly was at the root of the mass deaths is still not entirely known. Then, in the waters around Campania and Sicily, a different *Pinna* infection was discovered, this one caused by a mycobacterium. This was a deadly relation of that most tragic of pathogens in humans, the *Mycobacterium tuberculosis*, that itself had killed close to two million people alone in the year before the demise of the *Pinna*. In 2020, in addition to the research that had already taken place, a group of Italian biologists reported that the *Haplosporidium pinnae* had in fact been recorded three years *before* the beginning of the mass deaths of the *Pinna*. It meant that the parasite would not be the *bête noire* of only the *Pinna nobilis* and its closest relatives, but might also have decimated others. What is more, the mycobacterium thought to be killing them was also found in *Pinna nobilis* and *Pinna rudis* that were living quite healthily in the sea. Four years on from the mass destruction, the cause of the devastation remained a mystery.

But then these scientists, led by researchers in Sardinia, also found another infection in the form of a bacterium of a species known as *Rhodococcus erythropolis*. Bizarrely, these bacteria have also been detected on the surface of the human eye. They are more typically found in soil, and are such astonishing organisms that they can thrive with or without oxygen, because where they cannot find nutrients they will generate their own. They can accumulate within themselves, and then degrade some radioactive materials, azo dyes, pesticides. They are being heavily researched as a natural treatment for contaminants generated by humans, polluted soils and marine oil spills. What the *Rhodococcus* are doing inside the *Pinna* is an intriguing question, and is a subject of much speculation among scientists. But in July 2007, after the merchant freighter *Don Pedro* sank off the coast of Ibiza in the Western Mediterranean, near its busy island harbour, marine biologists were presented with the opportunity to study its effect on the *Pinna*.

For in the ship's hold were between one hundred and one hundred and fifty tonnes of fuel oil, as well as around fifty tonnes of light diesel. When the accident occurred, this fuel spilled out into the sea. When such a thing happens, substances contained within fuel oils remain in the seas. They are persistent, and some of them possess properties that give them the potential to cause cancers and other damaging changes to the genetic make-up of animals. The effects of the spillage on the *Pinna* were studied because mussels cannot move. Not only does this mean that they are particularly subject to whatever humankind throws at them, but, being fixed in one place, as the very largest of mussels they filter whatever is present in the waters around them. They gather pollutants, concentrating contaminants inside themselves. The levels of polluting chemicals that end up in their bodies, therefore, are always higher than those in the surrounding waters. Our pollutants accumulate in the *Pinna*. Because they are immobile organisms, and because they have always taken in everything around them, they have adapted by developing a certain tolerance to contaminants – defence mechanisms by which they are able to detoxify themselves. One month after the *Don Pedro* shed its tonnages of fuel, chemicals were found inside the digestive systems of the *Pinna* studied. The animals were under acute stress. It would be a full year after the oil spillage before their bodies returned to normal again. It is a complicated scenario presented to them, by us, and still the reasons for their mass mortality are far from being fully understood.

What is interesting is that these parasitic infections are not working alone; that is to say, they are not entirely to blame for the devastation they have wrought. That blame must fall squarely on humans. The parasites attacking the *Pinna* may simply have chanced upon an excellent opportunity, because all the evidence suggests that the scenario in which new diseases are emerging is complex. They are linked with changes in the opportunities that pathogens have to interact with a number of animals, including people. They are associated with the temperature of the seas increasing, with how pathogens spread, and how far they do so; with how virulent they can now become. They are also able to kill with such impunity because the growth patterns of many animals, and the ability of their immune systems to protect them, are worsening. There is a constellation of reasons why this might be happening, but these are only now beginning to be described.

A study of one Spanish lagoon, for example, found that pharmaceuticals had also accumulated in its *Pinna nobilis* populations, among them beta blockers, asthma medication, analgesics, anti-inflammatories and psychiatric drugs. Other studies have found that while the natural environmental challenges the *Pinna* have always had to live with – adapting to different depths, managing the effects of changing wave direction – the hydrodynamics of the sea can and do affect the size of their shells and the direction in which they must orientate themselves. As even the ancient fishermen of the Mediterranean will have known, the larger the animal, the deeper its home. With climate change, the increase in storms and the strengthening intensity of waves are likely to disturb what *Pinna* now remain, dislodging them from the seafloor, pushing large individuals to greater depths.

But of all of these things, it seems to be the apparently minor human actions – the things people do simply for leisure, the anchoring of boats, diving and fishing – that have wrought the most change in the seas formerly replete with *Pinna* populations. Through human recreation, their numbers, the patterns of where they can be found and how big these largest mussels of the sea are ultimately able to grow, is now dictated by what we choose to do. And while we do this, the outbreak of new diseases continues to be recorded globally. The consequences affect entire ecosystems. *Pinna* filter the waters around them; they keep them clean and clear. Their shells are a surface upon which other organisms, epifauna, as they are called, make their home. These are tiny, simple, sedentary aquatic animals, little marine worms that inhabit calcium-rich tubes made by their own secretions, and that date back to the Middle Triassic, well over two hundred million years ago. Occasionally, too, sponges attach themselves to *Pinna nobilis*, which fossil records say itself dates back 245 million years. And then there is a multitude of colonies of encrustations composed of tiny bodies, each with just an abdomen and a thorax. It is easy to overlook the presence of such things that may seem inconsequential, but that fit so intimately with the *Pinna*'s ancient world.

Their loss represents more than that of a legendary animal of the Mediterranean Sea. It is the loss of an ecosystem. It means more than the disappearance of a rare and curious textile, or, indeed, of an unpalatable meat. There are branches of science in which biologists and engineers repeatedly ask the question: 'what is it nature can do that we still cannot?' In this, the silk of the *Pinna* and its relations, and the mother-of-pearl nacre of its shells, have been a source of incredible inspiration, though no one is precisely sure how they build themselves of such materials that science still cannot replicate. Their aragonite crystals, a type of calcium carbonate from which they construct their iridescent mother-of-pearl interior, are of a structure somehow both tough and elastic. It is laid out like brickwork that expands horizontally, layer upon growing layer, with a resistance to fracturing thousands of times higher than should be possible just by their make-up alone. The paths of any fractures they do sustain merge and annihilate each other, even over large expanses of the shells. No one is sure exactly how its structure gives rise to such astounding physical and optical properties. Its sparkling iridescence can still be seen in the world's oldest fossils with aragonite like the *Pinna*'s, in reflective blues and greens and purples of shells still bright after three hundred million years. Theirs is an unparalleled strength, one so remarkable that attempts are being made to mimic their structures to fabricate body armour.

As for its silk, in life its anchoring threads self-assemble in a groove of the mussel's foot, before they are secreted as a liquid, and harden when in contact with water. If they become damaged, they can heal themselves. Somehow, they remain adhesive in a watery environment, able to firmly attach to a variety of different surfaces. They have become an archetype for bio-inspired polymers, a little like nylon or rayon, except that these are intended to regenerate themselves. They have inspired the development of new synthetic materials, extremely tear-resistant threads, adhesives for foetal surgery and synthetic self-healing polymers; for repairing the lost or damaged tissues of other animals.

In January 2021, *Pinna nobilis* was added to the International Union for Conservation of Nature's Red List of Threatened Species. It now falls under the category of 'Critically Endangered', alongside nearly 37,500 other species also threatened with extinction, a number which includes nearly half of all amphibians, a third of reef-building corals and of mammals, and just over 10 per cent of all birds. *Pinna nobilis* can no longer be fished, bought or sold, or, indeed, harvested for their silk. Little more can be done right now, except to monitor them, to map the locations in which they are becoming sick. To continue to record where they are dying.

When they die, they do so still standing, anchored by their silken threads. They are entered by marine animals that eat their dead flesh, while their empty shells offer havens in which octopus shelter from predators of their own. The rows in which they once stood become graveyards, with their upright shells for headstones. When their silken anchors disintegrate, these shells collapse into halves, and are washed wherever the currents take them.

Every ecosystem has its decomposers, those organisms in the business of recycling, of biodegrading what is no longer needed. Natural silks, biodegradable for the proteins of which they are composed, will also slowly be taken apart and changed into another form, useful to another organism. Under the Mediterranean Sea are such silent workers. There are around 1,500 species of marine fungi that can convert dead matter into nutrients to keep themselves alive. In turn these fungi are eaten by zooplankton and other organisms. They are fascinating in their own right. Some, found on driftwood, could adapt to degrade plastics. It is worth watching which of them inhabit our Great Pacific Garbage Patch, the disturbing vortex of trash that swirls in two giant collections of marine debris spread over nearly two million square kilometres of our North Pacific Ocean. But for remnants of sea silk of the *Pinna*, such fungi may be fascinating for another reason, too.

. . .

It was in 1978, in a damp basement in Saint-Denis, in the northern suburbs of Paris, that a cloth object was found during the excavation of a former abbey that had been the final resting place of the kings of France. Its twisted threads were tattered, but it remained intact enough to have held its shape. Knitted in a stocking stitch, it was a head-hugging, brimless cap crafted from threads in shades of gold and brown. This cap was dated to the fourteenth century, and it is unique. It may be the oldest European knitted object yet found. The only older examples of knitting originate in eastern Syria and North Africa, notably a pair of 1,600-year-old Romano-Egyptian socks, still a startlingly bright orange-red, and with toes split, ostensibly for wearing with sandals. Those socks had been excavated in the burial grounds of ancient Oxyrhynchus, a Greek colony on the Nile in central Egypt. But the Saint-Denis cap is now also the very oldest article made of sea silk that still physically exists, or at least that can be found, and it is held very securely in the Musée d'art et d'histoire de Saint-Denis.

From physical evidence, what was known of the use of the *Pinna*'s sea silk for textiles before this cap was only because of the dress of the Aquincum mummy, which, much like the oldest pieces of knitting, was possibly of Egyptian or Syrian origin, and dated to around a thousand years earlier. After the Saint-Denis cap, the next finds, or else explicit written records, would require a wait of another four hundred years. Writings mention many places of recent historical sea silk production – Calabria, Corsica, Dalmatia,

Malta, Tunisia – but no objects made of these threads have actually emerged from any of these places. There is certainly much evidence of the small-scale manufacture of sea silk from the end of the eighteenth century, from Sardinia, where there are physical remains, and Taranto, as well as Sicily, and Andalusia, in the south of Spain. More than fifty objects of this more modern manufacture have been found up to now. Half of these items are gloves, but there are also stockings, caps, cravats, scarves, small pieces of clothing for children and several wall hangings. They had been knitted or woven, made of sea silk alone or mixed with other threads. Unspun beards of the *Pinna* were also used like fur, to make muffs, purses, caps, collars and cuffs, bags, hatpins and necklaces. All these have survived. But if the threads of the *Pinna* were used in more ancient times, from physical evidence at least since the early years of the first millennium CE, and even if its production was niche, why is there such a marked absence of them from then until the fourteenth century? If they existed then – and we know that they did – what happened to these threads over time?

The Pinnidae, the family to which *Pinna nobilis* belongs, includes other large-shelled molluscs, though none quite as large. Whatever their size, where they must anchor in order to grow impacts the type of threads they produce. The longest come from the shells that must root themselves firmly to the seafloor, rather than on rocky surfaces. They include the reddened, fluted *Pinna rudis*, which may have been the subject of Mycenaean sacramental frescos, and the *Atrina pectinata*. This is a mollusc that reaches up to only thirty-five centimetres in height, and which has a shell that is fragile, neither sharp nor spiny, almost smooth to the touch. Like the *Pinna*, *Atrina* can live in shallow subtidal areas up to twenty metres in depth, anchoring in muddy or sandy seafloors. Rather than in Mediterranean waters, it, and its close relatives, are common along the coasts of Korea, Japan, China and the Philippines. In all those places, it is a popular delicacy and one highly valued, particularly for its adductor muscle, a nutritious food, because that is where the animal stores most of its own energy reserves. In some places, like the coastal waters of Maqueda Bay in the Philippines, it is the main livelihood of local fisheries. Though its silk is remarkably similar to that of *Pinna nobilis* and *Pinna rudis*, there seems to have been no local tradition of the weaving of its silk into textiles. The silk is routinely discarded when its meat is extracted, perhaps because these threads are far shorter than those of the *Pinna*. They grow to only six centimetres, compared to the twenty to twenty-five centimetres of their Mediterranean relation.

It was the silk of the *Atrina* that would come to the attention of one weaver in Sulcis, a result of her search for an alternative to the critically endangered *Pinna* of her home waters, and in the hope that in some small way, the local traditions of Sant'Antioco might continue without adding to the already severe environmental damage. In around 2007, 23-year-old Arianna Pintus became interested in collecting the artisanal knowledge of Sardinia. Born in Carbonia, her paternal ancestry was of Sant'Antioco, and, like Italo Diana, and indeed Vittorio Alinari, she began studying regional knowledge, gathering research, reading, visiting museums, talking to expert artisans. At first her interest was anthropological, about the people, its places, and their designs, about how they had processed fibres of different kinds into textiles.

It was not easy for Arianna to find one teacher who could show her all the practical skills in which she had become interested, so she learned from many, and started experimenting herself. Sometimes, pleasingly, the solutions she came up with ended up matching practices that she came to realize had already been worked out in the past. Using only traditional and natural materials, wool, cotton and linen, when she encountered difficulties in attempting to replicate old practices using modern yarns, she would go back to the very beginning. She did just that with linen, dissatisfied with the quality of the fabric that was commercially available. And so, on land borrowed from friends she started growing the flax herself, harvested it, processed it and then wove it. It informed her early efforts to learn the whole process of making a textile. It wasn't easy, but to her it was more satisfying to see the results of fabrics where no part of them had been industrially produced. 'Raw and natural linen is much more fascinating than the industrial kind, because of several of its characteristics', Arianna says. 'I wanted to keep all of those traditions alive, they were something that were becoming lost . . .'

Of all the threads that Arianna used, sea silk had been the first. Because of her father's origins in Sant'Antioco, its history was the first she researched. As a result, she had learned to weave with what many consider to be the most difficult of threads of all to spin. Arianna speaks of threads almost as if they were people. 'Yes, it was difficult', she admits, 'but no thread is really more or less difficult than another – each has its peculiarities, its characteristics. Any material will be difficult if you do not know how to work it.'

For Arianna Pintus, like Italo Diana, these activities were never a matter of making the fabric and selling it. 'It is most of all to research and follow the history of tradition', she says. 'I looked to my family and ancestors who came from different areas of Sardinia, researched the colours, the techniques, the patterns, the drawings which are characteristic of Sant'Antioco . . . that was how I found the tradition of sea silk and got involved in it.' There is also a powerfully overarching ethic that Arianna has, one which Italo had not had to consider in the Italy of the 1920s. It is no longer possible to harvest the threads of the *Pinna*, though she has heard of several failed attempts to farm the mollusc. 'In the past there were attempts in Italy to grow *Pinna nobilis*, which would have made it possible for the tradition to be kept alive. It was planned, and talked about many times, but never put into practice. The desire to do this had come from people interested in the cultivation of *Pinna* for food. That was in Sardinia, and it was attempted many times since the 1980s. But not now', she adds, referring to the recent mass mortality events suffered by the mollusc, 'because of the protozoa . . .'

It is important to Arianna, and indeed to the other remaining traditional weavers of Sulcis, not to take from nature what cannot be replaced. Because so few of the beards of silk Italo harvested himself now remain, abandoned when all the island's looms were requisitioned by the Fascists, only small items interwoven with linen are now made on the island. Arianna also makes only small items of her sea silk, despite the fact that hers are not taken from the *Pinna* at all. Some years into her practice, she started her own research in the search for a substitute. 'I studied types of large molluscs. They are very different in how they attach themselves', she says, 'and when I saw the *pectinata* I understood that its silk had similarities to the *Pinna*'s. *Atrina pectinata* lives in the sand like *Pinna nobilis*. It is different from the ones that attach to rocks, and so it has a different byssus. It is also not possible to fish the *Pinna rudis* here. Their byssus is similar to the *Pinna nobilis*, but it is also protected.'

In a fortuitous turn of events, a friend of Arianna's undertook a journey to East and South East Asia, and told her of the fishing and eating of that mollusc in Japan, the Philippines and Thailand. From that connection she was eventually able to source a total of five hundred grams of the silk of the *Atrina*. 'There is not a great quantity of *Atrina* byssus, they are not long, and they break easily. It's a very slow technique. But it's quite enough even if it is little', she says.

Arianna's lack of interest in having a large quantity of this silk, and the reason she only makes small samples, mixed in with other fibres, is ultimately rooted in her sense that if a tradition must be preserved, it should not come at the expense of nature. 'Even if I used *Atrina pectinata*, if I made a whole garment of its bisso, in a way I would give the impression that it is still possible to do this as if it was in the past, which it is not. It is unethical to use huge amounts of sea silk, even if the animals are fished for eating.' But it is her hope that the tradition can continue, although, as she says, only in a small way. 'We can never make a large business, and I hope we do not. In a way this continues the original tradition, I hope it will be realized by small artisan artists. But not for large-scale production. I do not want the sea to be devastated and the animals to be killed in large proportions. That would be destroying the environment for money, because obviously in order to take their silk, the animals must die.'

The artistic traditions in which Arianna is interested are of different eras, and will have started on the island at different times. The making of sea silk into textiles is not one her research has told her is one of its oldest. It may even be one of the most recent, based on the dating of the Aquincum fabric to the fourth century CE. Given that the *Pinna* was always known and fished there, and as someone who so carefully observes materials from the natural world, it does surprise Arianna that it had not been used before. '*Sì, è strano*', she says. It does seem a strange thing to have overlooked. And she does not have a sense of where the first inspiration to weave it might have originated. But continuing into the future with its small-scale production feels a part of a tradition in which silk of the *Pinna* was never used industrially, despite attempts some had made towards this end, over the years. The time it takes her to produce each item tells her that it would always have been very expensive. 'It was reserved for very important, rich people of that time, who might commission it from an artisan. It was reserved only for a few', she believes.

But it is not Arianna's impression that it is impossible that this silk had been used in antiquity. The physical evidence is not there, and that makes any assumptions about how far back in time this cloth may have been made a matter of speculation. But Arianna works with these silken threads. She knows them intimately, and she senses that the fact that they haven't been found may not, in itself, preclude a tradition that may indeed go back millennia. 'Small pieces may have been lost', she says. 'Sometimes people say that bisso is as strong as a textile fibre, which is not true. If you compare it to a single fibre of wool or linen, those are much stronger and thicker. It is quite fragile, and if you think about the fact that it was made in only small quantities, this could explain why we don't have any remaining from the past. Because they were so fragile that they may have disintegrated. It is delicate, and natural, so it can dissolve, it can disintegrate.'

Marine biologists in Cagliari also speak of something similar they saw under the sea when the mass mortality event decimated Sardinia's *Pinna* population. Then, the silken threads that spread into the sands, wide and deep, but out of sight, did disintegrate into the waters sometime after the animals died. That was when the giant halves of the shells fell to the seafloor, or were washed up on the coasts of the Mediterranean. 'And it is also likely', Arianna says, much like the threads still attached to animals that sicken, whose silk ceases to be self-healing on their deaths, 'when the fabric comes into contact with humidity, even the humidity in the air, it ruins it, or can make it dissolve.'

The marine ecosystem of the Mediterranean, so finely orchestrated, and in which the giant *Pinna nobilis* and the tiny organisms that thrive on it, the bacteria and protozoa that infect it, and indeed the fungi that digest and recycle what is dead, will inevitably also play a part. The graves of the ancient dead, around what becomes buried over millennia beneath ruined homes and temples, are always replete with bacteria and fungi of many descriptions. Some of these were identified and named by the discoverer of the mysterious Aquincum mummy, in her disintegrating body and over the bandages that were meant to preserve her for all eternity. Those silken threads that in life anchor the *Pinna* so robustly, at some unknown point in our history were made into a delicate golden yarn. Despite all efforts, its woven cloth of sea silk may, like the giant shell, be fated to vanish with time.

But as these fade, yet other strange silks persist; threads continuously made by every one of the fifty thousand or so known species of spiders. It is among these that the silk of the most extraordinary strength is to be found.

Byssus of other shells, prepared by Arianna Pintus, Sardinia, 2021.

18

UPON THE USEFULNESS OF THE SILK OF SPIDERS

IN 1710, RENÉ-ANTOINE FERCHAULT DE RÉAUMUR WAS STILL YOUNG, still a mathematician, and – as he had only recently been elected to the esteemed Paris Académie des Sciences – still largely insignificant. But Réaumur had a mind that was both acquisitive and ambitious; so that when the Académie tasked him and another of their members with a study into a curious use of an arcane animal, he accepted the challenge with fervid absorption. Réaumur was not to be outrivalled – not even by the naturalist whose efforts had set that whole peculiar investigation in motion.

That had been the work of François Xavier Bon de Saint Hilaire, a minor noble just four years older than Réaumur, but who had been rudely torn from his natural history studies to fulfil an inherited role as the president of the Court of Accounts in Montpellier. While Réaumur renounced his own hereditary role to immerse himself entirely in science, Bon struggled with leaving his minerals, fossils, shells and animals behind. Whenever Bon could escape the drudgery of auditing finances, he preferred to spend his time in the study of nature, and in the company of the learned men of Montpellier's Royal Society of Sciences. In 1709, Bon had embarked upon a body of work on 'the Usefulness of the Silk of Spiders', the observations from which he was ready to read to the Montpellier Royal Society by December that same year. His report was sent north to the Paris Académie – where Réaumur got wind of it – and then to the Royal Society in London. Bon's premise, that if cocoons made by silk moths had been collected and unravelled with such spectacular success, the same use might be made of the threads with which common spiders wrap their eggs, sparked great excitement. 'You will be surprised to hear, that spiders make a silk, as beautiful, strong and glossy as common silk', he told his fellow scientists. 'The prejudice that is entertained against so common and despicable an insect, is the reason why the public has been hitherto ignorant of the usefulness of it. And indeed, who would ever have imagined it . . .?'

Inspired by such encouragement, Bon took it upon himself to carry out the experiments. He collected a great many 'bags': the silk-wrapped egg sacs of short-legged, common spiders, easily gathered, for 'these always find someplace, secure from wind and rain to make their bags in; as hollow trees, the corners of windows or vaults, or under the eaves of houses'. At first, Bon collected twelve or thirteen ounces, 'beat them well for some time' with his hands and a small stick to release all the dust that had gathered upon them, and washed them in warm water until the water ran clear. He steeped them for two or three hours in a large pot over a gentle fire, adding soap, saltpetre and gum arabic; washed them again, dried them over the following few days, and then loosened their threads between his fingers – much as was done with the cocoons of *Bombyx mori*. The silk was ashen to look at, but easily took up colour, and it was easy to spin. This was a thread, Bon believed, much stronger, and much finer than common silk.

To progress with his experiments, Bon required more of these silk-wrapped eggs than could be found in crevices. Surely such a thing 'would be no difficult matter, if we could breed spiders as they do silk worms'. So he issued an eccentric order, as only a man in his position might: this time all the large, long-legged spiders that could be found in those summer months of 1709 should be brought to him. Bon corralled them in paper cones, put them into pots and covered the pots with paper pricked with holes so that the spiders could breathe. He hand-fed the spiders with flies, and waited. For his trouble, most of his captives produced six to seven hundred eggs beautifully wrapped in the silken egg cases he was after. The further eggs he required he paid collectors to bring him, and such was his belief that this 'perhaps may one day be as profitable', that he paid them 'by the pound as for common silk'. There was enough, he was sure, to be found in the windows of every house in which these spiders left their silken creations – enough to make large pieces of fabric, and more cheaply than silkworm silk. 'And so much the more', he said, 'by reason of spiders bags, in respect of their lightness, afford much more silk than the others, as proof of which, thirteen ounces yield near four ounces of clean silk; three ounces of which will make a pair of stockings for the largest-sized man.'

Bon knew that was possible because he had actually made such stockings using the silk threads furnished by his obliging spiders. He had also had gloves fashioned, and both were finer – between three and seven times lighter in weight – than the same garments made from *Bombyx mori* silk. As Bon described his work to the Society he had passed silken threads of the spiders around the room, as well as the fabrics he had made of them. But more than that, Bon urged his peers against 'the fear and prejudice that some people might have against making use of the silk of spiders'; for these uses were not just for economic gain nor the luxury of an exquisitely fine silk against the fair legs of the French nobleman. 'Its usefulness is much greater, and more essential', he added, 'on account of the specific medicines that may be drawn from it.' Because, by the end of his trials Bon had made not just textiles from his spiders' silk, he had also distilled a large quantity of spirit and a volatile salt from it, embarking on well-tried chemical tests he had already used when studying corals in his youth. Now, dramatic colour changes had shown the by-products of his extracts of spider silk to be not just 'very active', but so much more so than the extracts of *Bombyx mori* cocoons, which, at that time, were converted by the same sort of process into a potion known as 'English drops'. That tincture had become famous across Europe as a balm for people who had suffered strokes or general listlessness, used in the treatment of 'apoplexies, lethargies, and all soporus diseases'. Bon was certain that his spider silk, which he named 'Drops of Montpellier', would be a more powerful rival. That he left to the chemists and physicians among his peers to pursue, should they so wish. But it was the garments of silk that most excited Bon's audience, perhaps because they had heard of how he had them sent as gifts to men even more powerful than himself: a pair of spider silk stockings for the Duke of Burgundy; delicate gloves for a minister of state. Both were incontestable proof that right there in France was a source of fine silk that Bon made clear was his invention; entirely new. It was high time that the 'despicable' and 'common' spider ceased to be overlooked.

And that much was taken as read by the men of the Académie des Sciences in Paris. The one remaining question, and the task, therefore, that had been set Réaumur was not whether it could be done, but whether such a thing really could turn a profit. After all, the gloves Bon had shown off in Montpellier with such pride had been regarded in Paris, as far as Réaumur was concerned, 'with the pleasure provoked by curiosities'.

It was seven years before news of Bon's work would reach him and by that time Réaumur had moved from his home in the north of France to Paris; and although his Paris addresses changed over the years, he also kept a country house just southeast of the city, in the village of Charenton where the Seine and Marne rivers meet. There Réaumur could house his growing cabinets of collections. But there would also be a living laboratory, a menagerie of insects upon which he could perform all manner of experiments, write up his keen observations and have illustrators draw the scientific images of them as Bon had, but that he, quite simply, could not.

Réaumur's insect menagerie with caterpillars, chrysalises, ants' nests, beehives, dragonflies and spider web.

It was not ideal, for, like Maria Sibylla Merian, whose works he so admired, 'the advantage of such a talent . . . is to have the ability to capture those unique moments that leave no time for recourse to the hand of an outsider whom one cannot have continually at one's side'. But Réaumur's personal wealth made up for his inability to draw, so he had one young man trained, another brought from the draughting table of the Paris Académie des Sciences, and a third, Hélène Dumoustier, who to Réaumur was the 'one especially, whose eyes I trust as much as my own'. Hélène's precise hand would only shake as she certified Réaumur's will, which he had made out in her favour in recognition of his great debt to her. She had moved into the house on rue de la Roquette, which would be Réaumur's last address in Paris. She was with him when he died. But apart from her 'very perfect drawings', Hélène was a natural historian in her own right. When he was delivering the results of his great experiments in Paris, she often stayed at Réaumur's country laboratory in Charenton, recording every step of investigation in his absence; when they were there together, they observed whatever wonderful living things they could find. Sometimes they sought out queen bees; at others 'we were looking for the spiders that had stretched these threads, trying to see them performing the operation'. At his country house, Réaumur had a place in which insects and spiders were plentiful, where could be found both the tools to study them and the trusted hands to expertly record the experiments with which he would re-examine in fine detail the findings of François Xavier Bon de Saint Hilaire.

It wasn't so much that Réaumur did not trust Bon's observations, and what he had been able to create with them, as the fact that his instinct was to observe the work of the spiders himself, first hand and in its entirety. So he replicated Bon's work, except that, at each stage, from raising the spiders to observing their physiology and their habits, Réaumur's team went one better. More spiders, different species, greater detail, more elaborate food, more sophisticated receptacles through which to watch their every move – and watch them more closely than Bon had.

He seemed determined not just to follow, but to exceed his brief to pursue an understanding of the natural history of spiders with an eye very firmly fixed on the economics of an industry based upon their silk. Quantity was everything: in his trials two to three hundred spiders would go into his boxes the size of a playing card, one hundred in others, and perhaps fifty in some – the space was large enough, he thought, for such little animals. But as they grew, the spiders he had so carefully fed began devouring each other, so he separated them; but then the job of feeding each became untenable. Still, while he had them close he studied their silk in fine detail. He observed the ways in which different species spun their silks; and confirmed Bon's observation that spiders in fact appeared to have many different silks, of varied thicknesses, some with which they made their webs, and others for the egg cases that his predecessor had so coveted. But Réaumur tested the strength of these silks by attaching a series of weights to their threads, by the end attaching eighteen times as many to the more robust fibres from the egg cases than to the fibres from their webs, before they snapped. Like Bon, he compared all this to the silk taken from *Bombyx mori* cocoons, except more obsessively. He concluded that Bon's belief that the finer spiders' silk was 'much stronger than that of common silk' was inaccurate.

The interpretation of their experiments disagreed on a number of other points. Bon had recorded that spiders 'multiply much more, for every spider lays 6 or 700 eggs; whereas the [moths] of silk-worms lay but 100, or thereabouts; and of this number we must abate at least half, on account of their being subject to several diseases, are so tender, that the least matter hinders them from making their bags . . . on the contrary, the eggs of spiders hatch themselves, without any care . . .' Réaumur's notes steered the other way. He had 'very carefully weighed many silk worm cocoons', and found 'it takes at least 2304 worms to get a pound of silk', while 'with the same care I weighed a great number of spider shells, and I found that about four of the biggest were needed to equal the weight of a silk worm cocoon'. All of it led him to conclude that to produce one pound of silk would need some 55,296 spiders, all locked up in tiny compartments to keep them safe from their voracious siblings. Making Bon's 'ingenious discovery' work, he decided, would require an effort that was not just overwhelming, but really very impractical.

Réaumur was sure his own trials with spiders had been better executed, and, therefore, more conclusive than Bon's. Bon, in return, took offence at the way Réaumur had contorted his work. Bon had made no claim that spider silk would prove profitable, and objected to Réaumur that he 'did not find his calculations correct'. Réaumur had restricted to small boxes animals that would live quite happily together in any house, whereas to Bon 'the best reason one can give to prove that spiders do not kill each other when they are at liberty, for instance in a room, is that one finds a great many of them, and that the egg cases are very close to each other'. Both men made sure that their studies were reprinted and publicized. Ultimately, had it not been for Bon's peculiar idea, Réaumur's work would not have become so celebrated that it would even reach the ears of the Xuanye, the bright-eyed and sharp-minded Kangxi Emperor of China who was so impressed that he ordered the translation of Réaumur's version into Chinese. For in the end, Réaumur did not close the possibility of spider silk entirely. His suggestion was to look elsewhere, to different sorts of spiders, and in particular to the Americas, where he had learned from sources, particularly the works of Maria Sibylla Merian, 'to whom we owe the drawings of the insects of Surinam', that in that place lived spiders far larger than could be found in Europe, ones that might create even more magnificent silks. 'Whatever the case may be', his notes ended, 'we must experiment; that is the only way to discover curious and useful things.'

19

ARANEAE

WHEN DR FREDERIC MOORE'S LIFE DREW TO A CLOSE ONE SPRING DAY in 1907, he left unfinished his gargantuan study on the moths of South Asia, *Lepidoptera Indica*, which had consumed twenty-five years of his life. If it had been a formidable task it was because the geographical scope he hoped to cover was immense: from the Himalayas to the north, the Sulaiman and Hala mountains to the northwest, across the Andaman and Nicobar islands and down to 'Ceylon on the South, and Burmah on the East'. But Moore needn't have been particularly concerned. Soon after his death, his work was embraced with great enthusiasm by Charles Swinhoe, a British lawyer who had taken the opportunity to make collections of the region's geology, plants and insects while serving as the manager of a bank in Upper Burma. Over time, Swinhoe's specimens had been amassed in his beautiful house and splendid gardens in Maymyo, a former British military station located in the somewhat ambiguous and flexible borderlands that loosely marked the end points of India and China. These were just the sort of liminal thresholds that did not work for a European version of Empire, because both conquest and the quest for the rich resources of foreign lands needed clear maps. Such maps required surveys, and in an area so removed from the sea and its shipping lanes, surveys allowed the planning of new railway lines to move lucrative commodities like tea and ceramics, opium and silk to and from British territory. Attempts like these, at drawing lines where they were not wanted, had already led to the heads of British surveyors being separated from their bodies by locals and displayed for all to see. But the border would eventually be drawn up by a group – among them a relative of Swinhoe's – who kept their heads, and instead cut a line between Burma and the landlocked Yunnan province of China that lay just to its east.

Swinhoe himself, meanwhile, had been assembling a particularly curious collection of objects sourced from a region called Kachin, close to the northernmost point imperial lines still marked as being within Burma, in a remote jungle of the Hukawng ('place of the devil') Valley. Curiosities of such peculiarity were only to be found in rich quantities in that place. For there, a very long time ago, had stood another tropical forest, this one dominated by coniferous trees. From their bark spilt copious quantities of a resin created in special cells that allowed those trees to seal areas of damage in order to create a defence against infiltration by fungi, insects and anything else that threatened them with disease or destruction. Many and varied were the unsuspecting ancient insects that would spend their last living moments stuck fast in that coniferous resin. That hardened gum would perfectly preserve grasshoppers and cicadas, dragonflies and wasps and cockroaches. There were millipedes, too, and larger organisms, or at least parts of them, trapped in the conifers' yellowish, viscous gum: snails, crabs, scorpions, the skin of a reptile, feathers; tiny wings from hatchling birds which had perhaps tumbled from their nests; frogs, lizards, snakes, and even the small foot of a gecko. All of these would tell of a forest teeming with ancient life. And the pristine marine shrimps and ammonites imprisoned in resin would also whisper that this place had, long ago, been a coastal area, not yet the landlocked expanse that the British would one day seek to cut through with railway lines.

Swinhoe was mesmerized by these ancient sea creatures but he was not the first European to find Burmese amber, nor, indeed, to note that it contained treasures from a long-past world. Those colonial surveys of eastern lands had also been designed to map the locations of any resource that might be exploited, and in Burma, as Swinhoe will have known well, the project of mining the region's coal, lead, zinc and nickel had also revealed the existence of its remarkable amber. It had been Fritz Noetling, a German mining engineer in the employ of the Geological Survey of India, who had first taken note of Burmese amber in 1892. Noetling had imagined that, like Baltic amber closer to home, 'Burmite', as it would become known, and the once living objects it contained, must embrace an enormous time span. That span, he believed, was some forty million years.

But then, from 1916, Swinhoe began sending his samples, acquired or purchased, to a zoologist based at the University of Colorado who carefully examined more than forty of the animals that had been frozen in time inside amber. 'The fauna is very remarkable', Theodore Dru Alison Cockerell would write, '. . . containing a large preponderance of types which are usually considered primitive'. Spurred on by his studies, and from reports of the depths and types of rocks that were cut through when the ten-metre-deep shafts of the amber mine were constructed, Cockerell began rethinking their age altogether. 'Judging from the fossils', he said, 'the amber might be actually very much older than Miocene, conceivably even Upper Cretaceous', but ultimately concluded that 'the evidence seems to indicate that the Burmese amber fauna is Eocene', though, 'older than the Eocene beds which have produced fossil insects in the south of England'.

These names given to geological periods encompass vast periods of time. While a Miocene date would mean that Swinhoe's amber was between twenty-three and five million years old – which Cockerell discounted as being too recent – an Eocene date pushed that back to somewhere between fifty-six and thirty-four million years ago. But both datings, would, in fact, prove a gross underestimation. Had Cockerell followed his initial instincts, he would have been far closer to the mark, because the amber Swinhoe had brought to his attention, and the fossilized animals it contained, were in fact born in a forest that once existed on a long-vanished coast during the middle of the Cretaceous period – just short of one hundred million years ago. This was a period in history when the climate was warm, green swathes of the earth's forests reached to the Poles, the high seas contained marine molluscs shaped like boxes, and ammonites, and dinosaurs dominated the land. In years to come, other naturalists would buy other Burmite pieces that would continue to make their tortuous way from Kachin over the border into Yunnan province. There, the bustling market in Tengchong would come to be called 'the city of amber'. One glassy fossil would hold a remarkable fragment of the tail of a feathered dinosaur, its skin, bones and plumage perfectly intact, just as it would have looked in life. But the market at Tengchong also produced other fossils of very great significance.

Like three of the amber specimens Cockerell had acquired from Swinhoe, these other pieces of Burmite contained arachnids. Arachnids are Arthropods, a group that contains within it the vast majority of the animals on earth: those with segmented bodies, external skeletons and legs that come in pairs. Silk moths and their caterpillars belong to the Arthropods, too, as do all insects, crustaceans and centipedes. Like insects, arachnids shed their exoskeletons to grow, usually five, but up to twelve times, expanding each time with blood pressure and then hardening their outsides again into a tough cuticle. While they are distant relations, the arachnids are not insects. It may be that their ancestors, which were marine, were already distinct some four hundred million years ago, at a time when oceans shallow enough for sunlight to glisten through covered large land masses and the first plants colonized the land.

The arachnids faced many challenges living on land, adapting their movement and support, how they breathed, the intricacies of their reproduction and other fundamental mechanisms in different ways from insects. Arachnids have four pairs of walking legs rather than three. They have no antennae. They have only two major body parts – the front for movement, the back for digestion and reproduction – where insects have three, and their simpler body plan carries mouth parts far less complex than the feeding apparatus of insects. Their digestion is odd. Many digest food outside their bodies, because they have a strong stomach that pumps in a rhythm in which they ingest only liquids or very small particles, vomiting and sucking back up digestive juices, back and forth over their prey until only hard, indigestible parts remain. Failing that, should they find no prey, arachnids have an astonishing ability to withstand starvation for weeks, months, for some even years, without any food at all. If they were to move towards their prey, or even to move at all, most have no muscles to extend their joints; instead, theirs is a skeleton that is hydraulic, so that they pump blood into each limb as it extends. But to see their world, early in their evolutionary history, arachnids lost the excellent vision of the compound eyes that their insect relatives retained; what was left to them was between one and five pairs of simple eyes like little dark beads, but with an acuity far inferior.

Within the arachnids are spider-like things: 'tick spiders' and daddy long-legs, 'wind scorpions' and 'whip scorpions' and real scorpions, crabs, mites, soft ticks and hard ticks; but this is also the animal group to which real spiders, called the Araneae, belong. They are diverse, and number at least 48,500 species. Just like insects, their main prey, spiders are also ancient. The first definitive spiders lived more than 150 million years before the dinosaurs, but their fossils are rare, a fact that makes those preserved in Burmite even more remarkable.

Inside one of these pale windows into a very ancient world, one spider, flanked by fifteen strands of silk threads, stood frozen at the moment it attacked a wasp, before both were drowned in resin. Inside another amber piece was a mite that had evidently also been caught by a spider. Though there was no spider alongside it, its presence was implied, because this mite had been wrapped in spider's silk.

The Araneae have made silk for some 380 million years. At the middle of their abdomens for some, and at the tail ends for others, are spinnerets, a body part that developed from what were once the gills of their aquatic ancestors. Spinnerets were there, too, in a tiny fossilized spider preserved in a piece of Burmese amber bought from the market at Tengchong, an incredible specimen of the most primitive spider ever found. Before this one, named *Chimerarachne* – because it looked like a chimera, that is, as though composed of parts of different arachnids – there had been no fossil found in which a spider bore a tail. This curious proto-spider did have a tail, one that was long and whip-like, a trait of an extinct order of arachnids. But it also bore the characteristic features of living spiders – pincer-like fangs with venom glands, short feelers known as pedipalps, positioned just ahead of its first pair of legs, modified to give males the ability to transfer sperm from its spinnerets to the pedipalps, easier to draw close to a female, kept in readiness to fertilize her eggs. There were three additional pairs of legs behind that. And there were spinning organs – two pairs of spinnerets, minuscule lumpy lobes, from which silk would have been extruded, and the threads very precisely deposited – both neatly protruding near the rear of its abdomen.

For any Araneae spinning silk is entirely dependent upon a highly specialized system of genes, proteins and glands, and also their behaviours. Behind those spinnerets would be silk glands, whose evolutionary origins are less certain. They may have arisen as something completely new. But they may also simply have started as a collection of cells adapted from glands configured to excrete waste; or else glands that secreted the proteins needed to build the spiders' external skeleton. Whatever the case, while it is only the larvae of insects that are able to produce silk and not their adults, just as the silk caterpillars make silken cocoons, but their adults cannot: the silk glands in these spiders retain that ability throughout their lives. Many insects produce silk, but each one only of one type, while a single spider might make as many as seven different types of silk thread, initiated in a variety of silk glands with diverse forms. From each of these glands comes a unique mixture of transparent, viscous protein, specific to that gland. This thick, clear liquid dubbed silk-spinning dope leaves the glands through ducts like tiny needles of different sizes and shapes – *spigots* that protrude from the spiders' lobe-like spinnerets. Each spigot allies with only one specific silk gland. And each silk gland will be of a particular type, deep within whose cells reside distinct genes encoding a sequence of proteins that create silk fibroins – *spidroins* – of which particular sets can be called upon to form varying structures, qualities and strengths. Such layers of complexity mean that there are silks in which to wrap their prey, just as that mite had been one fateful day, a hundred million years ago; others to beautifully line underground burrows complete with silken trap doors and trip lines extending like sunbeams. Other silks would be used to anchor their bodies while they leap for prey and to lift them into the air by casting out silken strands, and to make diving bells filled with air bubbles to allow them to spend time in underwater retreats.

What is more, just as the caterpillars of silk moths do, spiders like tarantulas and trapdoor spiders which retain a number of ancestral physical features, and the everyday spiders whose bodies have evolved more modern traits, both produce silk threads composed of more than one type of protein. Some spiders use up to three kinds of fibres they are able to make interchangeably and use for any purpose – building their burrows, making silken egg sacs, or constructing sperm webs on which they deposit sperm before transferring it to the pedipalps, which they then insert into the genital openings of females. Others, with very particular attention, use between four and nine kinds of silks whose fibres are composed of different combinations of proteins, which emerge from different glands: one for their burrows, another for their egg sacs, sperm, webs, for the nets on which they feed.

And then there are the silk threads used to build their webs. These are crafted from proteins whose configurations and combinations make them strong, flexible, elastic; coloured to attract insects, gluey to keep the insects once caught, woolly to support the weight of larger spiders. Some webs are used only in the daytime, others both day and night; yet others, those that capture unsuspecting moths, will be made every evening and removed at dawn. They are of extraordinary variety – webs that appear to be crafted from flattened, thick, silken plates, others like long tunnels or funnels covered in soil or debris; some that look like lace, or tangles, sheets or three-dimensional lanterns, triangles, tubes, aerial nets, or perfect orbs, some decorated with zigzag patterns, thickened bands, spirals, diagonal stripes that to insects' eyes may mimic their favourite food plants, luring them to their doom.

FIG. 99. Central decorations on orbs of Argyraspis.

Orb web decorations.

Some 110 million years ago, these orbs, built like wheels with spokes, took former horizontal web sheets vertical, snaring flying prey with ease. Across them, poor-sighted spiders feel any crawling, or ensnare animals through vibrations passed along the threads. But the impact of a flying insect on a fine thread requires the orb to be built of three elements. A framework of robust silk; radial silk threads, strong and supportive, which section the circular web like spokes of a wheel and meet at the centre; and a capture thread, shock-absorbing, elastic and resilient, spiralling round and round, interspersed with tiny beads of sticky droplets. Of the spiders that make these complex and beautiful webs, there are three types – typical orb weavers, long-jawed orb weavers and cribellate orb weavers – which are not able to make sticky silk, and instead wrap their prey in silk, covering it in regurgitations until its body liquefies enough to be ingested. These three types are spread across almost every part of the world, where they weave their orb webs in many various sizes. But in the interests of finding greater amounts of silk, Réaumur's idea of looking beyond Europe for the largest of these was sound. He had in his hands the drawings of Maria Sibylla Merian, among them a spider so enormous it attacked small birds in the forests of Suriname. Such was the scale of the sources of silk to be found in the Americas – spiders' 'egg sacs', their magnificent webs and even the spiders themselves – that efforts to extract the silk of wonderful new types of Araneae would become not just more brazen, but increasingly bizarre.

20

THE HOUSE OF THE SPIDERS

IT HADN'T JUST BEEN FRANÇOIS XAVIER BON DE SAINT HILAIRE WHO would disagree with Réaumur's conclusions that, as things stood, a spider silk industry had little hope of success. A number of his assertions were also to upset other natural historians who were attempting similar trials in places very different from the temperate homes of the French elite. But few perhaps had taken Réaumur's work so seriously as Raymundum Wittermayer, a Dutchman who worked as a merchant in Cádiz until he converted to Roman Catholicism, and, at the age of 27, became Father Ramón María Termeyer, of the Society of Jesus.

In the long arms of Spain, and the Church, the world became his oyster. A Spanish force led by Don Pedro de Mendoza had explored the Rio Paraná and its tributaries exactly 227 years before Termeyer's ordination. Within the subsequent two decades, a series of Spanish fleets would follow, claiming for their country a region almost two thousand kilometres as the crow flies, covering the lands that stretched from the mouth of the Paraná to the upper reaches of Paraguay. Where the Rio Paraná begins its flow is a vast region known as the Gran Chaco. It is hot and dry and home to the white carob tree from whose fruit was brewed a beer that had made the earlier wave of Spaniards feel particularly welcome.

When Termeyer left Spain for Buenos Aires he was a mere nine months into his priesthood, but the vial of *Bombyx mori* eggs he had carried with him attested to the fact that by then he was a self-avowed naturalist and already five years into his study of silkworms. It is not clear whether mulberry trees had preceded him to the provinces of Paraguay, nor what became of his silkworms. But once he settled, some 180 miles from the Gran Chaco, Termeyer began in earnest the study of those other silk-producing animals, in the very place Réaumur suspected there were enormous spiders that would better oblige a new genre of silk industrialists in Europe. It was there that Termeyer 'read for the first time the notes of Mr Réaumur'. He determined to undertake new studies on silk of the spiders of Paraguay once he had seen with his own eyes that such large specimens really did exist there – ones he also quickly realized made an abundance of silk. There was, in particular, *Aranea latro*, a striking orb-weaver spider. 'They were large, with an extremely large abdomen, ferruginous in colour, and an oval thorax, hairy and ashy', whose 'abdomen had markings of different colours, and quite short legs covered by dense hair'.

It was two years after his arrival in South America that the *latro* first crossed Termeyer's path, as he made his way one day through a carob forest on church business. Or at least he had tried to follow a path, but at every turn he 'stepped into extremely frequent and hard spider webs, that often would get in the way of me and my horse and made my hat fall from my head, unless I took care to break them with a rod'. At first, Termeyer doubted that such webs could be the work of spiders. But his annoyance was to change to surprise, happiness even, when he realized that around the webs was 'an immense multitude of cocoons' as large as the spiders themselves.

Whatever the official business the priest had set off on must have been done distractedly, or at least with those spiders and their silk on his mind, because as soon as it was finished he prepared a bag with clothespins, soft pads and paper, took 'some friends and servants' towards the woods and began collecting a large number of the spiders. The friends and servants in tow 'both for help and for defence, since those woods are dangerous because of savage Indians and bears, tigers and other fierce beasts', and the pins and pads 'to catch [the spiders] by the legs without hurting them, and some paper to wrap each of them individually in a small paper bag'.

Termeyer's first thought was how to feed them, but only because Réaumur had found that so trying. He developed his own method, one that he had 'found neither expensive nor complicated'. But that was not yet good enough, in his opinion, and so he tried a new experiment. In a wonderfully laid-out garden of vegetables and fruit near his house, on a plantation of pomegranate trees eighty-five metres across and the same wide, Termeyer deposited his spiders 'so that they may work on it as they did in the wood of Chaco'. He made note of how he 'attached the paper bags to the tree branches, and opened them'. 'With great delight I saw that all had adapted, part in the bags and part on the branches where they had begun their webs. No one ignores that trees, especially in summertime, are the house for millions of insects and indeed, without any other need, the colony of my spiders was able to take care of itself.' 'In this way', Termeyer proclaimed, 'I solved the problems that so much had afflicted Mr Réaumur.'

Termeyer also worked, or at least would have attempted to work, with other spiders of Paraguay, among them 'those very large spiders', *Aranea avicularis*, that lived upon the branches of trees. '. . . Hairy and bristly . . . two inches and one-fifth in length . . . furnished with eight eyes, smooth and raised from the head . . . is indigenous to almost all South America; where it is called Abamdui, or Nbamduguazu, that is the *great spider*'. Because of Maria Sibylla Merian's iconic painting of a South American spider eating a small bird, Carl Linnaeus' name for this spectacular tarantula drew on the Latin *avicula*, 'little bird' – with which Termeyer agreed, 'because they carry away even hummingbirds from their nests'. Their 'cocoons' – that is, the silk around which the female wrapped her eggs – he noted, 'weighed as much as six cocoons of the silk worm when they were unwashed, and as much as three or four after having been washed'.

Such specific detail would continue to inform two volumes of research on his experiments with the silk of spiders, which seemed increasingly written in response to Réaumur, almost as a dossier of measurements he had taken which directly contradicted the French scientist's own. Though 'the authority of the French entomologist is certainly of great weight . . . first of all', it began, '. . . anyone can see how obscure and indefinite is [the] style of description of Réaumur's', and so Termeyer went on, until he had addressed each point Réaumur had found to be an obstacle, from the difficulties of catching, feeding and holding spiders, to their cannibalism and the inferiority of their silk. And, Termeyer concluded, 'the difficulties proposed by the celebrated Réaumur, in the way of a profitable culture of spiders for the purpose of obtaining silk from them, are either surmountable or unreal.'

Termeyer's enthusiasm for his spiders became increasingly palpable, and the way in which he described these spiders and their silk began verging towards the obsessional. He had spent so much time in their pursuit or cultivation, he wrote, 'I felt that, in their own way, they would talk to me, and would ask me to vindicate them from the injustice received by Mr Réaumur, since he had placed them in oblivion and contempt with his *Examination of spiders' silk*; they were considered useless animals by the whole world from which nothing useful may be obtained, thereby increasing hatred against them, and inducing all to kill them without pity.'

Termeyer grew increasingly certain of their usefulness. For the production of silk, it was not just the egg sacs accumulated by Bon and Réaumur which drew Termeyer's attention. To him, their silken webs were things of beauty, variety, utility; and the suppositions in his notes were often prescient, or at least not far from the facts that had not yet been determined by science. 'I think', he wrote, 'the spiders have different repositories for silk of different colours and adopt now one and now another, not interlacing the colours by design, but according to need and circumstances.' He also noted that it had been observed 'that the silk of which they weave their circular webs, is of different kinds, the radii, stretching from the centre to the circumference, differing from the threads which form the concentric circles; the second are viscous, but not the first. It is also known to entomologists that the spider has six spinnerets . . . whence the silk issues. Why may we not believe that from each comes a silk, different either in colour or in some other property?'

And so it was as a man possessed that Termeyer gathered an abundance of spiders. He had found and bred so many that he could say, in good conscience, what might otherwise have come across as the vain boasting of an ageing naturalist. For in the making of his iconic sequel to the work of Bon, 'Réaumur never made so great a collection . . .' as his. Unlike Réaumur, Termeyer had prevented any cannibalism, preserving his specimens quite intact, because, like 'President Le Bon', he 'had also been able to make use of such simple boxes', detailing his habits, how he was 'accustomed, on finding the cocoons of a spider known to me, which I wish to select, to take them, to cut them across superficially in order to ascertain the quantity of eggs; and to replace the latter upon cotton in a box well protected from dust and insects. There, in due time, I see them come forth, and place them where I wish to feed them . . . I made cases so that each spider could occupy his own little house and not extend his dominion beyond it . . .', and then 'having completed the collection I set the spiders at liberty in the places where I had taken them'.

Of course, in other instances Termeyer had allowed the spiders to remain in their own worlds 'upon the trees, in gardens and fields' – which was just the sort of system by which the silk of wild silk moths had been gathered in India from time immemorial. Termeyer and his friends and servants had collected nearly 2,500 'very large' *latro* spiders from the Gran Chaco, placed them in a pomegranate plantation, and from them harvested '2,013 great cocoons of the best yellow silk'. As would become his habit, Termeyer had then taken the eggs out of the cocoons, 'which, exceeding nine million in number, would have given me as many little spiders the next year'. But then events took a strange turn for the man who was supposed to be converting the locals to Christianity. In 1767, Charles III expelled the Jesuits from Spain. The effect on Termeyer's life and work was dramatic: he would neither be able to continue his studies in the Americas nor return home. His parting act was to take the confession, one last time, of the people of the nomadic Mocobí who inhabited the immense Gran Chaco region when the Spaniards had first arrived with their ships and crosses.

Termeyer had been informed that the priest who would replace him and his fellow brothers, who had kept as many records of the people as had been written on their spiders, would make no use of the Mocobí grammar book that Termeyer had taken the time to create. So, with the sacrament complete, on 16 May 1768

Termeyer and the Jesuits sailed from Montevideo to Spain, from where they were promptly exiled to Italy. Termeyer then found himself in Faenza, a stone's throw from Bologna and its scientific minds, and eventually settled near Milan.

There he resumed his peculiar investigations, this time on the extension of the life of beetles, and observed the large black Scarabæus as they made cocoons of fine white silk that floated on water and held their eggs. He published prolifically on insects and physics, and on agriculture. On a caffeinated herbal tea called yerba mate he had seen brewed by indigenous people in Paraguay. On their local techniques of weaving the wool of a relative of the llama known as the guanaco. On the electrical properties of a species of South American electric eel from the Saladillo River, on which he had previously performed extensive dissections and eccentric experiments with the help of an electroscope made of two small balls of elderberry pith, a spinning glass globe for an electrostatic generator, a Leyden jar in which to store its high-voltage electric charge, various conductors, and an isolating stand. On the reproduction of European spiders: *Araneas marmorea*, *formosa*, *curcubitina*, *conica*, *domestica*, and, most helpful to him, 'the female of the species called by Linnaeus *diadema*'.

This was the European garden spider that had also been gathered indiscriminately for the works of Bon and Réaumur, 'the domestic spider always in the corners of walls, the *diadema* under balconies, the *angulata* among bushes . . .' And though there was nothing to suggest that he had mentally put aside those enormous spiders of South America, in their absence Termeyer took the opportunity presented by his exile to take objection to one more of Réaumur's conclusions. 'Without seeking the American spiders, I have found myself in this country the spiders [called] *Aranea speciosa* and *Aranea pulchra*, which make such cocoons that three alone . . .

weigh as much as one cocoon of the common silkworm. I will also add that having verified my observations on the cocoons of *diadema* spiders, I have found constantly that six of these, and not twelve as Réaumur would have it, are equivalent to one cocoon of the silk worm.' Prohibited from returning to the Americas, Termeyer could no longer gather its spiders, and so, convinced that a serious prospector of spider silk need not seek out any more exotic species than there were in Europe, Termeyer once again gathered around him some two thousand spiders. His house in Milan became a 'nest of spiders', causing concern to his neighbours. But what concerned Termeyer was the criticism he anticipated. He asked himself difficult questions about the ultimate aim of his obsessive work, an internal dialogue that now consumed a mind that before had been focused on experimentation: '*why, since you have now been occupied with this subject for forty years, have you not made stuffs and netted goods and other fabrics in great abundance, whence some profit might have accrued, and the incredulous been convinced . . .?*' After all, Termeyer had in his possession a number of orb-weaver spiders producing millions of silken egg sacs of which Bon and Réaumur could only have dreamed.

And so, in a house filled with spiders, he would come up with a device that would circumvent the need for collecting spiders' egg sacs entirely. It was now time to once again consign the whole model of reeling silk from cocoons to silkworm producers. Future spider silk producers would have no need of the wrappings of spiders' eggs, because Termeyer invented something entirely new.

To do that he first had to make one concession to Réaumur: to agree with him 'that by reducing the cocoons of the spider to the state of coarse sewing silk, they lost their native brilliancy'. But Termeyer had an idea, that 'the thread of the spider can be wound also in its natural state', so that 'it becomes more brilliant than a

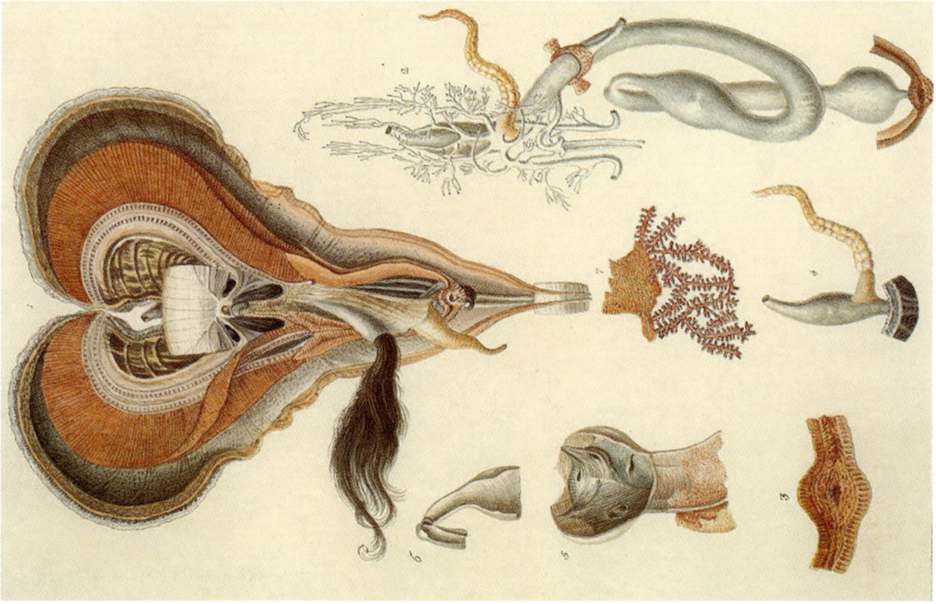

Anatomy of the *Pinna nobilis*, showing the position of the 'foot' muscle attached to its silken byssus 'beard' as it would appear if a living shell were prised open.

Pinna nobilis are long-lived and can grow to over one metre in height. They play a key ecological role, filtering water and providing a surface on which algae and benthic invertebrates make their home.

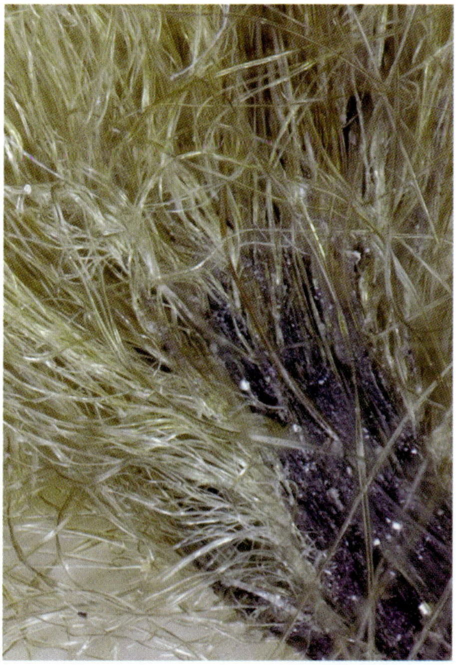

Golden byssus threads where they join the dark 'foot' of the *Pinna nobilis*, a muscle attachment towards the bottom of the shell that firmly anchors it to the sea floor.

Dead *Pinna nobilis* on the Mediterranean Sea floor. In January 2021 they were listed as critically endangered on the International Union for Conservation of Nature's 'Red List of Threatened Species'. Once they die, their silken anchors disintegrate and the shells collapse.

A ‘beard’ of byssus fibre, harvested in Sardinia in the 1920s, still attached to the withered muscle that would have anchored it inside the *Pinna nobilis*’ shell.

In cross-section, the byssus silk fibres of the *Pinna nobilis* appear elliptical, a shape that is not seen in any other natural fibre.

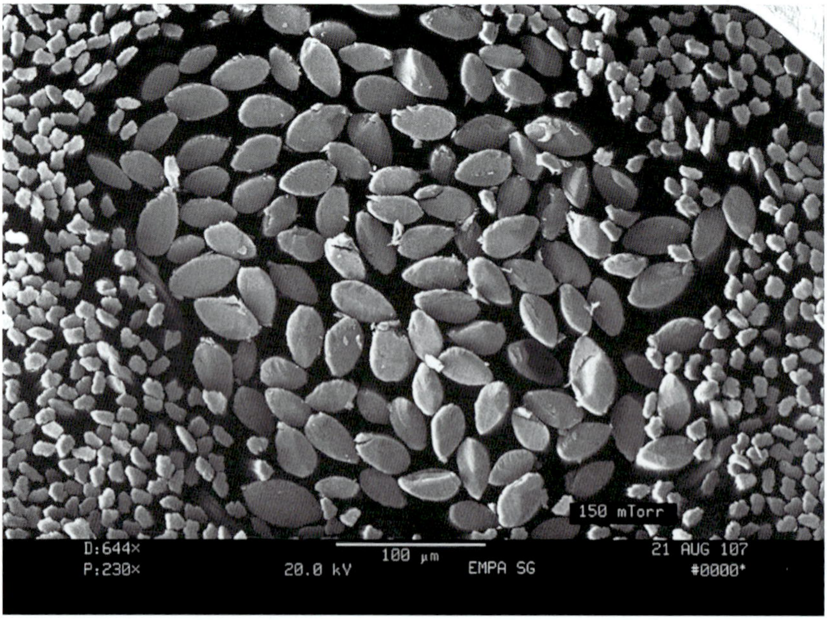

Sometime between 97 and 110 million years ago, in the Hukawng Valley, Myanmar, this male parasitic wasp flew into an orb-weaver spider's web and would have become its prey, had both animals not become trapped in resin. Fifteen strands of the spider's silk were also present inside this piece of amber.

This image of a bird-eating spider illustrates behaviours observed by Merian in Surinam, informed by information given to her by local peoples. Published in *Metamorphosis insectorum Surinamensis* in 1705, it was criticised by men of science who doubted her records, disbelieving that predation of a bird by a spider could occur in nature.

N. inaurata madagascariensis, the red-legged golden orb-weaver spider of Madagascar, produces webs over one metre in diameter, formed of golden-yellow threads capable of being woven.

Termeyer's eighteenth century apparatus for reeling silk directly from the bodies of spiders.

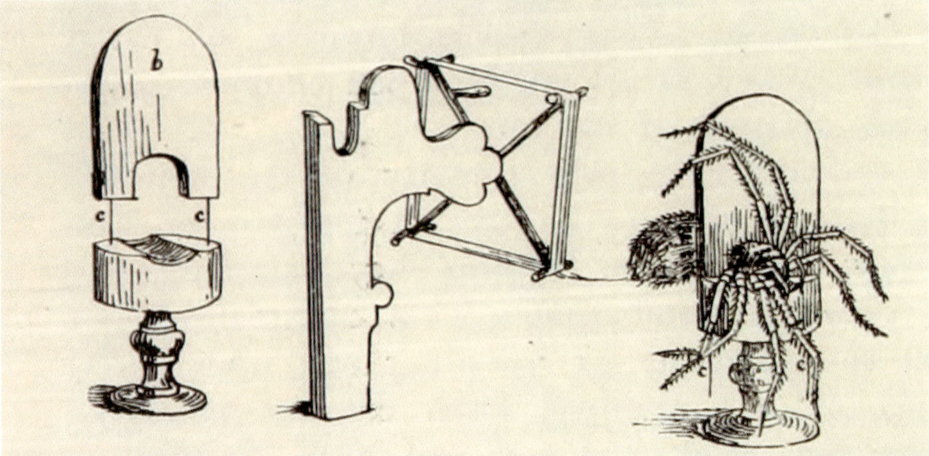

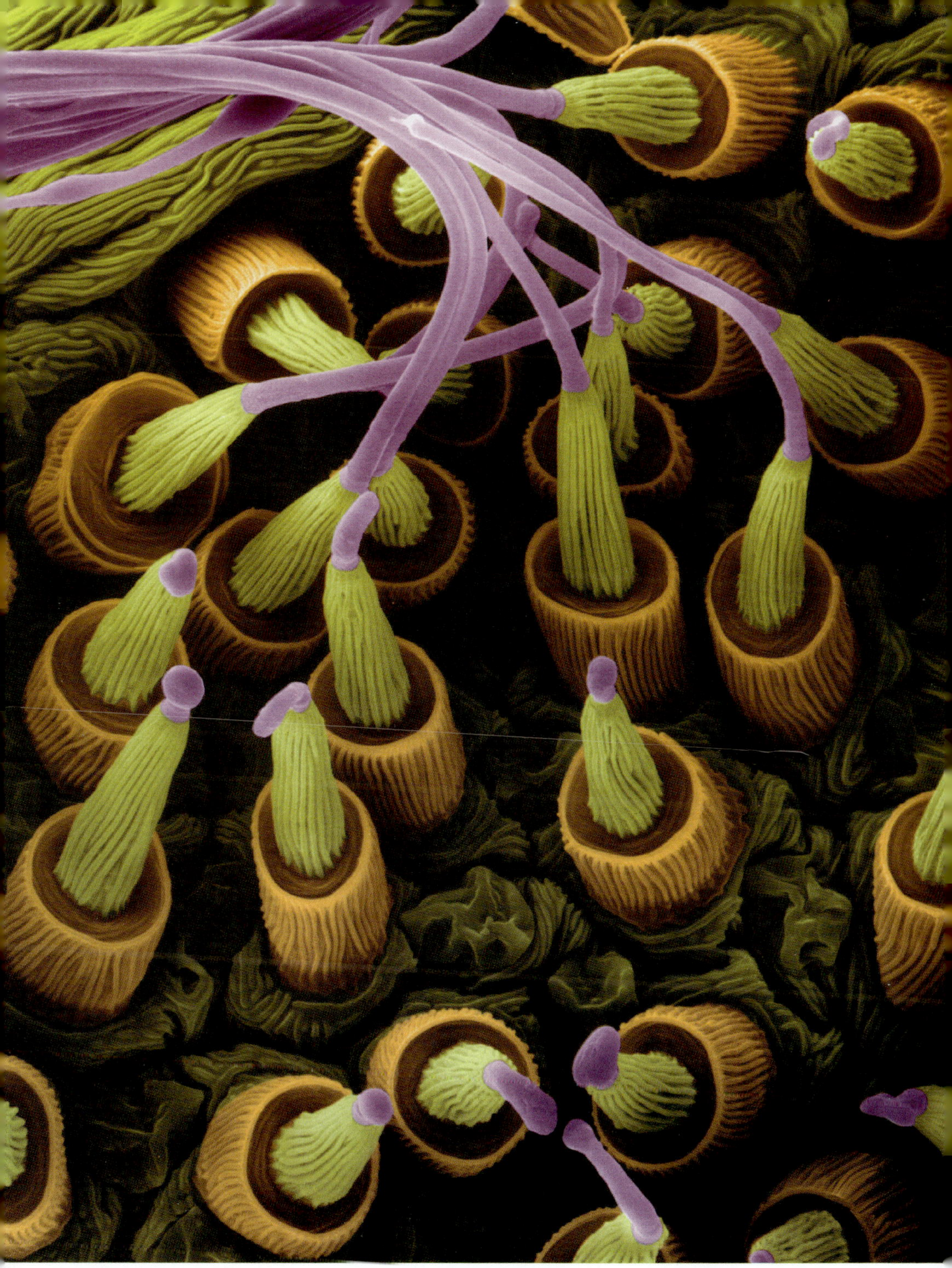

Coloured scanning electron micrograph of an orb-weaver spider's silk gland spigots through which silk is being secreted. Spigots protrude from spiders' spinnerets, and are like tiny needle ducts of different sizes and shapes. Each spigot allies with only one specific silk gland. From each emerges a unique mixture of viscous silk protein, specific to the silk gland from which it is secreted (magnification: x470).

In May 1941, Crete was the site of a paratrooper attack by Germany's 1st Parachute Regiment. Some of the 2000 *Bombyx mori* silk parachutes were found in the rubble after the attacks, this one hooked onto an awning in Heraklion's Lions Square. They would eventually be refashioned into dresses, handkerchiefs and scarves after WWII.

A member of the Women's Auxiliary Air Force uses a Singer sewing machine to stitch a bundle of parachute silk, circa 1942.

thread of any cocoon whatever'. At first, and with infinite patience, Termeyer had attempted to wind the silk by drawing the thread from a cocoon, but he could never manage to extend it more than a foot before it broke.

His trials were rudely interrupted by the invading Napoleonic army besieging a fortress near his spider-filled home, and in his haste to save himself and salvage his belongings the twenty-two ounces of silk he had extracted were either lost or stolen. Those trials would not be repeated. Perhaps it was the threat of war, or the uncertainty of the times that particularly concentrated his mind upon the machinations of spiders, because it was also during those days that Termeyer was able to make another observation, which led him to an even more fortunate experiment. He had noticed that when *Aranea diadema* captured an insect, 'it drew out from the spinner placed at the extremity of the abdomen some large threads, and enveloped it in a brilliant white web formed at an instant, and so strong that the insect lost all motion'. The speed with which that silk was produced made Termeyer consider that if he himself could draw similar threads directly from their spinnerets, the spiders' bodies would do the work for him, and, with little effort on his part, he could have in his hands an unbroken string of strong, beautiful silk.

Initially, Termeyer managed to hold the spider tightly in his fingers, touch its spinneret and draw out a strand of silk. But then he saw that the spider seemed to contract its spinneret, and with its long legs cut the perfect thread emerging behind it. Termeyer knew he could not prevent the spider from contracting its spinneret, but he did find a solution for the second problem. He held the spider again, this time in such a way that it could not use its legs to reach its abdomen at the point at which its silk emerged. And then Termeyer went one step further. To save his fingers the trouble and his spiders the inevitable struggle, he devised a 'little contrivance' – a simple, yet elegant spider silk-reeling machine. It was made using a circle of cork into which he carved a small cavity and placed upon a pedestal-like stand for height. He then cut a sheet of tinplate with a semicircle of the same depth as dug out from the cork – about an inch wide.

To that, he soldered two iron pins and, using them, dropped the tinplate over the piece of cork, so that the circular cavity created in the spaces carved out of cork and tinplate securely held the cephalothorax of a captured spider – the part of the spider's body to which all of its legs were attached. Thus immobilized, the spider's legs could no longer reach either its abdomen or the spinneret, and so could not cut the emerging silk.

Next, Termeyer worked out a way in which the immobilized spiders' silk could be drawn out with ease from their spinnerets. He presented the clamped spider with a fly. The spider seized it with its pedipalps and began turning the insect in readiness to wrap it in silk. At that moment, Termeyer touched the spinneret, once only, for that was all it took for the silk threads to begin to emerge, and in an incredible abundance. Termeyer caught the end of the silk, and attached it to a little reel precisely four and a half inches in diameter, equipped with cylindrical glass arms that he slowly turned, winding onto the reel perfect strands of thread. Should that thread have become broken 'by the caprice of the spider, or for any other reason', he patiently attached it again to the reel in the same way that strands of silkworm silk are lifted up and reeled from its wet cocoons as they are boiled in soap and water. He did in fact reel the silks of both animals – if only because 'the comparison shows evidently how much more brilliant and beautiful' spider silk was – 'so bright that it appears more like a polished metal or mirror than like silk'. He took those shining strands of reeled silk and spun them on a spindle. It gave 'a fine and brilliant thread, which had such elasticity as to stretch considerably without being broken, and to return to its first dimensions, which will be very useful when there shall be a sufficient quantity to weave, or of which to make a netted, or knitted fabric'.

When, and indeed how, Termeyer met his end is uncertain, but it was some time not long after 1814, by which time he had induced his reluctant spiders to produce for him items not so dissimilar to those made with such pride by Bon just over a hundred years earlier. Apart from the collection of spiders he had sent to the court in Madrid – which induced great excitement, though perhaps not of the same type that Termeyer felt for the animals – there were the stockings made of *Aranea diadema* silk sent to grace the royal legs of King Charles III, despite the fact it had been his edict that parted Termeyer from his beloved Paraguayan spiders. At one time or another there were requests for the same silken items from Empress Catherine the Great of Russia and the Archduchess Maria Elisabeth of Austria, and he would even produce a shawl for Napoleon's first empress, Josephine, which was put on show in Milan. Another request came for the ever-popular stockings, this time for Napoleon himself, despite the fact that it had been his battles that, for a second time, had stopped Termeyer's spider research in its tracks.

Having survived the vicissitudes of rulers and the whims of his spiders, Termeyer had hoped for more. His next step would have been adaptations to his simple contrivance that would allow it to accommodate multiple spiders, 'to draw the silk from all the spiders at once, and to do it so that the threads uniting would twist to form a single thread, as is done with the threads of the [silkworm] cocoon'. Until that time, he said of his research, 'it is enough if the readers of this are persuaded that here is a branch of industry and commerce little attempted as yet, and little known, from which those will be able to profit who have industry, energy and determination'. But, as this most eccentric man knew only too well, 'whoever undertakes it must be prepared first of all to be regardless of the ridicule'. In the years to come, and perhaps in places that Termeyer could never have imagined, such people would certainly emerge.

21

NEPHILA

AT AROUND THE SAME TIME THAT RAMÓN MARÍA TERMEYER PACKED HIS priestly robes and spiders and compendium of Mocobí grammar onto the ship that was to take him east from Paraguay and into perpetual exile from his beloved spiders, a Spanish military engineer named Félix de Azara was preparing a route in the other direction, ready to map a frontier. The Spanish and Portuguese now wished to legitimize, between them, which parts of the continent they had appropriated could properly be called their own. The resources of South America were ripe for a lucrative new export economy for Iberia, and that meant that the mountains of Paraguay needed to be measured, its serpentine rivers mapped and its animal specimens collected.

That was how Azara became the first to write home to Europe about another remarkable spider, this one twice as large as Termeyer's *Aranea latro*: dark, with red markings and equally hairy, fat legs. But the webs of these, *Parawixia bistriata*, were far grander. In the daytime they spread flat like the Spaniards' bivouacs, and upon them whole communities rested. At sunset, orb webs were painstakingly constructed by each member of their group upon a scaffold built specially for the use of the entire community: a place of shared feasting upon prey larger than themselves. The second sighting of these colonies was made in Argentina, this time by an English naturalist when he alighted from the *Beagle* and also witnessed webs of incredible size in Brazil, ones that may well have knocked off Charles Darwin's hat. For just as Termeyer had in the Gran Chaco, Darwin found there that 'every path in the forest is barricaded with the strong yellow web of a species belonging to the same division with the *Epeira clavipes* . . . which was formerly said . . . to make, in the West Indies, webs so strong as to catch birds'. This species of spider had been variously named *Epeira* – 'on wool' – from the ancient Greek by Charles Athanase Baron de Walckenaër, a Frenchman whose personal wealth enabled him to spend so much of his leisure time with spiders that they had been called his protégés; or else *Nephila*, from the Greek *philía* for 'love', and *neo* for 'thread, or weave', because of the great care they took with their magnificent webs. The males were diminutive, but females could become as large as five centimetres in length, with the spread of their lissom legs doubling their size.

Darwin had read Azara's accounts with interest, but he was less pleased about the travels of Alcide d'Orbigny, a French naturalist who, he growled, 'by ill luck the French government has sent . . . to the Rio Negro – where he has been working for the last six months, & is now gone round the Horn. – So that I am very selfishly afraid he will get the cream of all the good things, before me.' In fact, d'Orbigny had beaten Darwin to Venezuela, Colombia, Ecuador, Peru, Bolivia, Chile, Argentina, Brazil – and Paraguay. And that was where he was said to have ordered a pair of trousers made by its indigenous people from the silk of one of their great spiders.

In Java and New Guinea equally enormous spiders were spotted weaving immense webs 'several yards in diameter and of incredible strength and solidarity'. In Vanuatu, the locals had long made it a tradition to felt those golden webs of their large and lithe *Nephila plumipes* and *Nephila pilipes* into a fabric which covered a person's body entirely or else formed a headdress. They also used them in rituals related to ancestors; the transferring of leadership roles; funerary ceremonies; and for the making of effigies. In the north of New Guinea's Sepik Valley, webs harvested on a stick were put to use in the hunting of cicadas, and in Vanuatu as well nets of spiders' webs were made for hunting small birds, much as the great spiders did themselves. In several islands across Melanesia, knowing that these threads would not dissolve in water, people used them as bait, as fishing lines, or else nearly complete webs some two metres across, mounted on curved bamboo and immersed as invisible snares in which to capture fish. In the Trobriand Islands, to the west of New Guinea, such nets could weigh over a kilogram. And in all those places, the people who harvested the webs would take only part of what the spiders produced, so that the great arachnids, with which they maintained respectfully little contact, might have enough of it left to effect a repair, a base upon which to begin their weaving again.

Further east, in China, François Garnier, a French naval officer, reported a spider from Yunnan from which was being made 'satin of the eastern sea' – a fabric peculiar to that province. A fellow countryman, the maritime tax collector and naturalist Albert-Auguste Fauvel, would corroborate Garnier's sighting while making the first detailed description of the Chinese alligator, having also witnessed this spider 'which weaves in the pines webs of yellow silk so strong that small birds are sometimes taken therein'.

Similar spiders would be seen, too, in Australia, along the west coast of Africa and on the banks of the Congo, just as large, with webs just as golden. In 1863 a French doctor, Auguste Vinson, sent a beautiful and detailed study to the Académie des Sciences in Paris. It was entitled *The Araneides of Réunion* and was a fine work on the orb-weaver spiders of Réunion, the island on which he was born, as well as the neighbouring islands of Mauritius and Madagascar. It was on the palm-like Pandanus trees of those islands, Vinson wrote, 'which ascend skywards . . . that our gigantic *Epeiræ* attach their long silky threads and establish them from one tree to another at a distance of several yards. In these strong webs, multiplied and very broad, they are counted by hundreds, living in communities and in perfect harmony. They are found of all ages and sizes. They consist of the species known as the golden *Epeira*, which are so good commensals that [they] establish themselves upon their great webs in order to capture small prey thereon . . .'

Those great webs, complex disks a metre and a half or so in diameter, suspended by thick, twine-like golden silk stretching up to eight metres across, were clearly a striking sight for those who sought dominion in any of the warm places that were home to enormous *Nephila* spiders. What was stranger was that the copious numbers of small prey captured upon them had mostly seen those webs, too.

The *Nephila* had built their orbs perhaps not so much with love but by using a wonderful repertoire of elastic, sticky threads of various types of silks, embellished with glue-like drops of protein. Woven together, glinting under a brilliant sun, they sparkle in the compound eyes of insects. Yellow chemical compounds emerge from their many silk glands in varying amounts, changing the gold of the threads depending on the light: whitish to pale yellow, bright yellow to threads of an almost orange tint. The colours reflect the light much as the leaves behind them do, meaning such a choice of colours can sometimes camouflage the webs to insects' eyes. But sometimes their colours do not disappear into the foliage. Their small prey with their acute eyesight see such webs, and know they should be avoided. But their colours are too enticing. They shimmer in hues of yellows like flowers, like succulent young leaves, these golden orbs whose temptation many insects fail to resist.

That draw of the golden orb was also how many came to observe and collect the *Nephila*, soldiers and priests and scientists who braved forest paths strewn with their immense webs. But in so far as history remembers, after Termeyer there would be two in particular who took that encounter further. Who thought as he did. Who saw that the *Nephila* presented an opportunity that even Réaumur would not have turned down. To whom finding a way to work the golden silk of this great spider was a temptation too enticing to resist.

. . .

Whenever and due to whatever ailment Father Ramón María Termeyer had been given the last rites and died, both he and his work might have been largely forgotten had it not been for the fact that his writings on spiders had twice been found by chance, and sent on to someone else equally obsessed with such animals.

The first time that had happened was in 1833, perhaps ten years after his *Researches and Experiments upon Silk from Spiders* had first been published, though no one can say for sure. In that year, the book had been sent to Charles Athanase Baron de Walckenaër, the scientist whose name had been famously attached to a species of *Latrodectus – Latrodectus Walckenaër*, better known, and feared, as black widows – spiders with venom so neurotoxic that they appropriated not just insects and crustaceans and other arachnids for their meals, but also immobilized larger animals: lizards, geckos, and mice. Fortunately for Walckenaër, their venom mostly gripped human victims with nausea, cramping and twistingly severe muscle pains. On balance, this was a small price, for the various silk glands of the females and males of spiders like these appeared to produce some fifty proteins creating at least three major types of silk, as well as others related to the formation of silk, though quite what they were, and what they did, would remain unknown.

Thirty years later, Auguste Vinson would quote Baron de Walckenaër – whom he held in immense regard – in his own work on the *Nephila* spiders of his island, and of neighbouring Mauritius and Madagascar. Vinson had made no specific mention of the elusive Termeyer in this study. Perhaps that was because Walckenaër had not known what to make of the Jesuit's exertions himself. And yet, in among the lines written by the doctor in *The Araneides of Réunion* resonated the spirit of Termeyer's very peculiar experiments.

'If industry ever turns its eyes towards the useful exploitation of the threads of our spiders', Vinson wrote, 'it is assuredly to these black Epeira, gold Epeira and the large Epeira Madagascar. Walckenaër . . . already pointed out, following their description, that this last species gives yellow threads capable of being woven. These very strong, very long threads resemble the richest orange or gold coloured silk that China sends us. It is enough to take the voluminous, ovoid, elongated abdomen of the spider between the fingers and to twist this thread on a spindle or on a reel: the source seems inexhaustible. After having thus drawn from this insect an abundant quantity of silk, it does not seem to suffer from it, and can be set free.'

Vinson also made particular note that it was 'with the threads of this [Madagascar] Epeira that in Mauritius, the elegant Creoles hand-wove a splendid pair of gloves which they sent in homage to the French Empress. A witness, who saw this masterpiece of colonial industry, gave it the highest praise . . .'

These *Nephila madagascariensis* females, the same enormous *Epeira Madagascar* in which Vinson saw such potential, might not have crossed his path had it not been for the fact that, in the course of his research, he had been sent by Napoleon III to Madagascar for the coronation of their new king, Radama II, who succeeded his mother, the formidable Queen Ranavalona I, who had opposed economic and political ties with France. Her son was not so minded, so that when, on 10 November 1882, another Jesuit priest arrived in Madagascar, his experiments with the magnificent *Nephila madagascariensis* were in no danger and nor was his presence likely to end in exile.

Queen Ranavalona II of Madagascar (1829-1883).

Jacob Paul Camboué, a man who had achieved a baccalaureate in science at 16, was told by his teachers that he was not very good at science and then turned to law instead. He swore thc oath of a lawyer in the appellate court in Paris aged 19, enlisted as a soldier aged 21, and then, two years later, returned from military service to find himself knocking at the door of the novitiate of the Jesuits of Toulouse. They took him in. Ten years after that, Camboué was dispatched to serve as a bush missionary, working in rural outposts to the west of Antananarivo, Madagascar's capital, the kind of places where the forest paths were littered with animals that might knock a priest's hat squarely to the ground. Throughout the African continent to Madagascar's west were many animals that produced silk, and from which its peoples produced prestigious fabrics. They formed the embroidery on the flowing Babban Riga gowns of the Hausa people of West and Central Africa. In the Sanyan Aso Oke woven textiles of the Yorubas of Nigeria, woven of the beige silk cocoons of the Anaphe moth whose wings are criss-crossed like contrails and which is also found in Cameroon, the Democratic Republic of the Congo, Equatorial Guinea, Kenya, Malawi, South Africa, Tanzania and Gambia. And in the wild silk tombe toun strips incorporated into the wraps made and worn by Dogon women of the Tommo and Tengukan areas of Mali.

Spread as it was across the sclerophyllous forests of Madagascar's central highlands, Camboué could not have failed to take note of the tapia tree, upon whose leaves feasted Landibe larvae, the caterpillar of a wild silk moth named *Borocera madagascariensis*, or *Borocera cajani*, by Vinson. That was the point at which Camboué dispensed with his teachers' best advice and embarked upon a scientific study of the moths that Madagascans had long used to loom their own fabrics of silk, creations like the lamba, a cloth of a rectangular shape, used as shrouds for the dead. The silk of *Borocera madagascariensis* was reserved for this purpose; it was, after all, famous for being rot-proof; but there were others, too. Camboué himself named the *Borocera bibindandy*, whose male looked remarkably similar to *Borocera madagascariensis* but whose female was very different in colour, and larger in size; and *Borocera madinyka*, smaller, and a violet brown.

Even though Camboué then put away his studies with the wild silk moths, his love for natural science and for experimentation had instilled in him the fervour of the newly converted. Very quickly, he moved on to imagining working with the threads of spiders instead. For that lamba made by the Madagascan people was not just woven of the silk of their *Borocera cajani* wild moths. It was also their tradition to interlace the silk of the moths with the threads of their great golden orb spider – the *halabe*, or 'great spider' – *Nephila madagascariensis*. Just as Vinson had read Walckenaër, and Walckenaër had read Termeyer, Camboué now read Vinson. And that, as far as it appears, was the basis upon which little contrivances of his own making would be created. And they were contrivances that would have made Termeyer very, very proud.

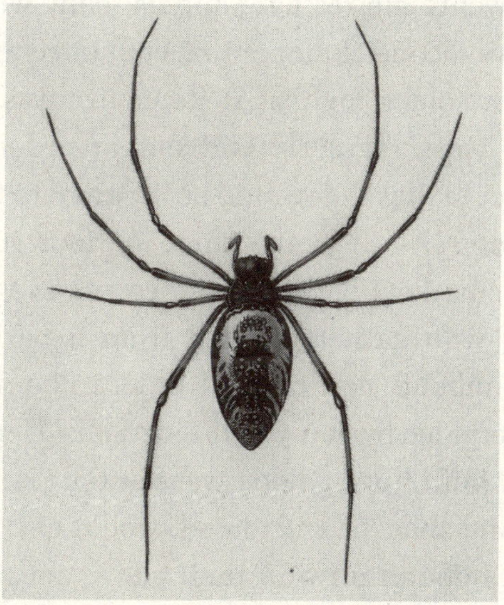

Nephila inaurata madagascariensis
aka the Madagascar Golden Orb spider.

For Camboué's spider studies were based upon the fact that the *Nephila* was a well-established producer of a usable silk, and one far more remarkable than any produced from a silk moth. And so he set out to attempt their breeding. In order to do that, he sent specimens to four abbots back in France, men who, between masses, would attempt to acclimatize *Nephila madagascariensis* in that mecca of European silk production, Lyons, as well as in Ardèche and the Cévennes.

Through these experiments he hoped to work out the quantities of silk threads the enormous female *Nephila* might ultimately produce, and, of course, how to replicate, in France, the conditions that were necessary for her survival. At the same time, Camboué was attempting his own *Nephila* breeding in Antananarivo.

In 1898, upon a long sacred enclosure on the hill of Rova, in a place forbidden to Europeans, he ordered the construction of a bamboo cage, twenty metres long and as many wide. With it was also constructed a second chamber that contained an area to protect the spiders from colder nights. At its centre was a pit in which scraps of meat were regularly laid out in order to attract the immense number of flies that would be required to feed the spiders. The spiders themselves – some three or four hundred – were brought in osier baskets with wooden covers every day by young Malagasy girls, who gathered them from a park near the site forbidden to Camboué, and readied them to be divested of their silk. There, surrounded by many well-fed *Nephila* females, Camboué watched as they built huge golden webs at the rate of a centimetre every second. And that, he calculated, would also be the speed at which he could hope to unwind their silk – not in the formation of any web, but, this time, directly onto his spool.

Camboué's next step was to immobilize the spider, as Termeyer had. To isolate its abdomen. To unreel an unwilling spider's threads until she was spent. First, he placed each spider in a matchbox, with her abdomen exposed. He tested each to gauge the length of the longest unbroken thread he might expect to extract and was pleased to note that the spider threads compared most favourably with those of a number of silkworms. His measurements were based upon criteria communicated to him by the silk research laboratory in Lyons: upon ideal measures of the threads' weight, their elasticity, diameter and their resilience. He calculated that the spider silk as he reeled it was fifty-two times finer than what was being extracted from the cocoons of *Bombyx mori*, but its delicacy was deceptive. The silk of the *Nephila* was nearly three times stronger, more elastic and more durable than the moth's.

Besides these miraculous qualities innate in the spider silk, Camboué's method was productive. The *halabe*, he reported, multiplied with extreme rapidity. What was more, they gave him between 150 and 700 metres per reel. That meant that in the course of one month alone, with five to six unwindings, on average, before the spiders died, he would have persuaded them to provide some four thousand metres of silk. Meanwhile, back in France, the unravelled threads of *Bombyx mori* offered only between 1,200 and 1,500 metres within the same period.

The obvious next step was to scale up his operations. Camboué built the prototype of a machine designed to be a complete system for the extraction and reeling of spider silk, and to harness many spiders at once. That machine was taken as far as it could go with the support of the director of the Professional School of Antananarivo. It was the 'native girls', reports said, who did the work.

It was the school's deputy director, M. Nogué, who improved the machine again to make the process even less labour-intensive. The new apparatus twisted together the silken strands of twelve immobilized spiders. A tray held twelve separate 'guillotines' to imprison each spider so that its abdomen was exposed, with its long legs kept safely clear of its spinnerets. In every section a metal rod with a hole at one end lay exactly thirty centimetres from the guillotine. These collected the twelve threads as they emerged and united them into one piece. Those threads wrapped around a coil that, like a bicycle wheel, spun with two rotational movements, rolling up the threads and turning them in on themselves, all at the same time, so that it was possible to double them, producing skeins of twenty-four strands. This was a machine so efficient that it generated 200,000 metres of twelve-strand silken skeins every year.

It was from these threads that an enormous bed canopy, one that would float from a *ciel de lit*, as well as a fireplace screen were made and sent from the Indian Ocean to the 16th *arrondissement*, across the Seine from the Eiffel Tower. There they were to be exhibited at yet another great display of the works of the colonies – the 1900 Paris Exposition Universelle. With the irascible spirit of an artist, M. Nogué complained that the precious fabrics had sustained irreparable damage from exposure to the salty conditions in the ship's hold as they sailed to France. The reporters from the newspaper *Le Matin* appear not to have noticed any such damage. They wrote of a fabric of paradoxical lightness and thinness, vaporous, almost unreal – one of most extraordinary curiosities that had been displayed from anywhere in the world. 'Will this . . . masterpiece of strength, lightness, and elegance . . . be the silk of the future?' asked *Le Magasin pittoresque*, for 'its thread might be employed in electricity on account of its insulating properties and furnish useful aid to meteorology . . .' But as the journalists marvelled, the passing visitors simply walked by, and noticed nothing much at all.

Golden Orb spider silk production in Madagascar, 1900.

PART THREE

REINVENTION

'It pays to know there is just as much future as past. The only thing that does not pay is to be sure of man's own part in it.'

– Loren Eiseley, *The Immense Journey*, 1957

22

THE KHAN'S UNDERCLOTHES

AT LEAST UNTIL THE SPRING OF 1221, MERV, NOW IN TURKMENISTAN, from which the tiny eggs of *Bombyx mori* had moved to Persia and the lands to its west, was still a most splendid city. Around 6 March of that year, its splendour was to end. Genghis Khan had taken its golden throne and ordered that the city should be burned to the ground. Its sweet watermelons were no longer cut into strips and dried on its washing lines; scholars put down their pens and abandoned its libraries; astronomers scattered from the observatory; poets forgot their words; and weavers left their looms still interlaced with unfinished fabrics of silk and cotton and ran from their workshops along the still waters of the Majan Canal. All Mongol soldiers were issued a decree from the Khan such that each was to end the lives of three to four hundred distraught souls. 'That city', it was said, 'which had been embellished by great men of the world, became the haunt of hyenas and beasts of prey.' Smoke rose over its palaces and groves, gardens and streams. Books which had held the learnings of centuries blackened and curled in the intense heat, before crumbling into ash. Its canals were destroyed, orchards of its celebrated fruit trees felled, oasis fields that produced its sweetest watermelons salted. Genghis Khan ordered a call to prayer from a minaret to root out anyone who had found a clever place to hide and had them slaughtered; and then he ordered a count of the dead that came in at 700,000 bodies of all ages, or, perhaps, parts thereof. 'It was the last day of the lives of most of the inhabitants of Merv', pronounced a Persian historian who had allied with the Mongols. By the end, only a small number of its sophisticated citizens would survive. Those who did had been intentionally kept alive. And all of them, it is said, were artisans.

Over its long history, many had seen and coveted the bountiful treasures of Merv. Occasionally, its walls had failed to deter these others who, before the Mongols, had also sought its wealth or its political prestige. Some seventy years before Genghis Khan and his son plundered and murdered their way through Merv, it had been the turn of the Oghuz, or Ghuzz Turks, a people whose descendants would found the Ottoman Empire. For three days they helped themselves to the contents of Merv's treasury and stores. Nothing of any value was overlooked, but it was on the first day that their chests were filled with what they considered most precious. Along with the city's gold, the very first things to be pillaged were its famed silks, loomed of threads pulled from boiling cocoons between the long fingers of its artisans.

When Genghis Khan died in 1227, perhaps even greater than the vast empire he had forged was the complete dominion of the network of roads that came with military conquest. Across these silk roads – as, many years later, they would come to be known – traders' caravans travelled no less efficiently than the Mongol blade, moving porcelain and jewels, gunpowder and horses, slaves, Marco Polo and the bubonic plague. There was also paper, an incredibly valuable commodity that had been invented in China some thousand years before Genghis Khan was born. And, of course, traded along these roads for magnificent profit were bales of perfectly crafted silks from China, as well as from wherever *Bombyx mori* feasted on mulberry leaves across Central Asia.

But for Genghis Khan, such people as he had studiously kept alive in Merv – its artisans – may also have had a significance beyond the spoils of war and the trappings of wealth, one upon which the very survival of his warriors might depend. Theirs were swords that would not rust and horses that could not rest, and their soldiers – all males older than fourteen who were neither doctors nor priests — were provided with armour designed to keep them light enough to stay agile and yet strong enough to return safely to the horde, to prevent casualties among their own. Breastplates and backplates of leather were sewn together like scales, with a leather-covered shield and helmet usually made of much the same. It weighed nowhere near the fifty kilograms or so of the iron mail worn by European cavalry at that time, putting additional weight on their already burdened horses. Much of a battle against Genghis Khan's hordes would take place after a soldier dismounted, or was dismounted by the iron tip of a Mongol javelin, the terrifying momentum of a swinging axe, or any of the sixty arrows with which Genghis' men were also armed. If this Mongol armour that speeded them onto golden thrones had no need of chains wrought from iron wires it was because of what was under its leather-scaled cuirass. It was something better than other types of under-armour which were made of linen quilted with wool or horses' hair, because it was smarter. The idea for the Mongols' choice of fabric had been appropriated from Chinese warcraft. It was to take the extraordinarily light thread extruded from the insect that Neolithic China's farmers had domesticated so long before, and with it craft an undershirt, standard issue, of tightly woven *Bombyx mori* silk. Compared to the promise of cold, hard metal armour, and although it may have been layered, the sheerness of silk cloth seemed to offer little deterrent against the sharp ends of enemy weapons, even if it did allow them more rapid onslaughts and escapes. But it was extraordinarily effective.

Were the leather body armour to be penetrated, the fine silk undergarment would wind tightly around the heads or points of sharp missiles that might otherwise have pushed deeper into limbs or through them. More often than not, an arrow would not actually break through this fabric so surprisingly delicate to the touch. Removing an arrow, particularly one that was barbed, inevitably caused a larger wound than the offending object itself had, and with it, extensive bleeding out. But when an arrow had embedded itself first in silk, the tightly woven threads around the wound would be pulled instead, turning the arrowhead, gently teasing the weapon out – minimizing further damage. As the Mongols herded the newly enslaved or slaughtered those who were unfortunate enough to be in their way, the lives of their own soldiers were much less likely to be lost thanks to their undershirts.

But the doctors serving the armies of the Khans may have also noted that the wounds into which fine *Bombyx mori* silk was dragged by the sharp end of an arrow might also have been better equipped to mend themselves. Simply breaking the skin is to create a crack in the wall of the body's strategic defence, an opening of which the forces of infection take full advantage. Where there is a wound – warm, and moist, divested of the first line of defence of intact skin – there is also an ideal opportunity for bacteria to invade and colonize. This attack the immune system must find a mechanism to avert. Under the broken surface, the journey of a physical trauma that heals is an intricate, programmed process built of an exact sequence of steps that the body completes through the conversations of myriad cells. Here are hormones, signals and the fine architecture of tissues that must work in concert in a precise order. The constriction of blood vessels, a spike in heart rate and in the cells that work to inflame and so repair, cells that move and recruit others to help, that rebuild broken blood vessels and new tissue in the place of the old – in which the matrix that formed the cavity of the wound slowly remodels into a new structure that seals, regenerates and binds broken muscle and nerves, bone and skin.

In one sense, the cocoons of *Bombyx mori* are not so different from skin. The cocoon exists to protect, not just because it forms an impenetrable layer that covers important structures within, but in the deep structure of silk appear to be embedded proteins that are antiviral, and yet others that can damage the fortressing walls of bacterial cells. These are defences that protect the silkworm pupa as it metamorphoses into its adult form, but they are also retained in the silk unreeled from its cocoon, spun by human hand into yarn. Silk fabric woven from those threads made in exactly the same way that the Chinese had developed it so long before: first stripping from it, by special boiling, the part called sericin, the cement that binds the strands of silk protein as it emerges from its silkworm, so that silk can interact with every stage of the complex healing process. Both the fibroin that forms the silk and the sericin that binds it can hasten the healing of wounds. But with sericin intact, an inappropriate, heightened immune response might be sparked in the injured, one that could induce an allergic reaction. The Chinese already having removed this cement, as far as can be told, had been spinning silk threads to suture wounds for around two thousand years by the time the Mongol campaigns began, and as dressings whose threads could stimulate the cells that repair and rebuild to convene and proliferate in the wound bed.

In a future time, some eight hundred years after the death of the Khan, silk without sericin, and even the sericin routinely discarded in the manufacture of silk, will be manipulated by doctors and engineers. They will create sponges and gels, films and mats of silk as scaffolds that seek to support wounds that struggle to heal; as matrices for the regrowth of blood vessels and broken skin; in formulations to attract cells as they migrate and regenerate. And all of this from the sophisticated manipulation of the extracts of a little silkworm. But before all that, the simple silk underclothes of the Mongols had only been intended to prevent the death of one more fighter, to stem the catastrophic loss of blood from an agile horseman riding into the path of an enemy arrow. That it was even possible for the fine threads of an insect's cocoon to halt the flow of blood, and even the flight of a missile designed to kill, would be backed up by observations made, quite by chance, and published exactly 660 years after the death of Genghis Khan, over six thousand miles away, in Arizona Territory in the American Old West.

23

CONSCRIPTION

THE CURSE OF FORESIGHT THAT HAD BOTH BLESSED AND BLIGHTED Ramón María Termeyer was matched only by the curse of hindsight for Dr Burt Green Wilder. In 1866 he became the scientist who would resurrect Termeyer's study of spider silk from the copy that had belonged to Baron de Walckenaër, a book that was sold with his estate, and then purchased by a Dr Cogswell for the Astor Library in New York. It was then sent to Wilder, because Cogswell had heard of Wilder's own investigations into spiders, which were as fastidious as Termeyer's, and equally closely resembled madness. Wilder was in fact far younger when he had begun to record observations of living spiders. Aged only 14, these were studies so astute that the child was invited to Harvard by the celebrated Louis Agassiz, a contemporary of Charles Darwin who had studied living fish and fossil fish and glaciers. His conclusion that 'the phenomena of animal life correspond to one another whether we compare their rank as determined by structural complication . . . or with their succession in past geological ages . . .' was one that in Darwin's mind accorded with the theory of natural selection. But Agassiz begged to differ. His mind instead heard these natural connections 'proclaim aloud the One God', that after every global extinction of life, God had created every species anew.

Despite being Agassiz's protégé, Wilder had been born into a family whose shoulders had broadened from swimming against prevailing currents. His was a home run by strict vegetarians, people who actively opposed oppression on racial and other grounds; who were committed to societal improvement. From his mother he inherited an unwillingness to sacrifice principle to expediency; from his father a hopeful spirit and tendency to seek new facts and to devise original methods. And so Wilder grew into a perpetually curious man of independent thought. In 1862 he enlisted as surgeon in the American Civil War, serving with the newly formed black 55th Massachusetts Volunteers.

That took him to South Carolina, where he pored over medical textbooks, treated the wounded and discovered the existence of an orb-weaver endemic to the area that Linnaeus had called *Aranea clavipes*, later called *Nephila clavipes*, and later still, in honour of Wilder, *Nephila wilderi*. So taken was he by this 'striking example of feminine superiority and domination' that he would refer admiringly to her when he came to pen challenges 'to expose the fallacies lurking' in the discussion of women's suffrage that were to come. Wilder lived during a time in which measurements of the weight of people's brains would increasingly be used to justify such glorious varieties of discrimination that were restricted only by the human imagination. But, Wilder would write, the enormous *Nephila* 'female not only makes the net and catches the prey', 'but weighs at least one hundred times her mate; that is as if the average man of one hundred and forty pounds should attach himself to a woman of seven tons'. In the main, however, Wilder's keenest interest in the works of this spider was the orb of fine golden silk upon which he found her. Her great web so impressed Wilder that he, with two colleagues, patented the most elaborate spider-silking machine yet.

And then the envelope arrived for him from Dr Cogswell. Inside it was Termeyer's text, which had been written in Italian, and so Wilder had it sent off to be translated. But within those pages were also images of Termeyer's machine that looked back at him like a mirror of his own work, almost in exact detail, yet, somehow, from a hundred years in the past. Those images needed no interpretation. He found them exceedingly interesting, 'the representation of a process . . . differing only in details from that employed by me at various times and with various modifications . . .'

The new discovery of Termeyer's very old invention might have presented Wilder with a sticky problem. Every scientist knew that to gain a patent not only must an invention represent something new, but also be *inventive* – not simply a modification of something that already existed. At first, Wilder's machinery had seemed to him to be entirely original. After all, it had been deemed so, he said, 'even to the experts at the Patent Office in Washington, so that a Patent was readily granted for the *idea or process of obtaining silk directly from living spiders or other insects by a reeling or circular motion applied to the insects themselves*'. But now that Termeyer's design had emerged from the century over which it had evanesced, Wilder was gracious in admitting that the novelty of his instrument was 'of course invalidated'. 'But', he added, 'is it not a little remarkable that an idea so novel, yet so simple, and, one would think, so readily suggested by what we may see on any summer's day, should have been conceived and carried out a hundred years ago, and yet there should be no reference to its nature, scarcely an allusion to its author, and, so far as I can ascertain, no knowledge of its having been published . . .?'

Remarkable it may have been, but the same scientific ideas do occur to different people, repeatedly, across continents, spanning millennia. Wherever delicate and beautiful threads were seen emerging from the bodies of other animals that surrounded humans – anchoring them to the floors of shallow seas, draped like nets across forests, egg-like cocoons from which winged insects emerged – these were sometimes harvested gently; at others, aggressively extracted; and, nearly always, someone, somewhere would attempt to corral them into farms.

Indeed, the same silks, or at least astonishingly similar ones, were also innovated, evolved and developed quite independently and on multiple occasions inside the bodies of these animals themselves. Among the insects alone, silk was 'invented' twenty-three times; and, separately, in spiders, once. Whether insect or arachnid, and although the glands in which their silks were stored might have developed by repurposing other cells of different origins, these silks themselves would evolve similar protein sequences, and be processed, liquid to fibre, under similar conditions within the animals. And yet they emerged from those bodies with diverse structures and a suite of varying properties: sticky, stretchy, flexible, strong. Perhaps, like the contrivances of Termeyer and Camboué and Wilder, ultimately the number of ways biology could come up with a silk fibre was limited. But in the uses to which its animals put them, the success of each silk showed how remarkable they had been in their ability to adapt, survive and persist over hundreds of millions of years.

On a tighter time scale, that was also really what Wilder had hoped for his contrivance, that it would not fade into the deep obscurity to which Termeyer and his work had been fated. And he seemed almost confident of it: 'so far from dragging out a precarious existence for forty years and then dying of neglect as it did in the Old World, this idea shall, in its present resurrection in a freer atmosphere, live to be what sober, cautious men already expect of it – a means of luxury, of comfort and of national wealth'.

If only Wilder knew how often those words, too, had been spoken before.

Wilder was known as a humane man, a lover of animals of every description. His had been one of the first scientific accounts of the gorilla. He said of himself that this was a passion he had also inherited from his mother, a 'tenderness towards animals which prevented his hunting for sport and restricted his physiologic experiments to such as are painless'. Sure enough, he even suggested the use of anaesthetic for the direct reeling of its silk from the body of the silkworm, rather than unravelling its cocoons. Somehow he did not think to render the formidable *Nephila* more comfortable by similar treatment, even in his next theoretical step with the spiders, which was to trial a method for reeling silk from many of them at once. It is unclear why his work with spider silk ceases there, for Wilder does not seem to have done that experiment with a spider horde. Like Camboué's, like Termeyer's – like all the spiders restrained in guillotines themselves – perhaps Wilder's little contrivance died first of fatigue.

After that, it did die of neglect, because at some point Wilder became preoccupied with the other field of science to which he committed himself to research, teach and defend. From his knowledge of neuroscience, he was outspoken in divesting those invested in the maintenance of discrimination from the ability to claim the backing of science. To neuroscience, he would leave a number of legacies, one of which was the first images which referred to a 'right brain' and 'left brain'.

Another was the witty, if macabre, joining of the hemispheres of an illiterate black janitor and a white jurist and politician who 'had probably condoned . . . the race riots', to illustrate that the brain of the educated white man was, in fact, the smaller. The third was a collection of 1,600 brains, of which 430 had belonged to human adults and children, and one that, ultimately, would be his. In homage to the spirit of the man while living, his brain, once dead, was compared to that of the suffragette Helen H. Gardener, and both were reported to weigh precisely the same.

Wilder would have been wryly amused at such an illustration of equality between the sexes; or, at least, between what had been contained in their heads. And yet there were two things that, in life, Wilder had done that seemed entirely out of character. The first had been the ultimate abandonment of his work with spiders and their silk, and this after the trials and patents and the burning fervour with which he had promoted it. The second was his authorship of *Health Notes for Students*. Despite his educated questioning of the scientific and societal bases upon which discrimination on the grounds of skin colour and sex were built, these writings contained a series of his opinions, distinctly not based upon evidence. What was more, they began with the words 'Sterilization of the unfit (under proper safeguards of course) is advocated by me', and ended with a quote from the first president of Cornell University: 'Paupers and criminals should be prevented from marrying. The tramp and the malingerer should be stamped out; they need not exist. It is as harmful to bring insane children into the world as it is to drive them insane by bad usage. The habitual criminal man or woman should be deprived of the power to procreate.'

To which the man who had once served as a surgeon added only that the president's last sentence might have included 'by operative procedure to express the most radical opinion of today'. Wilder's 'today' was 1883 and opinions were about to become even more radical.

In 1910, the British Home Secretary Winston Churchill penned voluminous correspondences concerning how 'the unnatural and increasingly rapid growth of the Feeble-Minded and Insane classes, coupled as it is with a steady restriction among . . . superior stocks, constitutes a national and race danger which it is impossible to exaggerate'. And then he formally asked the British government to consider a proposal for a new law based upon those passed in Indiana in 1907, that is, one that supported the sterilization of 'the insane, the epileptic, the imbecile, the idiotic', and, of course, 'the confirmed inebriates, prostitutes, tramps . . . as well as the habitual paupers'.

In the 1930s, Churchill warned his country to act against a Germany led by Adolf Hitler, who, among other things, was busy passing his own Law on Citizenship and Race; with the rounding up of beggars, prostitutes, homosexuals and alcoholics; and, of course, with a bespoke Nazi euthanasia programme codenamed Aktion T4, which translated to the systematic murder of institutionalized people with disabilities – all so that, as Churchill clearly articulated in his desire for the betterment of his own country, 'their curse died with them and was not transmitted to future generations'.

While the two men's differences were being settled on the beaches, on the landing grounds, in the fields, the streets and in the hills, through the dog days of war that followed, ministers of Adolf Hitler's Third Reich came together to find a solution to some of the challenges presented by the modern theatre of war. That solution was not extermination, but breeding; not of *Übermenschen*, but of *Bombyx mori*. The docile and pliable silkworms would now become wartime animals, allies in a new era of silk cultivation. At the same moment that Churchill steeled Britain's air force to wage war in the skies, Hitler recruited silkworms to the Nazi aerial warfare effort, for the production of parachutes.

The silken fabrics made of their threads were not just lightweight, tear-resistant and water-repellent, they were largely fireproof as well. For the cultivation of *Bombyx mori*, millions of mulberry trees were planted along roadsides and railways, in cemeteries and schools. Teachers trained to make silk suspended their cocoons over cauldrons of boiling water. They used them in experiments, dissected for the children's biological education. By return, students fed and attended to the silkworms. The little caterpillars were weaponized as instruments of biological instruction of 'racial hygiene'. It was easy to grasp. Even a child could successfully breed healthy silkworms, so long as all those that were weak, or sick, were removed and destroyed as soon as they were identified. *Bombyx mori*, inbred for millennia – or, in other words, pure of race – failed the test of Nazi eugenic fitness. Still, the scale of their industrialized programme of silk production meant that thousands of silken parachutes were made. On 20 May 1941, on the island of Crete, one of the war's great theatres of combat, two thousand of these parachutes darkened the skies. After Hitler's soldiers massacred and burned, and were finally beaten, the women of the island, who cultivated silk of their own, cut up those parachutes and worked them into handkerchiefs.

And then, just as the *Bombyx* had been, the spider was unwittingly recruited to military service, too. The peculiarities of its silk in particular were needed, not for parachutes, but for something far more precise. Astronomers had long used a single strand of spider's silk gathered in much the same way as François Xavier Bon de Saint Hilaire had, and from around the same time. Placed as crosshairs inside telescopes, these threads were a blessing for their consistency of thickness, being as good as weightless but almost impossible to break. Just such a thread had fixed the problem that in 1782 the celebrated astronomer William Herschel had found with its main competitor. Through the eyepiece of a telescope, 'the single threads of the silkworm' became, he found, 'so much magnified that their diameter is much more than that of many of the stars'.

More than that, *Bombyx mori* silk fibres are triangular in form, and while that triangular, prism-like structure allows silk cloth to refract incoming light, endowing it with exactly the shimmering appearance that made it famous as a textile, it did not work at all well in viewfinders. Nor would the threads of the wild *Antheraea* silk moths have, for they are flat and ribbon-like. But spider's silk is round, and, when drawn out by a spider, has a given, controlled diameter that remains constant over lengths that span metres. And that was the sort of consistency needed for crosshairs: reliably sized, extremely fine and yet tough enough to be handled. That was why spider's threads, in contrast to other silks – or hair of any description – allowed a clear line of sight so that the angles of stars and the distances between them might be measured with precision, and yet, somehow, remained fine enough not to obscure the line of sight.

Two hundred and sixty years after Herschel, the war that enveloped Europe meant that spider silk would be sought again, this time not by astronomers but to fulfil the need for crosshairs of bombsights, gunsights, telescopes and microscopes that would give armed forces far-reaching capabilities, which, in turn, rendered the spider indispensable for fine markings and sight lines. Military precision required silk that was either 1/10,000th of an inch in diameter – some ten times thinner than a human hair – or even far finer than that. In 1939, this call to arms with a spider's web was answered by a woman born in Tennessee fifty years after Burt Green Wilder had started life in that same state before eventually ending up in California. There, Nannie 'Nan' Songer raised two children, enrolled in biology classes at the University of California, and then put aside her childhood collection of arachnids for a house full of black widow spiders and other large species that crossed her path from then on.

Songer's spiders would be glorified as war-working spiders, spiders that toiled and spun for national defence. To encourage them, she devised a technique that would once again be hailed as novel, but was by now nearly two hundred years old: pinning the spiders belly-up onto a piece of cork, tickling their spinnerets until silk emerged, collecting those strands with a fine hook and then wrapping those threads onto a frame. But Songer's efforts succeeded where Termeyer, Bon and Camboué ultimately came unstuck. She counted among her clients the government of the United States of America. The couriers who collected the reams of silk from her home handcuffed briefcases containing the precious cargo to their wrists so that they could not be stolen. Nan Songer's products were precious. By the end, using week-old spiders and magnifying lenses made to her own specifications, she had managed to collect from her little protégés threads that seemed barely even there, 1/500,000th of an inch thick, and yet that she still found to be 'possibly one of the strongest materials made by a living creature'. When the lips of Hitler and his officers pressed down onto the thin glass vials of cyanide they'd kept close at hand and the battles of the Second World War had ceased, instead of the military, Songer's spider silk supplied the finest of crosshairs for the telescopes in which their use had begun, as well as microscopes and medical instruments. Showing that the threads of the spider might help to heal as well as they had helped to kill.

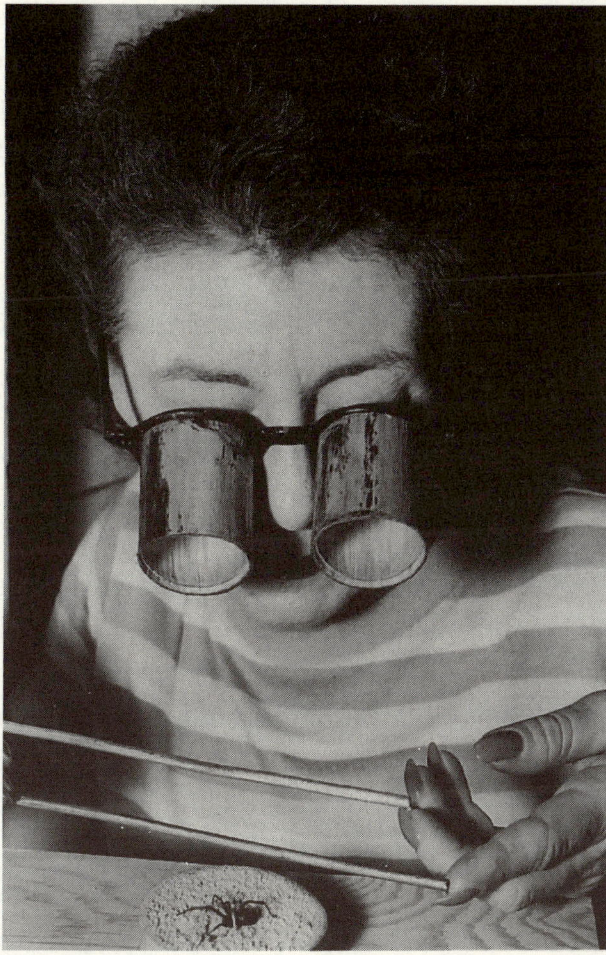

Nan Songer silking black widow spiders, 1940s.

It was widely known by then that the webs of various spiders had long been collected and used to stem the bleeding from deep wounds, and for the healing of ulcers, by ancient peoples. Such applications went back centuries; in the seventeenth century William Shakespeare referred to knowledge of just such a use by a weaver with a donkey's head in *A Midsummer Night's Dream*, in case he were to cut his finger. But the use of the processed, woven silk of a spider for healing was not mentioned until around 1891, and then only obliquely, first by the pen of Émile Jean-Marie Gautier, a French journalist who reported on scientific matters for the newspapers, which was how he first came across someone referred only to as Mr Stillbers. He was an Englishman who had gathered and worked the silken egg cocoons produced by enormous South American and African spiders. He had corralled five thousand of these into octagonal cases, fed them with insects and laid and wrapped their eggs amid the haze of a heady cocktail of chloroform, ether and fusel oil left to evaporate in a corner of the room so that they were kept in a perpetual state of mild intoxication. Stillbers thought they spun best in such a state. Any further detail as to his methods was closely guarded, but the end result was fabrics bleached brilliant and smooth, that were employed as surgical cloths, and that were being extensively manufactured.

Though Nan Songer had certainly found enough spider silk for her applications, and Stillbers claimed to have had sufficient, the generation of the quantities of spider silk that would be required to make full use of its precious qualities for medicine and technology remained a problem for which no immediate solution would become apparent.

But it would not be for want of trying.

24

TOMBSTONE

IT WAS IN 1881 IN A FRONTIER TOWN CALLED TOMBSTONE, AT ABOUT three o'clock in the afternoon on the last Wednesday of October, that a thirty-second gun battle claimed the lives of two outlaws, wounded the town marshal, a special policeman and grazed the shoulder of a gambler, gunfighter and dentist known as Doc Holliday. It was to go down in history as the Gunfight at the OK Corral, the most famous shootout of the American Wild West. It was by no means an isolated incident. Guns were rife, trigger fingers loose, and much was to be gained for those with the bravado and sufficient gunpowder to attempt to take it. Anyone – outlaws, lawmen, opponents who duelled or, indeed, those who simply stood on the sidelines – might feel the sharp end of a bullet. But it induced a particular type of pain for doctors, despite the fact that the offending firearms also undoubtedly kept them in work.

Tombstone had been so named by a restless prospector warned that he would find nothing in that place but his own tombstone, a fact which had evidently amused him when he struck silver there instead. Three years later, several million dollars' worth of precious metal had accumulated, and Tombstone had become a roaring town with a population of two thousand people that boasted three theatres, at least five churches and regular meetings of a Microscopical Science Society run by its doctors and mining engineers. Despite these graces, it was better known as 'the condensation of wickedness', due to the liberal hands of its gunslingers and opportunists. It was into that milieu that a 25-year-old diploma-bearing doctor called George Emory Goodfellow arrived. He was a symmetrical man with a middle parting to prove it, an impressive if unkempt moustache and eyebrows that arched as sharply as a taut bow. Though he often sported a military jacket, and had married a woman by the name of Colt, who – not without some irony – was a cousin of Samuel Colt, the man who made the mass production of firearms possible, he seems only to have been charged once with carrying a concealed weapon, for which he was fined twenty-five dollars. Goodfellow was of a clear conviction that 'war is pure barbarism, even though made under the specious pretense of humanity . . .' Instead, he had long made his fists his weapon of choice, and, even then, predominantly within the confines of the boxing ring.

As a scientist, Goodfellow had a particularly polymathic yet understated experimental brilliance. His firsts would include mapping the ruptures of a large earthquake that began in the mountains of northwestern Mexico and sent aftershocks all the way to Tombstone; and analysing the toxic effects of the venom of the Gila monster, including by acquiring a number of them and inciting one to bite him – which it did, severely, on the forefinger of his left hand. He was unharmed, which vindicated his suspicion that some of the reported victims of the venomous lizard, on whom he had performed autopsies, had in fact perished from the effects of acute and chronic alcoholism.

In Tombstone, where saloons were difficult to avoid, Goodfellow was not one to turn down opportunities for merriment, and even took an office above an infamous bar called the Crystal Palace. From that office, for the next eleven years, he would gain, as he wrote, in his typically modest style, 'a somewhat extensive experience in the gunshot wounds of civil life'. Not only did he regularly remove from the bodies of men infatuated with courage bullets from revolvers bearing his in-law's name; but the bullets he extracted from the OK Corral lawmen that day in October would foster a certain dark humour, and a prominent career as doctor and coroner to the 'festive or obstreperous citizens who delighted themselves with toys such as the .44 or .45-calibre Colt revolver . . .' The damage he saw on autopsy tables in the aftermath of these citizens' delights sealed his reputation, and soon he became known as 'the gunfighter's surgeon'. 'Their maxim', he noted, 'is "shoot for the guts," knowing that death is certain, yet sufficiently lingering and agonizing to afford a plenary sense of gratification to the victor in the contest.'

At midnight one evening in that little mining town, however, Goodfellow decided he would attempt to change the inevitability of that maxim among the men of Tombstone who would not bring themselves to get worked up about the death of a rival. It was a decision which also seems to have made him the first surgeon to cut into an abdominal cavity and actually save the life of a man who had taken a gunshot to the gut. The ungodly hour and circumstances of his first such case meant that he had to perform that surgery without the assistance of anyone with even the most basic medical expertise. 'I was alone entirely', he wrote, '. . . therefore was compelled to depend for aid upon the willing friends who were present – these consisting mostly of hard-handed miners just from their work on account of the fight.' These dusty men held lamps close to the victim's limp body, brought hot water and watched as a barber administered the strongest anaesthetic he had to hand. Through a single cut that ran from the man's sternum to his navel, Goodfellow identified and stemmed the source of a haemorrhage that would otherwise have claimed his life upon the dining table of the restaurant that also served as Goodfellow's operating theatre.

By 1887, the good doctor had flushed the blood from enough gunshot wounds to enable him to make a curious observation, and one, no doubt, that might have made even Genghis Khan proud. It was based upon the injuries or deaths of three men: a gambler at the Oriental Saloon by the name of Charlie Storms; an outlaw called Billy Grounds upon whom a deputy sheriff known as 'Helldorado' unleashed a hail of buckshot, full in the face; and a cattle rustler from the Mexican border who was shot from less than three feet away, by a ball from a standard-length .45-calibre Colt revolver.

The first victim had been shot in the left breast with a sawn-off Colt and with a force that had sent the gambler staggering back some twelve feet, in full view of Goodfellow, who was trying to have a quiet drink in the same saloon when the altercation began. No more than half an hour later the doctor had Storms' body moved away from the crowd and stripped of his clothing, at which point he stood back, bemused. Goodfellow 'found not a drop of blood had come from . . . the wound in the breast', and observed a silk handkerchief protruding from Charlie Storms' chest wound. At first, he presumed that somehow, in the ruckus that followed the incident, Storms' friends had the presence of mind to stuff the fabric into the wound to stem the flow of blood. But as he had already seen up close, there had been no blood. As Goodfellow withdrew the silk cloth, the bullet emerged with it. 'It was then seen', he reported, 'that [the silk] had been carried in by the ball.'

That bullet he then tracked through the left ventricle of the heart, down the aorta and all the way through the body of the unfortunate gambler's vertebra, which it had fractured before lodging itself in the spinal canal. Storms had been wearing a light summer suit, in which, Goodfellow realized, 'a silk handkerchief had been placed into its breast pocket'. In its passage from the breast pocket through the body and to the inside of Charlie Storms' spine, 'examination of the handkerchief showed only two slight tears or cuts in it, they being on the outside of the fold containing the bullet, where it had struck the bones of the vertebral column, no ribs having been touched . . .' He noted that there were two thicknesses of silk covering the bullet, no doubt due to the sartorial habit that left the deceased wearing an elegantly folded pocket handkerchief on his last day on earth. 'Had the handkerchief not been in the way', Goodfellow concluded, 'the bullet would have gone entirely through the body.'

The reason this had so surprised Goodfellow, as both doctor and coroner, was that he had seen illustrated many times that a bullet fired from the distance at which Storms was shot 'ordinarily goes through the body, bones or no bones . . .' He had seen the bone of the upper arm and part of a vertebra that had been fractured from a distance of 120 feet, despite that bullet having to pass through its victim's overcoat, two shirts and the waistband of his trousers. And then there was another at a distance of sixty feet, a shot entering the largest part of the lower leg bone that then travelled up through the thigh, burying itself an inch deep into its bone, 'after piercing leather boot-top, canvas overall and drawers'. A sound scientist, Goodfellow had also set about forensic experiments outside the human body: a bullet fired into a four-inch plank of pine or redwood from the same distance at which Storms was shot, that 'readily passed through, and sinks into another a foot behind';

and one which 'at fourteen feet the same calibre ball penetrated a six-inch pine joist, and struck the ground some twenty feet beyond, with force enough to flatten the ball . . .'

And yet, Goodfellow had witnessed the bullet that had hit Storms with such force, 'propelled from the same barrels, and by the same amount of powder, penetrated the tissues described, yet failed to go through four or six folds of thin silk'. Evidently, Storms' silken handkerchief had not been enough to save the gambler, but that was the point. The fact that the silk was barely damaged while Storms had died – when wool, cotton, canvas and leather had proved no deterrent at all – now captured Goodfellow's full attention. He began noting the misfortunes of others who had silk on their person when they came, injured or dead, onto whatever makeshift operating table he happened to be using at the time. Those cases, detailed in a medical report, which he entitled *Notes on the impenetrability of silk to bullets*, would also feature other instances in which the silk had not been pierced at all. During the fight, when Deputy Sheriff 'Helldorado' sprayed Billy Grounds at a distance of thirty feet with a loaded shotgun, Goodfellow noted how four of the shots penetrated the frontal bone of the outlaw's head, flattening themselves against the back of the skull; 'more entered the face, piercing the facial bones, and some passed through the upper thoracic wall, thence into the lungs'. And yet, between the four to six folds of a red Chinese silk handkerchief Billy had tied loosely about his neck, Goodfellow found two of the pieces of buckshot that had rained down on him, 'neither of which had so much as cut a fibre of the silk'. Evidently a man who dressed up for a fight, apart from his fine Chinese silk scarf Billy had turned up with his fellow outlaws sporting a thick, Mexican white felt hat that was heavily embroidered with silver, with an inch-thick silver wire snake for a hatband. He also wore two heavy wool shirts, over which was the classic blanket-lined canvas coat and waistcoat of the Wild West. Even untrimmed, that fancy hat weighed in at twelve ounces – not far off half a kilogram. 'The thickness and weight of these hats', in Goodfellow's words, 'can only be realized by those who have seen and worn them.' Perhaps it was meant to double as a helmet, but it was through his metal hatband that two bullets had penetrated the man's skull, and through the heavy clothing that they passed into the sternum and deep into his chest. It was necessary to understand the outfit in which he died, the doctor stressed, because he had now seen beyond doubt that, somehow, 'a few layers of light silk . . . were enough to stop bullets that could pass through all the tissues mentioned'.

Tests of Zeglen's bulletproof vest.

Twenty-seven years later, in Sarajevo, then under Austrian rule, a silk bulletproof vest invented by a Polish priest, which may have been based on Goodfellow's research, was said to have found its way into the wardrobe of Archduke Franz Ferdinand, heir to the throne of the Austro-Hungarian Empire. If he did indeed own such a garment, on the morning of 28 June 1914 Ferdinand neglected to wear it; or at least no physical evidence of it was found on his person on that fateful day. At about 10.45 am, he was shot in the back seat of an open-topped touring car. The assassin was a disgruntled young Serbian named Gavrilo Princip who served a group known as 'Unification or Death'. Princip's bullet entered just above Ferdinand's right collarbone, hit his internal jugular vein and finally lodged, much like the ball that had killed Charlie Storms, in the Archduke's spine. Next to him, Sophie, Duchess of Hohenberg, had taken a bullet to her stomach.

But before their attendants could carry her from the car and lay her upon the Governor of Bosnia's chaise longue, Sophie was dead. It was for the governor that Sophie's bullet had been intended, but Princip had only a month's experience of using a gun. With little recollection of where he had even aimed, the nervous 19-year-old had, from a distance of about two metres, hit and killed his targets entirely randomly. In the immediate aftermath, Princip's cyanide capsule failed him, and he eventually died in prison of tuberculosis. A month after the assassination, on 28 July 1914, Austria-Hungary retaliated by declaring war on Serbia. Germany invaded France, via Belgium. In August, Britain declared war on Germany; and in Munich's Odeonsplatz a young Adolf Hitler cheered. Having studiously avoided conscription into the Austro-Hungarian army, he now voluntarily signed up to serve the German Bavarian Reserve Regiment instead. With his serendipitous shot, Princip had also helped trigger the outbreak of the First World War, a tragedy that caused the death of around forty million people, and from which Hitler would emerge with a few particularly pernicious preoccupations to heartily pursue in his future career.

. . .

Casimir Zeglen was born Kazimierz Żegleń in 1869 in a part of Poland which had long ago been absorbed into an expanding Austrian Empire. Like Hitler, he had no intention of being conscripted into the Austrian army; unlike Hitler, Zeglen was a pacifist who grew from a deeply religious child into a member of a monastic order. After some months in Rome, he was sent to America, where he began his service in Chicago's St Stanislaus Kostka Roman Catholic church. It was Chicago that would lead him to invent, and submit the first patent for, a bulletproof vest of silk, armour that was to be acquired by the kind of men who brought a glint to the eyes of assassins, from humble mayors, to elected presidents, to emperors across the western world. The German Emperor, the King of England and the President of France were said to own Zeglen's bulletproof vests. Zeglen first came up with the idea on the day the mayor of Chicago was shot on his doorstep, on 28 October 1893. Reports called the assassin 'a madman', and even in America – long accustomed to violent death by firearms – it was seen as a shocking crime. 'The sensitive priest was shocked more than most people', one journalist wrote, 'because it occurred to him that there must be some way to create bullet-proof clothing that would protect people who, by their position, are most vulnerable to fanatics' attacks.' Less than two months later, Zeglen began tests to create his soft body armour, with a hope, and no doubt a prayer, that he would be able to design a product of silk 'of great usefulness to the world'. After

Goodfellow-esque tests on planks of wood and more macabre ones on dogs and human cadavers 'dressed in Zeglen cloth', the priest also stood in the line of fire himself. By then he had seen, as Genghis Khan and Goodfellow had before him, that raw silk had the technical capacity to resist the puncture of a fast-travelling missile designed to kill, so long as it was correctly woven and thick enough. After he was shot point-blank five times, as requested, with a .32-calibre revolver and a .44-calibre Colt, Zeglen smiled and reported that these had 'produced a temporary stinging sensation, that was all', as if 'someone had poked him in the ribs with his knuckles'; and 'hurt no more than if someone had given him a light poke with a cane'.

It was a trial of which Archduke Ferdinand would have done well to take note, especially as Princip's assassination attempt was by no means the first. In 2014, a series of replicas of the silk vest Ferdinand might have had access to was made in England by the Royal Armouries to Zeglen's patent specifications. The ammunition and weapon were similar to those used by Princip, and it was amply demonstrated that the bullet would have passed clean through the wool jacket and the canvas and angora layers of the armour that padded the wearer against the full force of a bullet's impact. Zeglen's layers of silk – had the assassin's lucky shot not hit his victim above the collarbone – would have stopped Princip's 'shot heard around the world'. In the Royal Armouries' test, the silken layers had stopped the bullet in its tracks. As for Duchess Sophie, there is no doubt that, had she been fitted with Zeglen's silks, she would have survived.

It was not the first time that such an oversight had had a devastating effect. Thirteen years earlier, the twenty-fifth president of the United States of America, William McKinley, was greeting visitors to the Pan-American Exposition in Buffalo, New York, when one of them extended a gun instead of an outstretched hand. The president, who, like Sophie, was shot in the stomach, died soon after. Just a few weeks before, Zeglen had offered his armour to the White House. The presidential secretary, who was present at the assassination, had turned that offer down.

Zeglen had at times been secretive about his invention, which was not entirely surprising as his own business partner was eventually dismissed for patent theft. That silk was its key protective component, however, was never in any doubt. This partner, known as the 'Polish Edison', had described how 'the method of weaving adopted paralyses concussion by distributing the shock over the entire area of the garment'. 'Of course', he added, 'the material is especially selected for the purpose.'

In the wondrous metamorphosis of *Bombyx mori*, the four cycles of moulting and growing begin to be embellished by tiny amounts of silk as they start, and when they end. At the beginning of each stage that silk keeps the little caterpillars from falling from the place where they attach themselves to feed; at the end, it helps to hold them firm, so that they can cast off their old larval skins. By the time they craft their cocoons, they will have produced ten kinds of silk. These have distinct strengths and qualities. But in the making of all of them, deep within that silk slowly engineered through time by the desires of humans, are particular sequences and complexes of tiny building blocks that coalesce to build the chains of its fibroin protein. This sequence is a signature for the silk of this insect, in particular. Its chains come together in a determined ratio, with a hierarchy of structures arranged in a very specific pattern. Fibroin strands are the primary source of such strength and ability to stretch that allowed even the finest of woven silks to avert arrows, and then bullets – strands at a scale a thousand times smaller than a millimetre, at least four times smaller than the human eye is able to see.

The special selection of this material by Zeglen had begun further back in time than either he or his partner could ever have imagined. The astonishing properties of silk had been at least two hundred million years in the making; almost two hundred million years before the first stone-tipped missiles would ever be crafted. It had been a natural selection in the bodies of the ancestors of *Bombyx mori* that created silken strands with a structure so tightly and efficiently formed that it would withstand up to twice the force cotton could before it fractured. Even under the most precarious circumstances, these were threads more likely to deform than to break.

25

MIMIC MEN

AFTER THE MANY VICISSITUDES OF SPIDER SILK SPANNING CENTURIES OF trials, the 1970s brought a renewed interest, and by 1982, with a nod to the past and a firm eye on the future, two scientists at North Carolina State University developed a new 'apparatus and technique for the forcible silking of spiders'. For Robert Work and Paul Emerson this was part of a continuing programme of research on silk fibres produced from the major ampullate gland systems of orb-web spinning spiders. It is from those sac-like glands that 'dragline silk' emerges – the fibre that forms the radial lines that frame the web and acts as the safety line for a falling spider. Relatively easy to reel, flexible and lightweight, this dragline silk possesses outstanding mechanical properties, surpassing the most sophisticated man-made fibres – three times as tough as the heat-resistant aramid fibres used in aerospace, the military applications, and as fabric for ballistic-rated body armour; five times stronger by weight than steel. 'It cannot be known who first discovered that such silk also can be forcibly drawn from immobilized spiders', the scientists said – because they did not know about the studies of Termeyer, for he was a man destined to be forgotten. But they were aware of Wilder, stating that he 'described the method' in 1868 with the spiders he had found in South Carolina, a method which by the 1970s, for researchers at least, had become 'the normal means of securing large samples'.

For the scientists, the apparatus consisted of microscopes and illuminators, micro-dissecting kits and a motor-driven mandrel upon which to reel the silk. For the spiders, it was in the form of a tiny 'operating table' much like Termeyer's, with two staggered needles embedded in a wooden supporting rod, self-adhesive tape to immobilize their legs, tweezers to extend them, facial tissue to stop them struggling, and carbon dioxide, which was to anaesthetize them to prevent them causing injury to themselves. This step, which Wilder had not taken, made it more difficult to extract a silk strand to begin the process of reeling, because the sleepy spider would not respond to the stroking of its spinnerets. But what was more, it had become clear in the mid-1970s that the physical properties of silk extracted from a spider under anaesthetic actually differed from that emerging from an alert animal. But at least enough of it could still be teased out and reeled for later studies.

In 1990, Randy Lewis, a biochemist who had joined the Molecular Biology Department of the University of Wyoming, put in an order for some *Nephila clavipes* spiders, and, inspired by Work and Emerson's idea, designed an apparatus to draw a single silk fibre from one spinneret of the spider, wrapped it on a spool and pulled out around one milligram of pure silk with the help of a variable-speed electric drill. Lewis did not need much silk, because his interest was in understanding reasons for the unique mechanical properties of spider silk rather than the mass production of anything in particular. These were animals, he wrote, which were unique because of the use of silks throughout their life span and their almost total dependence on silk for their evolutionary success; which had been using protein-based nanomaterials with the ability to self-assemble into fibres and sheets for over 450 million years. Theirs were fibres that combined tensile strength with elasticity, which allowed a web to hold prey while being resilient enough not to break upon impact. And yet, it was still unclear quite how spiders were able to do this. Virtually nothing was known about the silk proteins themselves. So Lewis began determining the make-up of spider silk proteins; he worked on understanding how the distinct mechanical properties of different spider silks were specifically gained through the way in which their protein modules came together like building blocks to construct those very special threads. And he used genetic engineering to mix those modules in specific proportions, to begin to design new proteins, based upon the spiders', that had a defined strength and elasticity. In these would be the potential for new applications both in medicine and in engineering. It was an interesting approach to the problem of spiders not willing to be farmed for their silk due to their territorial nature, and because they were likely to eat each other. In the eighteenth century it was an issue that, for Réaumur, had proved insurmountable.

In the twentieth century Randy Lewis was encountering the same problem. Apart from which, the fact that spiders' webs were made out of more than one type of silk meant that the best strategy for collecting it was not from webs but extracting it directly from the spider. And that he found an incredibly tedious task, and one that he wouldn't wish on anyone. But, by the 1990s, scientists would have new tools to help them circumvent such spidery challenges, which was when efforts were made to generate spider silk proteins synthetically. Instead of spider farming, what Lewis and others were trying to do was 'match as best we can what the spider does, trying to mimic the production system of a spider'. And yet, outside of the tiny amounts needed for laboratory experiments, the eternal problem of insufficient quantities remained, because in reality only tiny amounts were being generated. For any industrial application, the quantities needed could not be produced, or at least not affordably. For Lewis, they were 'not even in the ballpark in terms of something that would be practical'.

And then, on 18 January 2002, a group of scientists based at Nexia Biotechnologies in Quebec, Canada, and the Materials Science Team of the US Army Soldier Biological Chemical Command, Massachusetts, published a study in which they had sought to mimic the process of spider silk production – except, this time, in a seemingly bizarre move, from cells taken from two mammals. There was sound rationale in those choices, however. The mammary cells of cows were selected because breast cells are already wonderful at secreting other things, like milk proteins; and also the kidney cells of baby hamsters, since these were already known to produce massive amounts of laboratory-modified proteins. These two cell types were made to generate proteins using instructions encoded by two key genes taken from spiders. They were known as MaSpI and MaSpII – which are spider silk fibroin, or 'Spidroin' genes. Specifically, they encoded the instructions needed to build structural proteins that form the immensely strong dragline silk.

In and of itself, the concept of inserting genes from one organism into an entirely different one was neither novel nor unexpected as a next move to force greater production of a desired protein. That type of experimentation went back to 1928, starting with the studies that showed a living cell could take up, and use, the genetic information from another cell of the same type. In 1972, proof came that this capacity could be extended to introduce foreign DNA into a mammalian cell; that DNA sequences from different species might be mixed and matched, regardless of how distantly related their species of origin might be.

And so, just as the scientific team that set out to mimic spider silk production had hoped, silk proteins similar to those observed in the spider's silk glands were indeed produced from the cells of both hamsters and cows. Furthermore, the researchers were then able to spin the harvested proteins they had constructed into small amounts of strong, lightweight fibres, succeeding where before there had only been disappointment, on the occasions where they had tried inserting the genes into bacteria, yeast and plants, in which their silk proteins merely clumped together, and could be persuaded only to become brittle fibres at best. The mammal cell experiments brought new hope to a decade of frustrated trials, which had been 'agonizingly slow', as a fibre-spinning expert with the US Army Soldier Biological Chemical Command had put it.

Randy Lewis was watching these studies closely, too, and thought that such work was highly encouraging because it now opened up not only new avenues for research but also for the practical use of the quantities of silk produced that way, which is what, after all, would have mattered to the military. These quantities of spider silk protein produced through this research, though still small, should have been enough for trials to create a few small structures that could be implanted into the human body: tendons and ligaments and sutures for eyes, or for use in delicate neurological surgeries where the extraordinary properties of thread fine enough for intricate work, that could biodegrade, and yet be strong, and smart enough to support the body's healing, might be put to use.

But the team's next steps seemed even more interesting, because these held new promise of generating amounts of spider silk proteins that would actually be needed to fabricate high-strength composites and soft, flexible bulletproof clothing that could be worn by soldiers and police, and in the quantities of which Wilder had only dreamed. It would need about sixty miles of spider silk to knit one thin shirt. Such a scale would not just involve the genetic modification of animal cells simply immersed in small, transparent laboratory dishes. This time, Lewis' lab began working with those scientists on what would become the next stage of their plans – to produce the modified spider silk genes from the mammary cells, into the udders, and out of the milk of actual living goats that would be dubbed 'spider-goats'.

Using only a partial sequence of the MaSpI and MaSpII spidroin genes, rather than the full run utilized by an actual spider, the beautiful white goats selected to be modified were short-legged and long-eared, less expensive to maintain than cows, and smaller, so that they could be accommodated more easily on the university campus. These particular goats were derived from animals once brought from the Saanen Valley in Switzerland, where they had been selectively bred as dairy goats for several hundred years, during which time they produced milk in quantity – and in that milk a desirable percentage of goat-milk protein. Now, of course, the idea was that those quantities would also include the spider proteins the goats' genes had been modified to carry, from which the strongest fibres of spider silk were formed, which could then be easily harvested when the animals were milked. From the liquid milk, the spider silk proteins would be separated out, dried and gathered. And then the scientists would have to redissolve it, and attempt to do as the spiders did – to spin liquid into fine fibres. It sounded relatively straightforward, except that there appeared to be something very particular that happened in the spinnerets of a spider when the liquid silk was turned into thread.

That process involved a fine folding of the silk proteins into particular patterns. And such patterns of folding were vital because they contributed to the exquisite properties of the webs the spiders produce. The problem was, Lewis noticed, that the goats were only able to go so far with the spider's proteins. When processed in the spider's own body, the same protein undergoes a completely different process. With the spider silk protein taken from the milk of these goats, 'clearly', he says, 'we have to isolate the protein, we have to purify it, and then we have to reconstitute it and spin fibres. And the answer there is obviously we don't know how to do it exactly the way the spider is doing it.' Although, at least mechanically, the liquid spider silk produced by some fifty little goats at Utah State University was a 'reasonable' version of another animal's silk, it was clear to Lewis that it was not as good as the natural version. That, he thinks, 'has much to do with the fact that the protein we have in the goats is not nearly as large as the natural one. It was far more truncated. It was one fifth of the natural length.'

And so the patented spider goats became famous, and then infamous, because after all the fanfare afforded these remarkable creatures, the like of which had never before existed, this experiment would ultimately fail to deliver what it had set out to do. If spiders themselves had proved uncooperative and unwilling to be farmed, a spider-goat herd of sufficient size would also prove impossible to bring together. Some twenty years after the idea had been conceived, the little white goats that roamed happily in Utah were being phased out as furry factories for spider silk. Some of their embryos, semen and eggs would be frozen to allow the system to restart, just in case, one day, the great obstacle to creating goats that could produce real spider silk could be overcome. Because, as efforts were made to improve silk production in the goats, Lewis found, the team also started running into other problems with the spider's genes not remaining stable outside the spider. Plus, trying to breed more goats from the ones found to be most productive for making spider silk protein in their milk was also proving trickier than had been anticipated. The trouble with trying to take just their best producing goats and breed them was that 'frequently the offspring were never as good as the parents . . .' The team even made clones. It was 'a set of three clones from a very high producing female – and none of them was as good as she was', Lewis says. 'And they were *clones*.' That was when the team conceded that it looked like it would be 'pretty unlikely we were going to be able to expand the herd and produce very large quantities'.

Part of the problem was that the goats, not being spiders, would have randomly inserted the specific spidroin genes into their genome and not quite have known what to make of them. Like all silks, those spidroin silk proteins read from the MaSpI and MaSpII genes have an architecture that usually consists of a long, repetitive structure at their centre. Their protein sequences are dominated by a pattern of building blocks repeated over and over again. It is extraordinarily monotonous to look at. And yet, the supreme strength of the dragline silk these give rise to is entirely dependent upon the monotony of that sequence.

That kind of pattern repeated in the silk of the spider is also seen in silkworms. And that repetition tells of a complicated evolutionary history in which the genes that encode silk became duplicated and then brought together. Over these past events, silk sequences combined to generate repeats over and over again.

That, Lewis says, was 'what hangs things up, that these protein and DNA sequences are very repetitive. And that causes trouble for organisms', by which he means mammals, like goats, in which silk production was destined for failure, because their cells did not know how to handle and process and fold the repetitive silk proteins. In one sense, they might have been able to process these foreign proteins, simply because they are so related to the keratin that forms our hair, skin, nails and connective tissues. And yet, the strength and properties of silk, moth or spider, are so unlike anything that mammals can naturally make.

And that was what took the quest for a factory for the extraordinary silk fibres of territorial, cannibalistic, generally unfarmable spiders, right back to the silkworms. After all, these little caterpillars were very good at being cultivated en masse; for *Bombyx mori* at least, they had been created, and bred, to do exactly that. In any case, Lewis thought, there'd already been a pretty impressive business built around them for a few thousand years. 'The silkworms are far more promising if you want to make fibres because you don't have to do anything. All you have to do is unwrap the cocoon and start the work . . . and that wasn't *our* invention.' So his team inserted multiple spider silk proteins into *Bombyx mori*, this time including not a partial gene, but close to a full-length sequence needed for the dragline silk protein, designed so that it was less likely to interfere either with the use of those genes by the silkworm, or the silkworms' own process of generating silk. Lewis was able to look at the structure of the spider proteins made from the body of the silkworm, and found that they basically looked the same as they did in the spider. And that meant that the silkworm appeared to be able to duplicate the particular way in which the spinnerets of spiders fold the silk proteins into an arrangement that gives the dragline such wondrous mechanical properties.

Despite that fact, one issue still remained – that this spider silk, now folded as though it had been made by an actual spider, was emerging not as pure spider silk but as a strange blend of spider silk, and silkworm silk. That was because what Lewis' team had found was that in order to assemble the whole thing they had to use some of the silkworm proteins. That was the only way to get it to assemble correctly. But for reasons that the scientists didn't fully understand, they could only put a certain percentage of spider silk into the cocoon. It was true that the end result was that the mechanical properties of the silk they got out of it were very similar to those of the dragline silk of the spider. But – the silk itself – that was only '30–40% spider silk and roughly 60% silkworm silk'. Still, the problem of making enough of it – whatever 'it' now was – became less of a problem because as much of it could be produced as they were willing to grow the modified silkworms. For the purposes of Lewis' lab, they were not doing it on any kind of a commercial scale. In order to be able to produce silk for their studies, they were routinely raising a thousand cocoons. That would provide between 600 and 900 kilometres of silk thread, although, as he had seen, less than half of that might actually be considered genuine runs of spider silk. Still, 'the silkworm clearly is the way to go, if you want to make fibres, but that's only for fibres . . .'

Such fibres that come from the spider-silkworm threads could undoubtedly be useful, and Lewis sees new uses for two ancient silks never before brought together in one organism. 'Combining the silk with other kinds of modifications we can make to the spider silk proteins to put new functionality – whether that's antibacterial, anticlotting, having a surface that's smoother than what we make now – I think there are lots of things we can do and still base it around producing it in silkworms, because we know that that's a cheap way to make fibres.' Because, as history has shown only too well, 'until you can produce it cheap enough, it's not gonna do the job'.

But generating spider silk, or at least parts thereof wrapped tightly into threads, creates another problem, because there is a limit to what can be done with ready-made threads. Silk's traditional use in merely weaving textiles or felting webs, or even using simple threads as surgical sutures, is not entirely what twenty-first-century scientists had in mind for such an extraordinary biological material. Instead, alternative formats like films and adhesives were anticipated, so that a variety of materials with numerous technological applications might be moulded, printed or formulated.

If small parts of spider silk from the udders of goats emerge as a liquid that can then be separated out, then trying to work backwards to separate out spider silk proteins from a mixed *Bombyx mori*-spider dragline fibre already wrapped into a silkworm cocoon, is, Lewis says, 'a bigger problem than anything else. I mean it's just never going to be possible to do that.' His forecast is that, except for using the fibres, really inexpensive production of any other applications is still not possible yet. 'So then you go back to how do you make it? Is there something we haven't figured out yet?'

The question of why the problems of producing quantities of at least spider silk that would see it widely and economically used for medical and technological applications hasn't yet been solved is one Lewis gets asked all the time. 'It's put off a lot of people . . . why, if you've been working on it for thirty years – why's anybody else going to be able to solve it? . . . I mean there is some truth in that', he concedes. But science does not always move rapidly. In fact, innovations that do may be the exception rather than the rule, or the result of very particular circumstances: wars, pandemics, moments when funds are thrown at a problem and minds become finely focused. More often, scientific progress is just tiresomely incremental.

Lewis' team may not have solved all their challenges yet; but starting from a background of knowing virtually nothing about silk proteins, to what they've been able to discover about all of them – being able to look at the protein sequences, to begin to understand how it is the spider uses them for various purposes – that, Lewis says, is probably what he has enjoyed the most. More than that, they had 'sort of got the fibre end figured out', and feel that in those threads is where real progress is possible. On other applications that require silk to be produced in forms like liquid, answers are yet to be found. 'So it will remain to be seen whether somebody comes up with the magic potion. You've gotta believe somebody's going to figure it out somewhere. It's just that nobody's done it yet, and fewer and fewer people are working on it.' As it has remained for some four hundred years, for spider silk to be put to full use in medicine and technology, Lewis maintains, the breakthrough is cheap production. This may come from his genetically modified *Bombyx mori* silkworms that now partially create arachnid silk along with their own.

Lewis' lab also worked with the genes of an even more bizarre animal, the slime-secreting, eel-shaped Atlantic hagfish. The hagfish experiments had come about because they had been contacted by the navy who were interested in its applications. It turned out that slime could actually be manipulated, made into a protein-based fibre or formatted into sheets. It was not quite as good as spider silk, they found, but it was not bad, with a strength of around 70 per cent of spider silk's. That, Lewis thought, for a biological fibre, was pretty impressive. Hagfish slime was usually secreted from a gland in the animal that, under normal conditions, produced only a small amount. Their next step was to develop a system to generate more of it, once again by taking hagfish genes, and putting another organism which would serve as a factory for it. Fortuitously, Lewis says, E. coli bacteria do this with great efficiency. 'We have no idea why, but they are very proficient at being able to make hagfish fibres.'

But when it comes to the silk of spiders, just as it had been with the scientists who came before him, Lewis remains pragmatic. 'No one ever really anticipated that it would be that difficult to produce it at a reasonable cost. If you'd asked me ten years ago, could we do it in five years? I'd have said I was sure we could. And you know, it hasn't happened. And it's not just us, it's everybody in the field.'

26

THE SILKS OF NEARLY ANYTHING

THE FIELD OF UNDERSTANDING THE INCREDIBLE POTENTIAL OF SILKS is not a particularly crowded place, but those who have embarked on its scientific study seem to become appropriately enmeshed in these threads of wonder. For even longer than Randy Lewis, Professor Fritz Vollrath has been studying its potential, and making the journey towards biomedical and other applications that began to emerge as his research developed. His silk lab at the University of Oxford started up around 1979. At that time, Vollrath wasn't focusing so much on silk as on the mechanics of spider webs. Those webs led him to a lifelong interest in the material of silk, which began in earnest around 1988. Vollrath first began working with *Araneus* spiders, and then the golden threads of the *Nephila*. Soon he was working on any species, studying 'the silks of nearly anything you could lay your hands on'. That 'anything' even included a small shrimp-like animal called *Crassicorophium bonellii*, which interested his lab because 'it basically spins a thread, but the thread itself is much more like a barnacle glue'. Specifically, in strength and in elasticity that glue-like material was somewhere between the kind of cement barnacles use to affix themselves to rocks and ships' hulls – and spider silk. The 'shrimp' processes that glue in a gland, much as liquid silk is processed internally in spiders and silkworms, and then it emerges via tiny openings near its leg, where it is spun into fibres.

And that was very different, Vollrath found, from the enormous *Pinna nobilis* mollusc and its mussel-like relatives, whose byssus threads are not actually spun, but blow-moulded in the foot, and then flipped out. That extrusion moulding of the byssus thread, the way *Pinna* makes it, 'that is very sophisticated precisely because they are not spun. They grow.' Indeed, in 2014, threads like that of *Pinna nobilis* had been used by another group of scientists at the University of California, Santa Barbara as the inspiration for creating a new polymer that could not only repair itself – 'self-heal' – if damaged, but do so underwater, under conditions in which adhesives would normally struggle to set.

Vollrath's main focus, however, would remain on his spiders. And then he also began working with the silk of the wild tasar moth, the *Antheraea*. He chose the *Antheraea* rather than the *Bombyx* because wild silkworms evolved independently from the domesticated *Bombyx mori* silkworm. While the *Bombyx* lost much that it would need to survive in the wild along the road to its domestication, wild moths continued adapting to cope with the trials of their natural environments. Adaptations occurred to protect their delicate, succulent silkworm pupae as they metamorphosed, defenceless, from the threats of physical attack from animals; from bacteria and other organisms that might bring disease; and from the endless other dangers to which they might be exposed. As a result, those silk fibres of the *Antheraea* displayed breaking stress and toughness of the same magnitude as spider major ampullate silks – that is, the coveted properties of the dragline silk of spiders that had so diligently avoided being farmed.

Vollrath's early interest was in collecting and studying silks simply to understand the science and properties of the material rather than to make anything with it. As word of his research spread, he says, 'slowly you have people asking, well, what can we do with it? Then you collaborate with people who actually will try to make things.' One of those things would become materials made from silk, and destined for the repair of damaged structures inside the human body. Having tested them in the laboratory, and finding them to be effective for such repair, Vollrath's silk innovations went into the clinic, at least as far as human trials, in which his silk was tested for use in the repair of cartilage. But it did not successfully get past those trials, and, therefore, never made it onto the general market. Despite this, because of its efficacy, it has since been used in nerve repair procedures in humans, an outcome that was only possible in cases of 'compassionate use', which means that it was adopted for use as a treatment option despite being unauthorized. That sort of application of a product still under development is only permitted under strict conditions, and only in patients who have a disease with no satisfactory, authorized therapies, and who cannot enter clinical trials. 'So you can't really publish that', Vollrath says. Publishing experiments is how science progresses, so that others can understand what Vollrath had done, exactly how he did it, and try to do it themselves, as a check on the validity of what might otherwise be nothing more than one laboratory's claim. Added to which, compassionate use will be restricted to a small number of patients. To say with any good probability that a treatment is effective usually requires closer to one hundred patients, and ideally even more than that. Nevertheless, the small number of patients who did have their nerves repaired using silk implants has been followed up. And it seems to work – but, Vollrath still cautions, 'you have to do it in proper trials. Or people do not trust it.' Even if a small proportion of people have an immune response to it, he says, 'even if it's one per cent, we would consider it small, but if you roll it out to ten thousand or one hundred thousand people, then one per cent is a lot of people, so you have to be so careful. Someone's quality of life is so important. Putting the silk in looks like it will work from animal trials, but humans have a very sophisticated immune system.'

That great advantage of silk, as harnessed by Genghis Khan in the East and Dr George Emory Goodfellow in the Wild West, is that it is an animal protein; that it is already related to the keratin protein that we produce and possess; that it can, therefore, easily be integrated into our own bodies; that it is biodegradable – all these can also become an immense disadvantage if that silk ends up triggering an unmanageable immune response once implanted inside a human. And if the silk were to integrate into our tissues, triggered an immune response and then could not be separated out, that would be unconscionable.

Knowing why and from which specific part of silk the immune challenge arises is key. That seems to be as the result of one particular component of the silk, that adhesive, or cement-like sericin protein that binds the two strands of silkworm fibroin proteins together. But the sophistication of our immune systems makes the whole issue of placing foreign objects inside the body with the object of healing, or repairing, a little bit more complex. It is not, for example, a case of all or nothing. As Vollrath puts it, 'you want a little bit of a challenge'. This, he says, is the interesting thing. The fact that the sericin challenges the immune system is in itself not bad, because that would raise an immune response locally. And that local response, in turn, may lead to tissue regeneration. 'But if it overwhelms the immune system then that's not good', he says. 'Then you have a fight there. Total non-challenging, or total inert, neither is the best way forward. So it's a tricky one . . . In the medical field *Bombyx mori* silk has been used forever as a suture material, obviously, and it's fine. If it was an eye operation, you just take it out. But if you put it deep inside the body and you want it actually to stimulate regeneration? You have to clean the sericin off, the question is how clean can you get it and that, really, is the issue here.'

The problem was that Vollrath found it very difficult to remove the sericin from *Bombyx mori* silk without affecting the structure of the material itself, the integrity, and therefore the properties of the fibroin silk strands. However, in the *Antheraea* there is a slightly different sericin, which he says still needs to be removed, and removed carefully. But there are ways of doing it. 'And we have managed to do it. So we can actually get it off, I think, so you don't have any on it. At least any that you can detect. But of course the immune system is much cleverer at detection than we are with our chemicals.' Still, it was for this reason that Vollrath's team focused on *Antheraea* – 'because it has properties that we think are more interesting for medical applications than *Bombyx* silk, and we believe that we can clean it so there is no evidence of sericin on it'. That, in turn, makes him feel more comfortable about taking wild silk into human trials than commercial *Bombyx* silk.

The thing about spider silk, however, and one of the reasons for which it holds hope for medical applications, is that it does not have sericin. The spider has no need of it. The silks of its web can be made sticky by other means. Orb web spiders hold prey on their webs using a viscid, elastic 'capture silk' fibre, on which are glue droplets arranged like beads on a string. This was something that Vollrath studied early on, something that his work demonstrated to be an entirely new class of materials. 'Initially when we published it people said, ah, this is really interesting. Then the physicists said it can't work, it's impossible.' But there it was emerging from the nether regions of a spider, for which it did work for its own purpose of capturing prey. It was this discovery that has made Vollrath most proud, that 'out of studying a strange silk in a spider you come up with a new class of material. And that has all sorts of potential applications for microtechnology for soft robotics. I don't know how. I don't know how, but somehow.

While these new discoveries are being made and applications for them identified, the quest to harness an old class of materials, the silk of spiders for textiles, has never abated. Quite spectacularly, in the mid 2000s, Simon Peers, a British textile expert based in Madagascar, and Nicholas Godley, an American designer, embarked on a project that would culminate in the production of a radiant collection of fabrics made entirely from the silk of the Madagascan Golden Orb spider. Peers had studied the old attempts of Camboué (and his predecessors, like Termeyer, and successors, like Wilder) carefully, and though Termeyer could only have dreamed of such a result, the rare copy of one of his works Peers found and purchased became a source not just of historic interest, but inspiration towards what he was about to create. It would take a team of over eighty people who spent years collecting the spiders, harnessing them, and extracting from their bodies threads hundreds of feet in length, before freeing them to go about their spiderly business. None of it was easy. Peers recalls early attempts in which women from the team would go out and fill baskets with copius numbers of spiders, only to return, open the receptacle, and find that 'only one, very happy-looking spider remained'. By the time issues of collection, trial and errors of extracting the silk, and cannibalism were solved, it had taken well over a million spiders, and some four years to collect enough of the golden threads to twist together and string onto looms. In 2012, the magnificent capes and traditional lamba shawls that shone in an astonishing shade of golden yellow were shown to spellbound visitors at museums and galleries around the world, including London's Victoria and Albert Museum and the Museum of Natural History in New York.

None of the extraordinary effort it took its creators had been in pursuit of a financial profit, through producing such quantities that could be sold as clothing. Because as had been the experience of every single prospector of spider silk in the past, the cost of acquiring enough silk to create textiles of any substantial size would scarcely make good business sense.

As a case in point, one business seeking to make sustainable clothing with the silk of spiders is doing that quite without the silking spiders themselves. Although there is no doubt that would come as some relief to these arachnids across the world, the aim of working with spider silk was part of their mission to identify materials to 'solve the problems of a resource-constrained world'. Bolt, founded in California in 2009, started with a team that included a bioengineer, a biophysicist and a biochemist, who had set out to create textiles kinder to the environment. Among them was a 'mushroom' leather, created from mycelium, a network of fungal threads, that they farmed in a vertical facility. It has already been used by Adidas to craft a new version of their classic Stan Smith trainers, and by Stella McCartney, who made a line of luxury, vegan-leather handbags launched on the atelier's runway in the summer of 2022. In a similar vein, Microsilk™ was to be their silk-like textile inspired by spider silk. Referred to as a biosynthetic fibre, its creation considered what exactly it was about the silk of spiders that gave its incredible high tensile strength, elasticity, and softness, and sought to apply that in a product that was not, at least directly, created by spiders. The research and development of their version of a material that hoped to incorporate these similar characteristics involved the fermenting of yeast with spider DNA. Whatever the composition of the textile produced in that process, it has now been used to craft prototype products, which were knitted from the threads produced. These included ties in shade of blue and pink and red, conceived as a nod to the wrapped neck cloth, presumably of *Bombyx silk*, worn in 210 BCE by Emperor Shih Huang Ti's Terracotta Army. It also nodded to Louis XIV of France, a man partial to colourful silk ties, in all likelihood made of the silk of the *Bombyx mori* his country had been so successful at cultivating, but which, the company says, was a look inspired by the garb of Croatian soldiers. There was also a knitted dress that, as if in tribute to the webs of the great Golden Orb spider, was finished in a golden yellow hue, and shown in 2017 at New York's Museum of Modern Art.

Though these creations are undoubtedly exquisite, sustainable, and, at least for Bolt, created without using spiders at all – Fritz Vollrath still thinks there is more potential for yet more incredible innovations to be drawn from its wonderous threads. A few clever ideas have surfaced over recent years, albeit producing only prototypes. In London, England, in 2016, a composite material that used strands of the golden silk of an Australian Golden Orb spider was used to impregnate the top side of a violin, which, its inventor found, enabled its acoustics to be customized, by exploiting the resonating properties of spiders' silk. In 2018, graphene, essentially a layer of carbon an atom-thick, and one of the thinnest, lightest, strongest and most conductive materials to have been discovered, was fed to *Bombyx mori* silkworms. The idea, once again, was to create a material with the properties of spider silk, but without having to deal with spiders. The aim was to craft a super-super-material, not just strong and sustainable, but conductive, and two uses of this creation were suggested. The first was a lightweight substitute that would reduce the weight of body armour against high-calibre rifle rounds and shrapnel. Inspired by reports that British troops preferred to remove high-tensile strength synthetic Kevlar fibre armour in a firefight, because Kevlar needed an outer layer of ceramic, which was weighty, and hampered their movement. The second use was for maternity clothing, in which the silk would incorporate sensors that monitored a mother's blood pressure, contractions, and the movements of a baby in the womb.

It is the new, non-clothing-related promise of silks that represents the future of these threads, for Fritz Vollrath. 'I think the whole question is not just of using silk as a sustainable material in textiles,' he says. 'It's always been that, in India since the Indus Valley, and in China, it's been around as a key material for a very long time. But I think it has a future both in biomedical and in smart materials.'

27

SMARTER SILK

FOR FIORENZO OMENETTO, THE FUTURE IN SMART MATERIALS – AT LEAST with the silk of the *Bombyx mori* – has already begun. A professor of Engineering and of Biomedical Engineering at Tufts University, Massachusetts, Omenetto started his career as a physicist and laser expert. As sometimes happens in science, it was a throw-away conversation in the lab corridors that led to the discovery that silk could bring technology and biology together in entirely new ways. That conversation had been with David Kaplan, a biomedical engineer. Kaplan was holding a small piece of silk, which was meant to become a scaffold to be used to rebuild a human cornea. But Kaplan was concerned that it didn't have great permeability, and asked Omenetto if a laser could be used to burn tiny holes in the silk's surface. In the eyes, corneas can have no blood vessels, because, for clear vision, they need to stay transparent. But they also need to stay alive, and that requires them to be permeable enough to absorb oxygen, nutrients from tears, and other substances, while rejecting dust or bacteria. An artificial, implanted silk cornea would also need to be porous enough to allow our own cells to enter it to allow it to regrow by using the shape of the silk as a scaffold, or mould. For people with corneal damage, this would allow them to use such an implant to regrow a new cornea of their own.

Omenetto says he put the laser on the film of silk from Kaplan, but he could not see the laser, 'which might have been just dumb luck, but to me', he remembers, 'it meant that the material was optically sensational'. What that meant was the silk film had a near-perfect transparency – superior to anything made of glass, or indeed any synthetic material available. Here was a material to potentially be implanted into the body, and encourage the body to repair itself. And then because Omenetto would work out how to program silk implants to self-destruct, this was also a material that could disintegrate when told to, as if it had never been there at all.

In the 1990s, when their new silk research began, David Kaplan had been studying spider and *Bombyx mori* silk at the US Army Natick Research & Development Laboratories. As his research developed, he moved to Tufts University and decided to focus on silk that *Bombyx mori* caterpillars spin out of protein and water, and work backwards, taking the silk threads back into their liquid form, as it had been the glands of the insects. This liquid, when exuded from the body of the worm, becomes solid on contact with air. Kaplan's idea was to work in the opposite direction. If he could get hold of the silk fluid itself, he could mould it into whatever shape he needed, and make completely new kinds of silk materials never before seen. Kaplan and, later, with Omenetto, thought that for a number of reasons this re-engineered material could make possible replacements for cartilage, and bone; packages for safely delivering medications deep into the body; artificial blood vessels made of silk for the repair of the heart and other organs; and dissolvable nuts, gears and bolts that could be implanted in the body for surgical repair.

By reversing the process that silkworms use, and by changing the way silk protein is processed from liquid silk, they also worked on creating new transparent materials of natural protein that could be used for a variety of functions. It could be moulded into tiny needles that cause no irritation to the skin. It could be used as flexible and biodegradable implantable electronics that record our brain signals. It could be an edible sensor we could safely consume to track our fitness or the nutritional quality of our food. Or it could be used to preserve and stabilize vaccines or antibiotics so that they can be safely transported across remote areas without refrigeration or as adhesives and reflector tapes. The potential uses went on – as data stores that allow credit card-size devices that could hold as much information as CDs; as holograms; or as natural optic fibres to create a new generation of technologies that will conduct light as information. These materials could even be used to create 'silk plastic' cups or bags, and silk electronics – a perfectly biodegradable antidote to plastic, as well as to the curse of electronic waste. With imagination, the potential seemed almost limitless.

In learning from nature, Fiorenzo Omenetto sees what he calls infinite scalable technology that we haven't yet harnessed. Among these biological materials, including the natural nanotechnology used by plants his lab now studies, silk is central to a range of future applications. To Omenetto, using silk to reinvent electronic–human interfaces that can sense what is going on in the body will be a massively transformative innovation. 'The fact that we start from a naturally based material drives us to put tech where tech normally doesn't go', he says. 'It really brings biology and technology together.' Fiorenzo is by no means convinced that a 'singularity' is coming –

that is to say a seamless merging of our bodies with technology. But it is something he does think about. Because with a material as natural and implantable as silk, and one that can be embedded with gold electronics or sensors that interact seamlessly with the body, we could well be one step nearer to such a future, both dystopian and utopian. Our phones might be crafted from silk implantables embedded with sensors and become part of our bodies. '. . . Or you could dip silk into a substance x or y, weave it, and when you wear it, it can tell you whether you are about to have a stroke.' Silk is also dissolvable, and its self-destruction can be made to happen at set times, which means, for example, that electronics could be sent into our bloodstream using it. Those electronics could pick up on how much oxygen or carbon dioxide, or other substances, there is in our blood. And what is in our blood, indeed, in our bodies, then becomes data, and data that can be transmitted out to, for example, somebody's mobile phone.

Whether this takes us towards a truly cyborg future or not, much of Tufts' SilkLab research is being applied in one way or another. Some of their silk innovations under development have been produced, like temperature-stabilized vaccines that require no refrigeration; penicillin that has been stabilized, using silk, for many months; and a chemotherapy drug that has also remained stable, and fully functional, at the Mayo Clinic for the last decade. Omenetto's lab has also developed a soft-tissue filler based on silk fibroin protein. That is in clinical trials for cosmetic use, to fill wrinkles. But it is already approved for the treatment of vocal cord paralysis.

'Medically right now they reconstruct vocal cords', Omenetto says, 'that's one of the things that I think I can chalk up as having accomplished. Because patients walk into a room for the procedure, and they can't speak, and then they walk out and they can. So this is actually a product that is available for therapy today.'

Still, he says, 'nothing is really easy. I think that the biggest difficulty is an economy of scale. To have enough material. For example, if you're thinking of doing commodity plastic substitutes . . . you need to play with prices and with volume, and so this has been honestly the biggest obstacle.' But at least with the silk upon which his innovations are built – that of the *Bombyx mori* silkworm, domesticated to become a mass producer over millennia – this obstacle has largely been overcome.

In the autumn of 2012, in the MIT Media Lab, Massachusetts, 6,500 *Bombyx mori* silkworms were plucked from their final feast of mulberry leaves and placed upon a giant scaffold. It was built like an enormous work of string art, by a robotic arm which rapidly attached silk thread wound off a reel to nails placed around the edges of aluminium frames of four, five or six sides. With the threads drawn taut, and the frames all joined together, the final scaffold looked much like a geodesic dome. On that open-thread structure, the silk worm horde crawled, sensing the topography and limits of their new space. And then they began spinning – not their ellipsoid cocoons, but instead, flat patches of silk across areas of the structure upon which they were placed. Around them was a protective fence – there was a drop cloth below them to catch them should they fall. After they had laboured for two or three days, the caterpillars were collected on the drop cloth, and so retired. They continued their metamorphoses into silk moths, to mate and lay their eggs, so that their cycle was complete.

Called *Silk Pavilion*, the project was the brainchild of the Mediated Matter Group at MIT, which was led by designer Professor Neri Oxman. Fiorenzo Omenetto, who, by now, knew the ways of the *Bombyx mori* well, was a key collaborator. Like Omenetto, Oxman's work brought biology, computing, and engineering materials together. But unlike Omenetto, Oxman had started life as a medical student and an architect, to which she also combined an artistic sensibility. Having observed that the silken creations of *Bombyx mori* caterpillars were affected by spatial and environmental conditions, meaning that, if they were provided with a particular frame, or flat surface, they would freely create shapes other than the standard cocoon, the team expected that the insects, now so close to metamorphosis, would work with any scaffold provided to them. That was exactly what they did, except this time, not in a small container in a laboratory, but in a large room, and on a grand, architectural scale. As someone who had designed buildings, Oxman saw this type of construction, made not with an assemblage of factory-made parts, but organically, as something more akin to the natural growth of a biological entity. Here was a way to bring together the industrial and biological, for the fabrication of human-scale structures. For the silk worms, being set to work in the way that they had also meant they did not have to be boiled or stifled inside their cocoons in order for designers to acquire their silk. Instead, like little, succulent, construction workers, they supplied their threads directly in the place it was needed. To the team, that represented a more sustainable, and kinder way of harvesting silk, without harm to the insects. In 2020, Oxman spectacularly repeated this idea to create *Silk Pavilion II*, this time with 17,532 industrious silk worms reared in Teolo, in the Veneto region of Italy, one of the largest centres of silk cultivation in Europe. When it was hung in New York's Museum of Modern Art, the creation rose six metres high and spanned five metres across. It was one illustration of how building materials might mimic what is made, used and decomposed in the natural world. In Oxman's choice to use silk in this way resonated her counsel, 'we must reorient ourselves with the natural environment, or else perish.'

It was no different for Omenetto, for as much as the medical potential he sees in silk, it is the social and environmental that really excites him. He foresees the development of 'an array of new sensors important at all levels of society, for global health, women's health' and in other applications that are socially important. Like Fritz Vollrath, he also sees a huge future value of silk in sustainable industries; in the potential of innovations based on silks in planetary science. That includes building silken alternatives for plastics, using silk to make substitutes for construction materials – sustainable substitutes that will replace adhesives, all technologies that are currently based on petrochemicals. That same vision was shared by another group of researchers, based at MIT, in the USA and at BASF in Germany. In 2022, the group co-developed a silk-based replacement for the type of microplastics routinely, intentionally added to micro-sized active materials, like vitamins, fragrances, herbicides, used in agricultural products, paints and cosmetics, from where they find themselves in air, water, and soil across the globe. The reason they are used, even though they are such pernicious polluters, is to protect certain key ingredients from being degraded when exposed to air or moisture. By using a silk protein – non-toxic, and able to naturally degrade – extracted from cocoons rejected in the production of textiles, and dissolving them, the scientists were able to coat, or encapsulate the commercial products. For one of these, a standard water-soluble microencapsulated herbicide product, the team's tests showed it worked even better than the polluting synthetic alternative, at least in a greenhouse, in which a crop of corn was being grown.

Even in similar form to the fabrics silk has always fashioned, there is still potential for its threads, made into textiles, to intervene in the impacts of the planetary crisis. In 2021, a team of researchers in Nanjing University, China, and in Stanford University, USA, were thinking of creative ways to develop methods of cooling the human body without any energy consumption. It is a pressing issue, exacerbated by the climatic changes the planet is increasingly seeing the effects of. Cooling the body is of course a problem which people, throughout history, have sought to solve in their particular environments by the choice of fabrics they wore. But none of our traditional fabrics, nor more recent proposed designs for new materials, have taken this cooling to a temperature below the ambient. That is, though they may help us feel cool, none can actually reduce the temperature of the body. But because of its particular microstructure, and the fact that silk has always been sought for its smoothness and comfort on the skin, the scientists decided to make a new attempt using engineered *Bombyx mori* threads. They embedded the fibres with miniscule particles of aluminium oxide, sized less than 100 nanometres – about one thousand times smaller than the width of a human hair. At that scale, those particles reflected away the ultraviolet wavelengths of sunlight. Their tests showed that silk treated in this way stayed 3.5°C cooler than the surrounding air, kept the skin 8°C cooler under direct sunlight than natural silk did, and 12.5°C cooler than cotton.

Omenetto's team is also working on materials for different types of thermal management, with the aim of reducing local heating effects due to climatic shocks. Those 'very interesting things on the planetary scale', he says, are 'the things that I'm most enthused about.' Working with Cambridge Crops in the USA, his team's SilkLab innovations have been applied to create edible food coatings, the impacts of which should not be underestimated. Because in this one technology lies the potential to minimize global food waste, limit greenhouse gas emissions and water waste caused by the food supply chain and reduce reliance on non-biodegradable plastic packaging. Their work has already stabilized cassava crops, in collaboration with farmers. Omenetto and his collegaues have worked with silk cottage industries in Kampot, Cambodia, in which local people partnered with Tufts' silk research and innovations.

Silk sourced at fair-trade prices from Kampot would make the kind of green high-tech products that could then be reincorporated into their own local environment. The vision was that the people there, having produced the silk that was then, for example, used to stabilize medicines, or foods, could be used right there in an environment where medical care was difficult to access and food and medicines hard to preserve.

Sustainability is part of the point of working with silk. Because, apart from humans, who have catastrophically broken the mould, Vollrath makes the point that nature tries to be as energy-efficient as possible, because, as he says, 'why waste energy on something that you could use for reproduction? The currency of life is energy.'

And our problem is that our currency ceased to be energy. 'It was cheap. We just burn it. We are not husbanding it. We are not looking after it well enough.' It has been by understanding the efficiency of energy use – the lack of obscene wastage in the production of silk – that the scientists working towards its future applications place a huge emphasis on learning from nature. In the natural world, Vollrath says, 'everything is recycled and that's the way it works.' Each of the animals that make silk evolved many very specific applications as a response to environmental pressures or availability of proteins from their food. 'Therefore, we have a lot of historical research and development – not by humans, as they did in the case of the silkworm, which was domesticated for six or seven thousand years, but in the case of all the other creatures, for millions of years. So there's a lot of embedded knowledge there about the protein, which is a biopolymer. And we have issues with polymers. We've got to get away from the bloody hydrocarbons.'

And that, to these scientists, is a very good reason to look to silk, because at least when it comes to the cocoons, or even the liquid silk from silkworms, they can be harvested from nature for diverse applications. The polymer chemistry and polymer physics that has become so well established, and upon which we have become so dependent – 'because humans now have been making plastics for a hundred years', as Vollrath puts it – also means that science understands exactly how to make a plastic, and, therefore, potentially, how silk polymers can be constructed. It is an apt transition back to an ancient material, because though traditional plastics, which are synthetic polymers, have been enormously useful, their continued production from unsustainable hydrocarbons is increasingly unconscionable.

It is in this kind of bigger picture problem-solving that silk-manipulating scientists see real potential for the future of silk, what Omenetto describes as more profound social implications than anything that happens in American or European curiosity-driven research bubbles. That is pertinent, because silk has never had only one source, and the animals that make it can be found in the wild on nearly every continent. Vollrath has been able to work with wild silks across the globe. In Bhutan and Kenya, local projects have been developed around the balance between sustainable practices and the exploitation of nature, which, after all, any co-opting of a material taken from an animal, or that leads to the repurposing of its natural habitat, is. 'If you use the mulberry, the normal silk, whether it's the *Antheraea* or even *Bombyx*, if you grow it', Vollrath says, 'it's a very environmentally friendly way of producing filaments, because it's a mixture of silviculture – maintaining forests where you don't cut it down, you don't till the ground – although you still need to fertilize, but you can do that with waste, cow shit or something. That is a very interesting way of producing large quantities of environmentally friendly material', as long as it is combined with the use of renewable energy for silk fabrication processes, like heating and reeling, for example. Such forms of silk production from wild silk moths are very labour-intensive, which might be considered problematic, but is something that Vollrath sees in a positive light: 'it's not bad if you have eighty per cent unemployment', he says. 'And if you then add to the value chain locally, don't just send their filaments away – but actually make things locally, it's an interesting model, for even normal silk, not just spider silk material.'

There is more environmental value in the maintenance of wild silk moths, because they require the preservation of entire ecosystems: the local plants, on which they feed, maintained in the forests in which they live. But, Vollrath says, even a field of mulberry trees, planted to allow local biodiversity to thrive, would be better than competing industries that clear trees. 'I mean cotton is a terrible material, if you think about it', he says, 'terrible for the environment. Otherwise it's great, I can throw the T-shirt in the compost. But the way it was made is unbelievably disruptive.' With mulberry trees, he says, 'what the Chinese did was use them for anti-erosion, and if you just harvest the leaves, but not the wood, you're binding carbon. And, of course, you're always binding carbon in the silk. If you have a million tonnes, roughly the annual production of raw silk cocoons – that's a lot of carbon that is bound for a very long time.'

In silk – its materials, its animals, its exploitation and its potential – is an echo of words written back in the wake of the 1969 moon landing, which are words that have always resonated, and perhaps always will, with any scientific and economic pursuit. 'A few years ago American scientists could state', René Dubos wrote, '"We *must* go to the moon, for the simple reason that we *can* do it . . ." Such statements are admirable to the extent that they express man's determination to accept difficult challenges . . .' Nevertheless, there remain many 'equally good scientific reasons for accepting the staggering human, financial and technological effort' required to undertake 'other kinds of difficult and challenging tasks . . . preventing the further desecration of nature, or dedicating ourselves to works of beauty and to the establishment of a harmonious equilibrium between man and the rest of creation.'

Though the mimicking of nature – those attempts to generate a thread that animals make so effortlessly – has proved infinitely more difficult for scientists, with all of our technology, to emulate, researchers across many countries, east and west, continue to pursue the challenge through great technical effort, in the hope of creating from silk new kinds of smart and sustainable technologies that promise to play an important role in promoting health and preventing the further desecration of our natural world. The converse, the extraction of that substance from living animals was, if limited in its applications, a simpler if sometimes brutal process, involving the immobilization of unwilling spiders, the boiling and stifling of *Bombyx mori* silkworms and the type of harvesting that contributed to the near-extinction of *Pinna nobilis*. In furnishing ourselves with fabrics, therapies and an extraordinarily versatile material, both methods have sought to co-opt a technology from the animal world that has built so much of our history, from political favour to economies, military capacity to medical capabilities. In silk is a fascination that will continue to inspire those who seek to understand the mysteries it still keeps, so that we may uncover the ample potential that it has yet to unfold. For silk was never just a cloth of luxury, or a conduit of trade. Across millennia, in the uses to which it has been put, in its animal sources which we have exploited, and manipulated, in this one material lies our protean relationship with the natural world.

Acknowledgements

I AM IMMENSELY GRATEFUL FOR THE GENEROUS TIME, DISCUSSIONS and support of many colleagues and friends, old and new who helped me think through the research and writing of this book. This work is built upon published research, lived experience, family histories, diaries and commentaries from diverse sources. I have tried to bring these together to recount the science and stories I have found so fascinating that they have sustained me along the long road to completing this book. In gathering this information there were occasions on which I have had to bridge factual gaps, contradictions, historical and current understandings. I have endeavoured to convey these tales as accurately as I could, and any errors that I may have made are mine alone.

I would first like to extend my heartfelt thanks to Prof. David Whitmore, William Dalrymple, Will Francis, Ian Bonaparte, Arabella Pike and Mauro diPrieta, without whom this book would never have been written. Thank you for your enthusiasm in the subject and faith in me that carried me through the research and writing.

For your immense help with my research, or for sharing yours, thank you to Dr Alessandro Giusti and Sarah Sworder at the Natural History Museum, London; Ariana Bishop and Laura Weinstein at the Museum of Fine Arts, Boston; Dr Tristram Hunt, Professor Lesley Millar, and Oriole Cullen at the Victoria and Albert Museum; Karen Stapley at the British Library; and Kat Harrington at Kew Gardens; Veronica Ranner, Prof. Fiorenzo Omenetto, Simon Peers, Dr Henry Noltie, Shyamal Lakshminarayanan, Dr Tom Young, Prof. Kay Etheridge, Prof. Dorian Fuller, Prof. Tim Williams, Dr Susan Whitfield, Prof. Randolph Lewis, Prof. Fritz Vollrath, Prof. Llorenç Alapont, Shree Priya Srinivas, and Roopjyoti Gogol.

Thank you for your stories on *Pinna nobilis*, and your generous assistance with my research in Sardinia: Felicitas Maeder, Assuntina Pes, Giuseppina Pes, Antonella Senis, Mariangela Foscalino, Filippo Foscoliano, Arianna Pintus and Prof. Guido Barbujani. In Greece: Dr Karolos Dedos, Dr George Bethimoutis, George Tsiakiris and Giannis Tsiakiris. In Hungary, Dr Orsolya Láng and Dr Anita Kirchhof.

And to my wonderful translators: Carlotta Farci and Dr Gianvito di Stefano in Sardinia, and Amina Shamim and Dr Humera Iqbal in Pakistan; and Tara Lumley-Savile and Prof. Giulio Cossu, for your help in deciphering those antiquated French, Italian and Latin texts.

I am very grateful also for discussions and comments from Nalini Persad, Jen Franklin and Fawzia Gibson-Fall; and to all my UCL Portico Drunkards, especially Ruairidh McLeod, Prof. Mark Thomas, Dr Catherine Walker and Dr Adam Rutherford. A special thanks to Nadia Owusu for her sage advice, sisterly empathy and fortifying encouragement in the course of putting together what has been a challenging book to write; and to Prof.

Florian Mussgnug and Dr Simona Corso for the inspiration I found on the terrace and the bookshelves of your beautiful home in Trastevere, where a third of this book came into being.

Thank you all.

List of illustrations

27: The transformation of the *Bombyx mori* silkworm, from Maria Sibylla Merian, 'Maulbeerbaum samt Frucht,' Der Raupen (The Caterpillars), 1679, Plate 1

79: Portrait of Georg Eberhardt Rumpf, in *D'Amboinsche Rariteitkamer*, 1741

83: *Antheraea rumphii rumphii*, from Georg Eberhardt Rumpf, *Herbarium Amboinense*, 1743

104: The tasar silkworm by William Roxburgh, *Transactions of the Linnean Society of London*, 1804

110: Helfer travelling on the *Euphrates*, from Chesney, *Narrative of the Euphrates Expedition*, 1868

121: Muga silkworm and moth, Asiatic Society of Bengal, *The journal of the Asiatic Society of Bengal*, 1837

157: Journal of the Soviety of Arts Thomas Wardle, History and Description Of The Growing Uses of Tussur Silk, Thomas Journal of the Society of Arts, 1890

160: Processing silk cocoons in Bengal, from November 2, 1895, issue of *Scientific American*

161: Some of the Indian artisans, from *Reminisces of the Colonial and Indian Exhibition*, ed. Frank Cundall, 1886

162: Larva, Journal of the Soviety of Arts Thomas Wardle, History and Description Of The Growing Uses of Tussur Silk, Thomas Journal of the Society of Arts, 1890

163: Cocoon and moths, Journal of the Soviety of Arts Thomas Wardle, History and Description Of The Growing Uses of Tussur Silk, Thomas Journal of the Society of Arts, 1890

170: *Pinna nobilis*, Charles Bevalet, public domain

196: Portrait of Italo Diana, Studio87

199: Fishing the *Pinna nobilis*, Taranto, 1793, Muschelseide.ch

221: Byssus of other shells, author's photo

226: Réaumur's insect menagerie, drawn by Philppe Simonneau for Réaumur's *Mémoires pour servir à l'histoire des insects*, 1734

239: Orb web decorations, from Henry C. McCook, *American Spiders and Their Spinningwork, 1889*

259: Queen Ranavalona II of Madagascar, Council for World Mission Archive, SOAS Library

261: *Nephila inaurata madagascariensis*, Auguste Vinson, *Aranéides des îles de la Réunion, Maurice et Madagascar, 1863*

265: Golden Orb spider silk production in Madagascar, *The Silk-Producing Spider Of Madagascar, Scientific American*, Vol 83, issue 9, 1900

287: Nan Songer, Yucaipa Valley Historical Society

295: Tests of Zeglen's bulletproof vest, public domain via Wikicommons

Plate sections:

Domesticated silk moth, DE AGOSTINI PICTURE LIBRARY/Getty

Maria Sibylla Merian wreath, public domain

Domesticated silk moth larva, Science Photo Library C029/0328 and C029/0327

Insect anatomy, seventeenth-century drawings, Science Photo Library C013/3530 and C013/3529

Golden-coloured filigree cocoons, author's photo

'The Manner of Feeding Silkworms', Print Collector/Getty

'Starling with Two Antheraea Moths, Caterpillar, and Cocoon', Minneapolis Institute of Art

Queen Anne of Denmark, public domain

Illustrations of shells, public domain

Crystal Palace Saloon, public domain

The weaving of Banarasi Sari, Dinodia/Bridgeman Images

A woman weighs a batch of silk moth cocoons, Hulton Archive/Stringer/Getty

A string of diseased silkworm cocoons, Science Museum, London

Silkworm cocoons arranged on trays, Ann & Bury Peerless Archive/Bridgeman Images

Anatomy of the *Pinna nobilis*, from Giuseppe Saverio Poli, *Testacea utriusque Siciliae eorumque historia et anatome*, 1791, Plate 26

Living *Pinna nobilis*, Hectonichus

Golden byssus threads, Felicitas Maeder, Projekt Muschelseide

Dead fan mussel, BIOSPHOTO/Alamy

The 'beard' of byssus fibre, author's photo

The byssus silk fibres, Picture Empa

Wasp and spider trapped in resin, Oregon State University

Bird-eating spider, from Maria Sibylla Merian, 'Metamorphosis insectorum Surinamensium', 1705, Plate 18

N. inaurata madagascariensis, Charles J. Sharp

Termeyer's apparatus, from Henry McCook, *American Spiders and Their Spinningwork*, 1893

SEM of an orb weaver, Science Photo Library

Bombyx mori silk parachutes, K. Mamalakis Archive

WAAF woman uses a Singer sewing machine, Fox Photos/Getty

Index

Achaemenian Empire, 59
Adidas, 320
Aerssen van Sommelsdijck, Cornelis van, 70
Afghanistan, 57, 89, 122
Africa, 256, 260, 288, 332
Agassiz, Louis, 277–8
Ahom kingdom, 120, 122
Akbar the Great, 111
Akrotiri, Santorini, 11
Alexander the Great, 84, 85–6, 180
Alinari, Vittorio, *In Sardegna*, 191–3, 195, 196, 216
Allard, Jean-François, 126–7
amber, Burmese ('Burmite'), 232–5, 236–7
Ambon Island, 78–80, 82, 96, 101, 102
Amsterdam, 19–20, 63, 64, 65
Anaphe moth, 260
Andaman Isles, 124, 128–9, 231
angora, 181, 298
Anne of Denmark, 29–30
Antheraea moths: *Antheraea assama* (muga moth), 120–6, *121*, 133–4, 135, 162; *Antheraea assamensis* Helfer, 91, 109–10; *Antheraea frithi* Moore, 103–4, 140, 141–2; and future sustainability, 332–4; metamorphosis of, 121, 315; by-products of, 123; Rumpf's moth (*Antheraea rumphii rumphii*), 80–1, 82–3, *83*, 91, 96; silk compared to that of spiders, 285, 315–16; strength and durability of silk, 123 *see also* tasar moth (*Antheraea paphia*)
Aquincum, city of, 182–5, 214, 219, 221
arachnids, 234–7 *see also* spiders
aragonite, 212
archaeology: ancient cocoon finds, 47, 50–1, 56, 91; Bronze Age sites, 54, 88; at Harappa, 86, 87–8, 89, 90–1; and the Indus civilization, 87–91, 124; at Knossos, 86–7; at Mohenjo-daro, 88–9

Argentina, 254
Aristotle, *History of Animals*, 179, 182
art: of Isabella Gilbert, 131–2; Maria Merian's works, 19–20, 21, 22–8, *27*, 81–2; topographical engraving, 20–1; watercolour techniques, 21
ArthaĐĐstra (Sanskrit text), 122
arthropods, 234–5
Arts and Crafts movement, 147–8
asbestos, 11, 185
Ashoka, 112
Assam, northeast India, 7, 91, 109, 120–6, 162
Assisi, town of, 203
Aurangzeb, Mughal emperor, 122
Australia, 140, 256
Azara, Félix de, 253–4

bair tree, 93, 94, 95, 99, 144, 150
al-Baiṭār, Ibn, 186
Banerjee, Rakal Das, 88
Banks, Joseph, 98, 99
BASF, Germany, 329
Bassi, Agostino, 115
Basso-Arnoux, Giuseppe, 199–200
bats, 94–5
beetles, 67, 94, 97, 105, 247
Bene, Rita del, 204–5
Bhutan, 332
Birdwood, Sir George, 144, 145–6, 151, 160
Bologna, 30, 31, 33, 34–5, 61
Bolt (biotechnology firm), 320–1
Bombycidae family of moths, 28, 49–50, 72–3, 120, 153; *Bombyx mandarina* Moore (ancestor of *Bombyx mori*), 50–4, 102, 136; *Rondotia menciana*, 48, 50 *see also Bombyx mori* (mulberry/domestic silk moth)
Bombyx mori (mulberry/domestic silk moth): adult form, 6, 27, *27*, 28, 53, 102; anatomy of, 34–9, 54, 61; under-armour made from silk of, 273–6; arrival in Europe, 60–1; caterpillar of, 5–6, 12, 24–6, 29–30, 35–9, 45–7, 52–4, 284, 299; cocoons of, 5–6, 7, 26–8, *27*, 37–8, 43, 52, 103, 225, 275; complete domestication of, 4, 10, 28, 46–7, 50–4, 58, 91, 102, 103, 273–4, 315; diet of white mulberry leaves, 4, 5, 6, 26, 28, 44, 53, 56, 284, 332–3; earliest allusion to in ancient writings, 17; eggs of, 5, 25–6, *27*, 35, 60, 228–9, 242, 271; evolutionary biology of, 43, 51–4, 102, 136, 300; and future sustainability, 12, 321–2, 332–4; global spread of, 7, 55–6, 57–61, 271; graphene fed to, 321–2; immune system, 43; in Italy, 34–5, 60–1, 114–15; James I's mulberry gardens, 29–30, 61; Linnaeus names, 4, 28, 50, 72; Malpighi's anatomical work, 34–9, 54, 61; *mandarina* as ancestor/origin of, 50–4, 102, 136; Master Xun on, 12; mating, 6, 25, 27; medical uses of silk, 318, 323–7; Merian's work on metamorphosis of, 20, 24–8, *27*, 54, 73; and MIT *Silk Pavilion* project, 327–8; as most well-known source of silk, 4, 7, 43, 83; Nazi breeding of, 283–4; in the Neolithic, 10, 43–8, 50–4; problems of inbreeding/disease, 114–15, 117, 119; pupae, 26–7, *27*, 43, 58, 275; removing of sericin from silk of, 58, 150, 275, 318; silk at Great Exhibition (1851), 138–9, 142; silk compared to that of *Saturnidae*, 123, 146, 152–4, 155–6, *157*; silk compared

to that of spiders, 224, 225, 228, 263, 285; silk found at Pompeii, 181; silk of compared to sea-silk, 174, 175; silk ties worn in history, 321; smart materials from, 323–34; specimens in Natural History Museum, 7; spider silk proteins inserted into, 309–11, 312; stifling or heating at pupal stage, 58, 59, 91, 103, 328, 334; strength and durability of silk, 6, 299; Termeyer's study of, 242, 250; and thermal management research, 330; tubular silk glands, 38, 39, 43, 54, 58
Bon de Saint Hilaire, François Xavier, 167, 222–6, 227–8, 229, 241, 245, 247, 251, 284–5
Bradford Technical College, 154
Brahmaputra River system, 120
Brazil, 254
Britain: Great Exhibition (1851), 137–40, 142; importing of raw silk, 114, 138–9, 152; and Indian silk, 114, 152; Liberty department store, 147; silk in Jacobean period, 29–30, 61; small-scale local production of silk, 138; Wardle's silk business at Leek, 142, 145, 147–8, 149–56, 159
British East India Company, 81, 84, 85, 93–6, 130–1; annexes Kingdom of Punjab, 137; Assam acquired by (1825), 119–20, 122; East India House, 103–4, 142; effective rule of India (from 1757), 91–2, 103–4, 110; and naturalists, 97–104, 112–14, 115–29, 131–5, 137, 139, 142
British India: Anglo-Sikh Wars, 131; Archaeological Survey of India, 85–9; Asiatic Society of Bengal, 110–13, 116–24, 131, 202; British racism/cultural assumptions, 87; 'Colonial and Indian Exhibition' (London, 1886), 160–2, *161*; Geological Survey of India, 233; and Great Exhibition (1851), 137–40, 142; the Helfers in, 107–11, 112, 113–14, 115–25, 131; India Museum, Leadenhall Street, 103–4, 142; 'Indian Collection' at Paris Exposition (1855), 140, 141; 'Indian hill coolies' to Australia, 140; Indians transported as free labour by, 87, 140; and Linnaeus's 'apostles,' 48–9; mapping and surveying, 231–4; Masson's journey across (1827), 84–5; mercantile value of natural history, 98–9, 102–4, 113–14, 116–25, 138–40, 142, 144–51, 152–60; naturalists in northeast of, 140–1; Wardle in, 143–4, 158–60; George Watt on silk from, 139–40 *see also* British East India Company
bubonic plague, 272
Budapest, 182–5
bulletproof vests/body armour, *295*, 297–9, 300, 306, 322
Burma, 231–5, 236–7
Burnes, Alexander, 85
Byzantine Empire, 59–60

Cabras, Assunta, 204
Calasetta, town of (Sant'Antioco), 190–1
Calcutta, 86, 87, 93–6, 97–103, 107–13, 115–24, 126–7
California, University of, Santa Barbara, 315
Camboué, Jacob Paul, 259–64, 319
Cambridge Crops (food technology company), 330–1
Canabis sativa, 10

Canada, 304
canningi (*Samia* moth), 124
Caribbean, 130, 254
Cassini, Giovanni Domenico, 32
castor oil plant, 8, 124
Catherine the Great, 251
Cerruti, Attilio, 201–2
Chalcosia pectinicornis moth, 133
Chandragupta, Emperor, 122
Chanhu-daro (Indus civilization site), 90
Charles II, King of England, 38–9
Charles III, King of Spain, 246, 251
Chicago, 297
China: ancient writings of, 17; *Bombyx mandarina* Moore in, 50–4, 102, 103, 136; border with British Empire, 231–5; domestication of silkworms in, 4, 10, 28, 45–7, 50–4, 58, 91, 102, 103, 273–4, 315; giant spiders in, 255; Han Dynasty, 185; Helfer on, 116–17; Henan province, 44–7, 51, 56; Huang He (Yellow River), 4, 44–7, 51, 54; Hwen-Thsang's travelogue, 86; invention of paper in, 272–3; Liangzu Neolithic sites in, 47; mulberry trees used for anti-erosion, 333; Qianshanyang (ancient site), 47; and removal of sericin, 58, 275; *Rondotia menciana* in, 47–8, 50; and sea silk (byssus), 185, 186; Shang Dynasty, 51, 54; Shanxi province, 48, 51; Shuanghuaishu (ancient site), 44–7, 50, 51–2; and silk's many forms of value, 11–12; silk/silkworm artefacts in, 45–7, 51; silkworms other than *Bombyx mori* from, 7, 47–8; Taixicun (Bronze Age site), 54; T'ang Dynasty, 44, 186; warcraft, 273–4; Xiyin Cun (ancient site), 47; Xuanye (Kangxi Emperor), 229; Yangshao culture, 46–8; Yunnan province, 232, 234, 255; Zhejiang province, 47, 51 *see also Bombyx mori* (mulberry/domestic silk moth)
Churchill, Winston, 87, 283–4
climate change/environmental crisis, 12, 13, 210–12, *320*, *325*, *327*, *328–34*
Cockerell, Theodore Dru Alison, 233–4
coconut palms, 82, 128–9
cocoons, silkworm: of Anaphe moth, 260; ancient remains/archaeological finds, 47, 50–1, 56, 91; automated cocoon-reeling machines, 155, 159; of *Bombyx mandarina*, 50–1, 52; of *Bombyx mori*, 5–6, 7, 26–8, *27*, 37–8, 43, 52, 103, 225, 275; bound by *sericin* cement, 52, 58, 73, 123, 132, 150–1, 154–5, 275–6, 317–18; broken threads caused by emerging moth, 6, 27, 58, 59, 91, 103; *Cricula trifenestrata*, 120, 142, 162; diseased, 114–15; egg-like shape of in India, 95, 96, 100, 139; of eri/arrindy silkworms, 8, 124–5; escape valves in, 125; Isabella Gilbert's observations of, 132–3; at Great Exhibition (1851), 138; Helfer's collection/study of, 117, 118; human unravelling of, 49, 56, 80–1, 91, 101, 103, 125, 155, 159, 250, 275, 281, 309; large size of Saturniidae cocoons, 72, 80–1, 83, 91, 95–6, 103, 121–4, 141; Merian and Rump's observations on, 67, 72, 73, 80–1, 83; of muga moth, *121*, 121–4, 142; at Paris Exposition (1878), 8, 140;

processing of in India, 146, 159, *160*; protective anti-viral proteins, 43, 275; specimens in Natural History Museum, 4, 7–8; spinning of by caterpillar, 5–6, 26–7, 37–8, 100, 132, 154–5; stifling or heating at pupal stage, 58, 59, 91, 103, 146, 159, 328, 334; and sustainable industries, 332, 333; of tasar moths, 95–6, 100–3, 117, 132, 141, 146, 149–51, 154–5, 158–9, *160*; weight increase due to domestication, 52, 53, 103, 141; Zain al-Din's depiction of, *95*, *96*, 99–100 *see also* metamorphosis
Cogswell, Dr, 277, 279
colonialism, European, 8–9, 13, 61–2; British in America, 30; British in Malay Peninsula, 127–9; British in South Africa, 99; in the Caribbean, 130; Dutch, 66–75, 76–81, 82; French, 258–64; perceptions of other cultures, 20–1, 87; Portuguese, 253; Spanish in the Americas, 241–2, 253–4; voyages of discovery, 20–1 *see also* British East India Company; British India
colouring/dyeing of silk, 52, 57, 58, 149, 151, 153–4, 158; and eri or arrindy silk, 125; natural dyes, 147–51, 162, 190, 200; and sericin fluid, 58, 123, 150, 154–5; spider silk, 223–4; and Thomas Wardle, 145, 147–54, 162; Wardle's fourteen 'gem colours,' 151
Constantinople, 60
Cosimo III de' Medici, Grand Duke of Tuscany, 79
cotton, 10, 11, 90, 138, 181, 333
Coussmaker, George, 149–51
Crassicorophium bonellii (shrimp-like animal), 314–15
Crete, 284
the Crystal Palace, 137–40, 142
cuckoos, 9
Cunningham, Alexander, 85–6

damask, 8
Darjeeling, northeast India, 124, 140–1
Darwin, Charles, 254, 277–8
Diana, Italo, 195–9, *196*, 202–4, 205, 216, 217, 218
Dogon people, 260
Don Pedro, sinking of (2007), 209–10
Drury, Dru, *97*, *98*, 103
Dubos, René, 333–4
Dumoustier, Hélène, 227
Dutch East India Company, 64, 77–8, 81, 82
Dutch West India Company, 77

ecology, 39
ecosystems, loss of, 211–12, 213–14, 332–4
Egerton, Lady Alice, 155–8
Egypt, 138, 187, 214
Eiseley, Loren, *The Immense Journey*, 269
electric eels, 247
Emerson, Paul, 301–2
Enome ampla moth, 133
environmental crisis/climate change, 12, 13, 210–12, 320, 325, 327, 328–34
eugenics, 282–3, 284
Euphrates River, 107, *110*, 177n, 186
evolutionary biology: of *Bombyx mori*, 43, 51–4, 102, 136, 300; embedded knowledge in, 331–2; emergence of winged insects, 40–1; of genes that encode silk, 308; of insect flight, 40–2; of insect metamorphosis, 41–3;

of *Pinna* and *Mytilus*, 173; of spiders, 235–40, 302–3, 308; and structure/types of silk, 280, 300, 315–16

fabric/textile production: and the Abū Ḳalamūn, 187–8; bio-inspired polymers, 212; from broken silk threads, 59; byssus (ancient world textile), 177–9, 177n; clothes made entirely of sea silk, 201, 203, 215; dyeing of wild silk cloth, 148–50, 151, 154; early history of, 9–10, 90–1; embroidered cloth, 8, 21, 30, 73, 106–7, 144, 158, 260; from eri or arrindy silk, 8, 125; European discovery of ancient silks, 8–9; evidence at Pompeii, 176–7, 180–2; fashionable designers of Victorian Britain, 147–8; and Great Exhibition (1851), 137–40, 142; hand looms in south of India, 4–5; long history of in India, 83, 90–2, 109, 120; new synthetic materials, 212; oldest examples of knitting, 214; from orbace, 192, 198, 204; on Sant' Antioco, 191, 192–4, 196–7, 198–200, 201–5; of Santal people, 144; from Saturniidae moth silk, 83, 144, 146–7; search for new ways to cool the body, 329–30; silk in late-Elizabethan age, 29–30; silk ties worn in history, 321; silk-like textiles inspired by spiders, 320–2; and social hierarchies, 11; from spider silk, 224, 225–6, 251, 254–5, 258–9, 264, 319–20; in Taras/Taranto, 200–2; tasar carpets, 158; tasar replacement for sealskin, 155–8; weaving of *Pinna* threads, 179–80, 183–4, 185–8, 191, 193–4, 198–200, 201–5, 214–15, 217, 219–20, 221
fagara silk, 123
Fauvel, Albert-Auguste, 255
First World War, 197, 296–7
flax or linseed, 10, 98, 178, 217; linen from, 10, 93, 151, 178–81, 187, 203, 217, 218, 220, 273
France, 28, 30, 61, 113–14, 116, 321; Académie des Sciences, 169–70, 222, 223, 225–6, 227, 256; colonies, 258–64; Lyons as epicentre of Europe's silk industry, 152, 155, 262, 263; Paris Exposition (1855), 140, 141; Paris Exposition (1878), 8, 148, 151, 152; Paris Exposition Universelle (1900), 264; and *Pinna nobilis*, 170–5; Saint-Denis cap, 214
Frankfurt, 20–1, 25, 28
Franz Ferdinand, Archduke, assassination of (June 1914), 296–7, 298
Friend of India newspaper, 126
Frith, R. W. G., 140–1
fungi, 183, 184; marine, 213–14, 221

Galileo, 34, 111
Ganges, River, 108–9, 143, 159
Gardener, Helen H., 282
Garnier, François, 255
Gautier, Emile Jean-Marie, 288
genetic modification, 303, 304–5, 306–13
Genghis Khan, 271–4, 317
geological history: of Assam region, 120; Burmese amber ('Burmite'), 232–5, 236; Cretaceous period, 234; Late Triassic, 3, 41; mass extinctions, 40; Permian period, 40
Gila monster, 290
Gilbert, Isabella (née Ross), 130–5, 142, 144, 162

Gilbert, Sir Walter Raleigh, 131
Gillanders Arbuthnot & Co., 87
goats, spider-, 306–9, 311
Gobi desert, 56
Godley, Nicholas, 319
Goodfellow, George Emory, 290–6, 317
graphene, 321–2
Great Pacific Garbage Patch, 213–14
Greece, ancient, 177–8, 179, 180, 185, 214
guanaco, wool of, 247
Gunfight at the OK Corral, 289, 291

hagfish, 312
Harappa (Indus civilization site), 84–6, 87–8, 89, 90–1
Harvey, William, *De motu cordis*, 29, 31
Hastings, Lady (Flora Mure-Campbell), 130–1
Hastings, Lord (Francis Rawdon-Hastings), 130–1
Hausa people, 260
Helfer, Johann Wilhelm, 105–11, 112, 113–14, 115–25, 131, 138, 142, 162; and eri or arrindy silk, 123–5; mission to Malay Peninsula, 127–9; on sea silk, 202; violent death of in Andaman Isles, 128–9
Helfer, Pauline, 105–9, 112, 113, 126–9, 131
hemp, 10, 98, 178, 181
Herschel, William, 285
Hindu Kush, 57
history, early human: domestication of animals and plants, 4, 10, 46–8, 50–4; Early Food Producing Era, 9–10, 46–8, 51–2; emergence of farming in the Neolithic, 9–10, 46, 51–2; emerging elites, 10–11; Neolithic societies, 9–11, 43–8, 50–4; sources/records, 12–13
Hitler, Adolf, 283–4, 296–7
Hollendonner, Francis, 184–5
Hukawng Valley, Burma, 232–5, 236–7
Hungary, 182–5
Hwen-Thsang (Xuanzang), 86
hydrogen cyanide (prussic acid), 147
Hypsa ficus moth, 133

immune system, human, 317–18
Impey, Lady (Mary Reade), 93–4, 95–6, 97, 101
Impey, Sir Elijah, 93–4, 97
India: author's childhood in, 4–5; and *Bombyx mandarina*, 50; cotton from, 138; early Sanskrit texts, 87, 122; genus *Samia* in, 124; Geological Survey of India, 233; Hwen-Thsang's travelogue, 86; Indian indentured labour system, 87, 140; Indus civilization in, 84–6, 87–92, 96, 103, 109, 120, 124, 322; and the Kushans, 59; and Frederic Moore's work, 136–7, 231; Mughal Empire, 111, 122; natural dyes from, 148–9; Roxburgh's botanical studies in, 97–103, *104*, 109, 123, 131–2, 134, 139, 141, 162; Santal tribe, 143–4, 146, 159; science, 111–13, 115–16; selective breeding of silk worms in ancient times, 91–2, 102–3, 116–17, 120, 246; silk from viewed as inferior in West, 119, 123, 139, 146–7, 152; silk moths from, 7, 91–2, 94–7, 98–102, *104*, 109, 116–24, 131–5, 144–7, 149–59, 162; take-off in exports of wild silk from, 142, 152; and the Tarim Basin, 55, 57; tasar moths in, 94–7, 98–102, *104*, 109, 116–17,

123, 144, 145–7, 149–59 *see also* British India
Indian Museum, South Kensington, 137
indigo, 147–9
Indonesia, 76–81, 82
Indus, River, 84
Innocent XII, Pope, 31
insects: and arachnids, 235, 236; evolutionary biology of, 40–3; farming of fungus/other animals by, 9; as first animals to fly, 40–1; Malpighi's microscopic study of, 34–9; Merian studies in Suriname, 67–8, 69–75, 134, 229–30; Merian's work on natural history of, 23–8; parasites feeding on, 9; Pterygota class, 40–1; specimens in Natural History Museum, 3–4, 7–9; Termeyer's study of, 247; wing development, 40–2
International Union for Conservation of Nature, 213
Iran, Sasanian, 59, 60
Islamic Empire, 60, 61, 187–8
Italy, 28, 30, 61, 155; Campania, 176, 207, 208; Fascist era, 191, 192, 203–5, 218; Sant' Antioco (Sulki, Slky), 189–94, 195–200, 202–4, 205, 216–21, *221*; Sicily, 61, 202, 208, 215; silk production in, 34–5, 114–15, 138, 328; Taranto, *199*, 200–2, 204–5, 215; Termeyer's exile in, 247, 248–52, 253; Venice Biennale (1928), 203

Jaipur, 111
James I, King of England, 29–30, 61
Jamestown, Virginia, 30
Java, 255
Jesuits, 241, 246–7, 251, 259–60
Jones, Inigo, 30
Jones, Sir William, 110–12
Josephine (wife of Napoleon), 251
Justinian, Byzantine emperor, 186

Kampot, Cambodia, 331
Kaplan, David, 323–4
kapok, 181
Karadong, 56, 57, 58–9
Kenya, 332
Kerameikos cemetery, Athens, 180
Kevlar fibre armour, 322
Koh-i-Noor diamond, 137
kohlli (*Samia* moth), 124
Kushan Empire, 59

Labadie, Jean de, 21–2
Lahore, 126, 137
Lepidoptera order, 3, 41, 49, 72; *Bombycoidea* superfamily, 72; Merian studies in Suriname, 67–8, 69–75, 134, 229–30; Frederic Moore's work, 136–7, 231; moth wings, 3, 6, 27, 28, 37, 41–2, 94–5, 100–1, 141; moths in Indonesia, 78, 80–1; Zain al-Din's depiction of, 94–7, 99–100, 102–3
Lewis, Randy, 302–4, 305–13
Liberty, Arthur Lasenby, 147
linen, 10, 93, 151, 178–81, 187, 203, 217, 218, 220, 273
Linnaeus, Carl, 4, 28, 48–50, 72, 97, 101, 134, 170, 244, 247
Louis XIV, king of France, 321
Loulan (Kroraina), 56–7

Madagascar, 7, 256–64, *265*, 319–20, 321
Madras, 130
Malay Peninsula, 127–9
Malpighi, Marcello, 29, 30–5, 54, 61; *De Bombyce*, 35–9

Marco Polo, 272
Maria Elisabeth, Archduchess of Austria, 251
Marseilles, 171
Marshall, John, 86–9
Masson, Charles (James Lewis), 84–5
Mastrocinque, Beniamino, 201
maternity clothing, 322
Mauritius, 138–9, 258–9
McCartney, Stella, 320
McKinley, William, assassination of (1901), 298–9
Mechi people, Nepal, 162
medicine: eye surgery, 318, 323–4; germ theory of disease, 115; Goodfellow's discoveries, 290–6, 317; Harvey's *De motu cordis*, 29; healing of wounds, 274–6, 317; Helfer's studies in, 105, 106, 113; Malpighi's anatomical work, 30–4, 54; Mycobacterium tuberculosis, 208; new synthetic materials, 212; Pasteur's vaccines, 115; plants in Suriname, 69–70; smart materials from silk, 322, 323–7, 334; and spider silk, 225, 286–8, 303, 305, 311, 312, 314, 318–19; and *Spongia officinalis*, 182; suture materials, 311, 318; traditional, 52–3, 67, 69–70; use of *Pinna nobilis*, 174, 185, 212, 315; use of silk, 6, 12, 212, 274–6, 316–18, 323–7, 329; Wilder as military surgeon, 278
Mediterranean, marine ecosystem of, 9, 171–5, 177, 179–82, 191–4, 198–205, 206–14, 217–21
Melanesia, 255
Mendoza, Don Pedro de, 241
Merian, Dorothea Maria, 19–20, 63–4, 65, 67, 74–5, 81
Merian, Johanna Helena, 19–20
Merian, Maria Sibylla: artistic talent, 19–20, 21, 22–3, *27*, 81–2, 226–7; brings Amerindian woman back to Amsterdam, 74–5, 81; death of (1717), 82; entomological diary, 23; family background of, 20–1; illustrates Rumpf's shells, 75, 81; at Labadie's community in Friesland, 21–3; and new study of ecology, 39; return voyage from Suriname (1701), 74–5; and *Rothschildia aurota*, 73, 82, 83, 91, 123, 134; sells her possessions (1699), 19–20, 63; in Suriname (1699-1701), 66–75, 80, 229–30, 240, 244; voyage to New World (1699), 63–6; work on insect metamorphosis, 20, 22–8, *27*, 34, 36, 39, 54, 73; works of, 19–20, 21, 22–3, 24–8, *27*, 32–3, 48, 81–2; *Metamorphosis Insectorum Surinamensium*, 81–2; *Wondrous Transformation*, 23, 24–8, *27*
Merv, city of, 60, 271–3
Mesopotamia, 59, 88, 89–90, 107, *110*, 186
metamorphosis, 5–6, 7, 14, 95; anatomical changes during, 26–7, 35–9; ancient veneration of, 45–6; *Antheraea* moths, 121, 315; and Buddhism, 59; construction of chambers/underground cells, 43; defences protecting the pupa, 275; of eri or arrindy moths, 134; evolutionary biology of, 41–3; four cycles of moulting and growing, 26, 299; Malpighi's work on, 34–9; Maria Merian's work on, 20, 22–8, *27*, 34, 36, 39, 54; partial type of, 41–2; Isabella Ross observes, 132–3; Rumpf's study of, 101; of Saturniidae, 72, 80, 121, 132–3, 315; seventeenth-century

studies of, 5, 20, 22–8, *27*, 34–9; vulnerability during, 43, 315
Mexico, 60
microscope, compound, 34
Microsilk (silk-like textile), 320–1
military technology: bulletproof vests/body armour, *295*, 297–9, 300, 306, 322; Chinese warcraft, 273; silk under-armour, 273–6
Minoan civilization, 86–7, 180
MIT Media Lab, Massachusetts, 327–8
Mohenjo-daro (Indus civilization site), 88–9
molluscs: at Ambon Island, 78; *Atrina pectinata*, 215–16, 218–19; marine in Cretaceous period, 234; murex, 180, 190, 200; *Pinna carnea*, 177; *Pinna rudis*, 173, 177, 208, 215, 216, 218; Pinnidae family, 172, 207, 215, 315 *see also Pinna nobilis*
Mongolia, 61
Montpellier, 222–6
Moore, Frederic, 133, 136–7, 140, 141–2, 231
Morris, William, 147–8
muga moth (*Antheraea assama*), 120–6, *121*, 133–4, 135, 162
Mughal Empire, 111, 122
mulberry, white (*Morus alba*), 4, 5, 6, 28, 44, 50, 53, 155, 242; ancient remains of, 56, 57; growing of in Europe, 29–30, 60–1, 284; King James I's mulberry gardens, 29–30, 61; sustainable production of, 332–3
al-Muqadisi, Muhammad ibn Ahmad, 187–8
Museum of Modern Art, New York, 321, 328
Museum of Natural History, New York, 320
mussels: hair-like strands of protein, 172–3, 177; *Mytilus* (blue mussel), 173, 201
Mussolini, Benito, 191, 203–5

nacre (mother-of-pearl), 171, 190, 212
Nanjing University, China, 329–30
Napoleon, 251
Napoleon III, French Emperor, 259
Natural History Museum, London, *3–4*, *7–8*
Nelson, Horatio, 200, 202
Neolithic societies, 9–11, 43–4, 50–4
Nepal, 162
Netherlands, 19–20, *63*, 64, 65, 81–2; and colonial brutality, 68–9, 77–8; empire of, 66–75, 76–81
neuroscience, 281–2
New Guinea, 255
Noetling, Fritz, 233
Nogué, M., 263, 264

Oghuz Turks, 272
Omenetto, Fiorenzo, *323–7*, *329*, 330, 331, 332
d'Orbigny, Alcide, 254–5
Orléans, Duke of, 171, 173–4
Ottoman Empire, 60, 272
Oxford, University of, 314
Oxman, Neria, 327–8
d'Oyly, Elizabeth Jane, Lady, 126–7, 130–1
d'Oyly, Sir Charles, 126–7, 130, 131

paper, 272–3
Paraguay, 241–6, 247, 253, 254–5
Paramaribo, 66–8, 71–2, 74
Parasa Isabella moth, 133
Parasa laleana moth, 133

parasites, 9
Pasteur, Louis, 115
Pausanias (Greek geographer), 178–9
Paxton, Joseph, 137
Peers, Simon, 319–20
Persepolis, city of, 88
Philippines, 216, 218
Phoenician people, 189–90, 192, 194
Pinna nobilis, 9, *170*, 170–5, 334; Aquincum mummy, 182–5, 214–15, 219, 221; Aristotle on, 179; as 'Critically Endangered' species, 213; failed attempts to farm, 201–2, 218; Helfer's knowledge of, 116; historical evidence of sea silk, 177, 180–1, 182–8, 214–15, 219–20; impact of human actions on, 206–7, 209–12; impact of pollutants/ contaminants, 209–10; *manu de ferru* tool, 198, *199*; 'mass mortality event' (from 2016), 206–12, 213, 217–18, 220–1; medical use of, 174, 185, 212, 315; nacre in shells, 171, 190, 212; Arianna Pintus's research, 216–18, 219–20; and Sant' Antioco, 190–1, 193–4, 198–200, 202–4, 205, 216–18, 219–20; strength and durability of silk, 9, 212, 221; and Taranto, 201–2, 204–5, 215; weaving of threads, 179–80, 183–4, 185–8, 191, 193–4, 198–200, 201–5, 214–15, 217, 219–20, 221
Pintus, Arianna, 216–21, *221*
plastics, 213, 325, 327, 329, 330–1, 332
Pompeii, 176–7, 180–2
Portugal, 253
Princip, Gavrilo, 296–7, 298
Prinsep, James, 112, 121
Procopius of Caesarea, 186
proteins, silk: antiviral/bacterial, 275, 315; biodegradable, 213, 305, 325; as a biopolymer, 331–2; and cement-like sericin, 52, 58, 73, 123, 150–1, 154–5, 275–6, 317–19; *fibroin* protein, 52, 58, 72–3, 123, 237–8, 275, 299–300, 304, 317, 318, 326; genetic codes/sequences of, 280, 299, 304, 308–13; and genetic modification, 304–11; and human immune system, 317–18; of marine molluscs, 172–3, 174, 177, 213, 315; related to the keratin protein, 309, 317; repetitive sequences of, 308–9; from Saturniidae moths, 91; scientific attempts to replicate, 6, 303–13; scientific study of, 303–13, 314–19, 323–34; silkworm's secretion of, 6, 38, 43, 52, 324; smart materials from, 323–34; of spiders, 237–8, 256, 258, 303–13, 318–19; *spidroins*, 237–8, 304, 306, 308
Prussian blue, 147
Psalis securis moth, 133
Punjab, Kingdom of, 137

Radama II, King of Madagascar, 259
ramie fibres, 10
Ranavalona I, Queen of Madagascar, *259*, 259
Ranjit Singh, the Lion of Punjab, 126–7
Réaumur, René-Antoine Ferchault de, 116, 169–75, 222–3, 225–6; house at Charenton, 226, 227; insect menagerie of, *226*, 226, 227; lack of artistic talent, 226–7; and Termeyer, 242, 243, 244–5, 247–8; work on spiders, 225–30, 240, 241, 242, 245, 247–8

religion/spirituality: Buddhism, 59, 86; Christian missionaries, 60, 260; Labadism, 21–3; use of silk, 11–12
Réunion, island of, 256, 258
Rhamnus jujube tree, 101
Rhizophora caseolaris (food plant), 101
Rhodococcus erythropolis (bacterium), 208–9
Rome, ancient, *96*, 122, 176–7, 180–5, 189–90, 203
Rosetta stone, 177–8
Ross, Major Thomas, 130
Roxburgh, Dr William, 97–9, 139, 144; and eri or arrindy moths, 124, 125, 134, 162; and *Phalaena cynthia*, 124, 134; study of the tasar moth, 99–103, *104*, 109, 117–18, 123, 124, 131–2, 141
Roxburgh, Mary, 98–9, 102–3
Royal Society of Arts, 155–8
Royal Society of London, 32–3, 34, 35–9, 64, 110, 223
Rumpf, Georg Eberhardt, 76–81, *79*, 96, 102; death of (1702), 81, 82; moth of (*Antheraea rumphii rumphii*), 80, 82–3, *83*, 91, 96; *The Ambonese Curiosity Cabinet*, 75, 82; *Herbarium Amboinense*, 101

Sahni, Daya Ram, 87–8
sal tree (*Shorea robusta*), 144
Samia fulva (*Samia* moth), 124
Sant' Antioco, island of (Sulki, Slky), 189–94, 195–200, 202–4, 205, 216–21, *221*
Santorini, 11
Sardinia, 189, 191–2, 193, 199–200, 208–9, 215, 216–21, *221*
Saturniidae family of moths: *Actias selene* (Indian moon moth), 132, 134, 142; anatomy of, 122–3, 135, 141; *Attacini* tribe, 83, 91, 133–4, 162; *Attacus* genus, 123–4, 133–5, 142, 162; caterpillars of, 72–3, 80–1, 134, 135, 159; *Cricula trifenestrata*, 120, 142, 162; eri or arrindy from Assam, 123–5, 134–5, 162; and fabrics of Indus civilization, 83, 91–2, 109, 120; and Isabella Gilbert, 131–5, 142, 162; Isabella Gilbert's moth (*Attacus atlas*), 133–4, 142, 162; Helfer's lectures on, 115–24, 142, 202; huge size of, 72, 100, 102, 122, 134, 159; in India, 91–2, 95–104, 109, 116–24, 131–5, 139–42, 144, 146–7, 149–59, 162; large size of cocoons, 72, 80–1, 83, 91, 95–6, 103, 121–4, 141; and Merian in Suriname, 71–3, 134; Merian's moth (*Rothschildia aurota*), 73, 82, 83, 91, 123, 134; named by Harvard librarian, 71, 82–3; Rumpf's moth (*Antheraea rumphii rumphii*), 80–1, 82–3, *83*, 91, 96; *Samia* genus, 91, 124, 162; *Saturnia pyri*, 116; *Saturniini* tribe, 83, 91, 96, 133–4; silk compared to that of *Bombyx mori*, 123, 146, 152–4, 155–6, *157*; silk of at Paris Exposition (1855), 140, 141; silk produced by, 73, 80–1, 83, 119, 123–4; take-off in India's exports of wild silk, 142, 152; and Thomas Wardle, 142, 144, 146, 147, 149–59, 162 *see also Antheraea* moths; tasar moth (*Antheraea paphia*)
Sawai Jai Singh II, Raja, 111
Scarabæus beetle, 247
science: beliefs in spontaneous formation, 25; and ecosystem loss, 211–12, 213–14, 332–4; European natural historians, 4, 8–9, 13,

19–20, 63–8, 69–75, 76–83, 96–104, 105–11, 113–14; food technology, 330–1; and future sustainability, 320–2, 328–34; Goodfellow's discoveries, 290–6, 317; Indian, 111–13, 115–16; Linnaeus' two-name system, 4, 28, 48–50, 72, 134, 170; Malpighi's anatomical work, 30–9, 54, 61; 'mass mortality events,' 206–12, 213, 217–18, 220–1; Merian's work on *Bombyx mori*, 20, 24–8, *27*, 54; microscopic study of silkworms, 28, 35–9; mimicking of spider silk production, 304–13, 334; and mutual global benefit, 13; and natural polymers, 212, 315, 331–2; neuroscience, 281–2; plastic/microplastic substitutes, 325, 327, 329, 330–1, 332; Réaumur's work, 169–75, 222–3, 225–30, 240, 241, 242, 245, 247–8; search for new ways to cool the body, 329–30; and sense of wonder, 6; seventeenth-century anatomists, 5, 30–9, 54; silken alternatives for petrochemicals, 329; smart materials, 322, 323–34; study of silk proteins, 303–13, 314–19, 323–34; thermal management research, 329–30; Fritz Vollrath's studies, 314–19, 321, 322, 329, 331, 332; Work and Emerson's research, 301–2 *see also* evolutionary biology

sea silk (byssus), 170–5, 177, 179–88, 191, 193–4, 198–205, 212, 214, 315; of *Atrina pectinata*, 215–16, 218–19; Italo Diana's work with, 198–9, 202–4, 205, 216, 217, 218; historical evidence of, 177, 180–1, 182–8, 214–15, 219–20; natural polymers created from, 315; Arianna Pintus's research, 216–21, *221*; Saint-Denis cap, 214 *see also Pinna nobilis*

Second World War, 183–4, 204–5, 283–4, 285–6

Serra, Mariannicca, 198–9

Shakespeare, William, 287–8

sheep, 10

Sicily, 61, 202, 208, 215

silk: African animals producing, 260; archaeological evidence, 44–8, 56–9, 90–1; British sources of, 114, 138–9, 152; broken threads caused by emerging moth, 6, 27, 58, 59, 91, 103; in bulletproof vests/body armour, 273–6, *295*, 297–9, 300, 306, 322; cultivation technology, 7, 52, 58, 60–1, 92, 113–14, 138–9, 146, 284; deep structure of, 52, 58, 275, 299–300; dragline silk from spiders, 301–2, 304, 308, 309–13, 315–16, 318–19; earliest production outside of China, 57–9; economic importance of, 38–9; *eri or arrindy from Assam*, 8, 123–5, 134–5, 162; European discovery of ancient silks, 8–9; European production of, 34–5, 57, 61, 114–16, 138, 152–3, 155, 262, 263, 283–4, 328; future value in sustainable industries, 6, 12, 13, 320–2, 328–34; Goodfellow's research on gun-shot wounds, 290–6, 317; and Great Exhibition (1851), 138–40, 142; Helfer on, 113–14, 116–24, 131; 'Indian Collection' at Paris Exposition (1855), 140, 141; and the Indus civilization, 90–2, 322; as item of very high value in early economies, 11; long continuous strands of, 52, 58, 80–1, 91, 103,

155, 250–1, 258, *262–3*; Lyons as epicentre of Europe's industry, 152, 155, 262, *263*; many forms of value of, 11–12; MIT *Silk Pavilion* project, *327–8*; natural polymers created from, 315, 331–2; Nazi production of, 283–4; as plastic/petrochemical substitute, 325, 327, 329, 330–1, 332; produced by muga moths, *121*, 122, 123–4, 162; social and environmental potential, 12, 13, 329–34; spider–silkworm threads, 309–11, 312; of spiders, 221, 223–6, 227–9, 236–40, 245, 247–52, 262–4, 280, 284–7, 301–5; take-off in India's exports of wild silk, 142, 152; use of in Second World War, 283–4, 285–6; use of in telescopes, 284–5, 286 *see also* proteins, silk; sea silk (byssus)
silk moths, wild: *Borocera* of Madagasca, 260–1; Camboué's study of, 260–1; eggs of, 99, 100, 117, 118, 135, 159; from India, 7; mating, 25, 27, 59, 102, 117–18; Merian's (*Rothschildia aurota*), 73, 82, 83, 91, 134; Moore's *Silkworm moths of India*, 136, 142; in Neolithic China, 47–8, 50–4; Roxburgh's study of, 98–103, *104*, 109, 123, 131–2, 134, 139, 141, 162; specimens in Natural History Museum, 7–9; George Watt on term 'wild,' 139–40 *see also Antheraea* moths; Bombycidae family of moths; Saturniidae family of moths; tasar moth (*Antheraea paphia*)
Silk Roads, 7, 272–3
SilkLab (at Tufts), 326, 331
silkworms: anatomy of, 5, 34–9, 41–3, 135; of *Bombyx mori*, 5–6, 12, 24–6, 29–30, 35–9, 45–7, 52–4, 284, 299; camouflage in the wild, 53; commercial possibilities of in colonial era, 98–100, 102–4, 113–14, 116–25, 138–40, 142, 144–51, 152–60; development of wings within, 37, 41–2; domestication of in China, 4, 10, 28, 45–7, 50–4, 58, 91, 102, 103, 273–4, 315; early breeding of in Europe, 61; emergence from their eggs, 5, 25–6, *27*, 35; liquid silk inside, 38, 43, 280, 315, 324–5, 332; Malpighi's anatomical work on, 34–9; microscopic study of, 28, 35–9; by-products of, 52–3; of Saturniidae family, 72–3, 80–1, 134, 135, 159; spider silk proteins inserted into, 309–11, 312; spinnerets, 3; of tasar moth, 91, 94, 95, 99–100, *104*, 123, 132, 144, *162*; tubular silk glands, 38, 39, 43, 54, 58, 72–3, 280 *see also* cocoons, silkworm
slavery, 68–9, 70–1, 87, 97, 130, 138
Sommelsdijck, Lucia van, 72
Songer, Nannie 'Nan,' 286, *287*, 288
Sophie, Duchess of Hohenberg, 296, 298, 299
South America, 20, 48, 65, 66–75, 80; Gran Chaco, 242, 243, 246, 254; Rio Paraná, 241–2; Spanish colonialism, 241–2, 253–4; spiders of, 66, 229–30, 240, 242–6, 253–5, 288
Spain, 60, 138, 187, 206, 215; colonialism in the Americas, 241–2, 253–4; Jesuits expelled from (1767), 246–7, 251
spiders: absence of *sericin* in silk, 318–19; of the Americas, 66, 229–30, 240, 242–6, 253–5, 278–9, 281, 288; anatomy of,

236–8; *Aranea avicularis*, 243–4; *Aranea latro*, 242–3, 246; Araneae order, 236–7; black widows, 257–8, 286, *287*; Bon's work on silk of, 223–6, 227–8, 229, 241, 245, 247, 251; Camboué's study of, 261–4, 319; and cannibalism, 319; 'capture silk' fibre, 318–19; 'common' spider, 223–6; and Darwin, 254; *diadema* (European garden spider), 247–51; different types of silk produced by, 228, 237–40, 245, 258, 303; dragline silk, 301–2, 304, 308, 309–13, 315–16; egg sacs ('cocoons') of, 223, 224, 228–9, 240, 243, 244, 245–6, 247–8, 288; enormous, 230, 240, 242–6, 253–7, 258–60, 261–4, 278–9, 281, 288; *Epeira* or *Nephila*, 9, 254, 255, 256–7, 258–60, 261–4, *265*, 278–9, 281, 302, 314; evolutionary biology of, 235–40, 302–3, 308; fabrics from silk of, 224, 225–6, 251, 254–5, 258–9, 264, 319–20; feeding of in captivity, 224, 228, 243, 244, 303; fossils of, 236–7; human unreeling of silk threads from, 248–51, 262–4, 279–81, 286, 301–3, 334; Randy Lewis's work on, 302–4, 305–13; liquid silk inside, 237, 280, 306–7, 312, 315; machines/devices for forcible silking of, 249–51, 263–4, 279–81, 301–3, 334; Madagascar Golden Orb spider, *261*, 261–4, *265*, 319–20, 321; medicinal use of silk, 225, 286–8, 303, 305, 311, 312, 314, 318–19; *Parawixia bistriata*, 253–4; poisonous, 257–8; production of silk by, 221, 223–6, 228–9, 237–40, 242–5, 247–52, 254–64, 278–81, 284–8, 301–13, 314–16, 318–21; quantities of silk produced by, 229, 262–3, 288, 304, 305–8, 311, 313, 319–20; Réaumur's work on, 116, 225–30, 240, 241, 242, 245, 247–8; scientific mimicking of silk production, 304–13, 334; silk glands, 237–8, 258, 305; silk proteins, 237–8, 256, 258, 303–13, 318–19; silk-like textiles inspired by, 320–2; spinnerets, 236–7, 245, 249, 250, 264, 286, 302, 306–7, 309; strength and durability of silk, 9, 228, 255, 264, 303, 305–6, 308, 320–1; tarantulas, 238, 244; Termeyer's study of, 242–6, 247–52, 258, 277, 279–81, 301–2, 319; trapdoor spiders, 238; use of silk of in Second World War, 285–6; Fritz Vollrath's studies, 314–16, 318–19; and Walckenaër, 254, 257–8, 261, 277; webs, 238–40, *239*, 242–3, 245, 253–7, 278–9, 287–8, 301, 303, 307, 314; Wilder's investigations, 277–81, 302, 319

sponges, 183, 211; *Spongia officinalis*, 182

St Basil the Great, 186

Stanford University, USA, 329–30

Stillbers, Mr, 288

sugar cane, 71, 73, 98

Suriname, 65, 66–75, 80, 134, 229–30, 240, 244

sustainable industries, 320–2, 328–34

Swinhoe, Charles, 231–4

Tagore, Dwarakanath, 127

Taklamakan desert, 56–7

tapia trees, 260

Tarim Basin, 55–9, 61

tasar moth (*Antheraea paphia*): adult moth, 60, 94, 95, 97, 100–1, 102–3, 118, *163*; *Antheraea frithi* Moore as ancestor, 103–4, 140, 141–2; caterpillar of, 91, 94, 95, 99–100, *104*, 123, 132, 144, *162*; and cement-like sericin, 123, 132, 150–1; cocoons of, 95–6, 100–3, 117, 132, 141, 146, 149–51, 154–5, 158–9, *160*, *163*; colouring/dyeing of silk, 147–8, 149–51, 153–4; diet of bair and sal tree leaves, 94, 95, 99, 144, 150; eggs of, 99, 100, 117, 159; evolutionary biology of, 94–5, 315–16; Frith's samples of, 140–1; and Isabella Gilbert, 131–2; in India, 94–7, 98–102, *104*, 109, 116–17, 123, 144, 145–7, 149–59; medical uses of silk, 317–18; reeling of silk, 154–5, *157*, 159; Roxburgh studies, 98–103, *104*, 109, 117–18, 123, 124, 131–2, 141; from *Saturniini* tribe, 133–4; 'seal cloth,' 155–8; sheen/lustre of silk, 155–6; silk not in Great Exhibition catalogue (1851), 139–40; silk of viewed as inferior outside India, 123, 139, 146–7, 152; stifling or heating at pupal stage, 103, 146, 159; strength and durability of silk, 152–4, *157*, 315–16; Fritz Vollrath's studies, 315–18; and Thomas Wardle, 144, 146, 149–60, 162; wings of, 100–1, 141
Termeyer, Father Ramón María, 241, 242–52, 253, 257, 258, 277, 279–81, 301–2, 319
Terminalia alata glabra tree, 101
Terracotta Army of First Emperor, 321
Tertullian, 185–6
tobacco, 30
Tombstone (Arizona Territory), 289–96
Toulon, 171, 173
Trabala Vishnu moth, 133
trade networks: emergence in the Neolithic, 10–11; major trading posts in Tarim Basin, 57; Mongol dominion over silk roads, 272–3; new routes in early centuries CE, 57, 59–60; silk as item of very high value, 11; Silk Roads, 7, 272–3
Trisula variegata moth, 133
Trobriand Islands, 255
Tufts University, Massachusetts, *323–7*, *329*, *330*, 331, 332
Turkey, 59–60, 114
Turkmenistan, 60, 271–3
Tuscany, 60–1
Twain, Mark, 11

United States of America: American Civil War, 278; cotton plantations in south, 138; Natick Research & Development Laboratories, 324; scientific mimicking of spider silk production, 304–13, 334; spider silk during Second World War, 285–6
Uzbekistan, 55, 57

Vanuatu, 255
Vats, Madho Sarup, 88
Victor Emmanuel III, King of Italy, 203
Victoria and Albert Museum, London, 320
Vinson, Auguste, 256, 258–60, 262
Vollrath, Fritz, 314–19, 321, 322, 329, 331, 332

Walckenaër, Charles Athanase, Baron de, 254, 257–8, 261, 277
Wardle, Joshua, 145, 147

Wardle, Thomas, 142, 143–5, 146, 147–59, 160; and 'Colonial and Indian Exhibition' (1886), 160, 161, 162; trip to India, 143–4, 158–60

wasps, 9

Watt, George, A *Dictionary of the Economic Products of India*, 139–40

white carob tree, 242

Wilder, Burt Green, 277–83, 302, 319

wings: in adult *Bombyx mori*, 6, 27, 28; aerodynamics, 40–1; anatomy of, 40–2, 94–5; of *Antheraea frithi*, 141; in the growing silkworm, 37, 41–2; Lepidoptera order, 3, 6, 27, 28, 37, 41–2, 94–5, 100–1, 141; Pterygota class, 40–1; structures to avoid predatory bats, 94–5; of tasar moths, 100–1, 141; varying forms of, 41

Witsen, Nicolaes, 64

women's perspectives: and Isabella Gilbert, 131–5; Labadie's community in Friesland, 22; lack of sources/records, 13; Royal Society admits only men, 32–3, 64

wool, 138, 180, 192, 247

Work, Robert, 301–2

Xun, Master, 12

Yiu Huan, 186

Yoruba people, 260

Zain al-Din, Shaikh, 93, 94–6, 99–100, 102–3

Zeglen, Casimir, *295*, 297–9, 300

zooplankton, 213

30 Years *of*

HarperCollins *Publishers* India

At HarperCollins, we believe in telling the best stories and finding the widest possible readership for our books in every format possible. We started publishing 30 years ago; a great deal has changed since then, but what has remained constant is the passion with which our authors write their books, the love with which readers receive them, and the sheer joy and excitement that we as publishers feel in being a part of the publishing process.

Over the years, we've had the pleasure of publishing some of the finest writing from the subcontinent and around the world, and some of the biggest bestsellers in India's publishing history. Our books and authors have won a phenomenal range of awards, and we ourselves have been named Publisher of the Year the greatest number of times. But nothing has meant more to us than the fact that millions of people have read the books we published, and somewhere, a book of ours might have made a difference.

As we step into our fourth decade, we go back to that one word – a word which has been a driving force for us all these years.

Read.